IMAGES
of America

FANNIN COUNTY

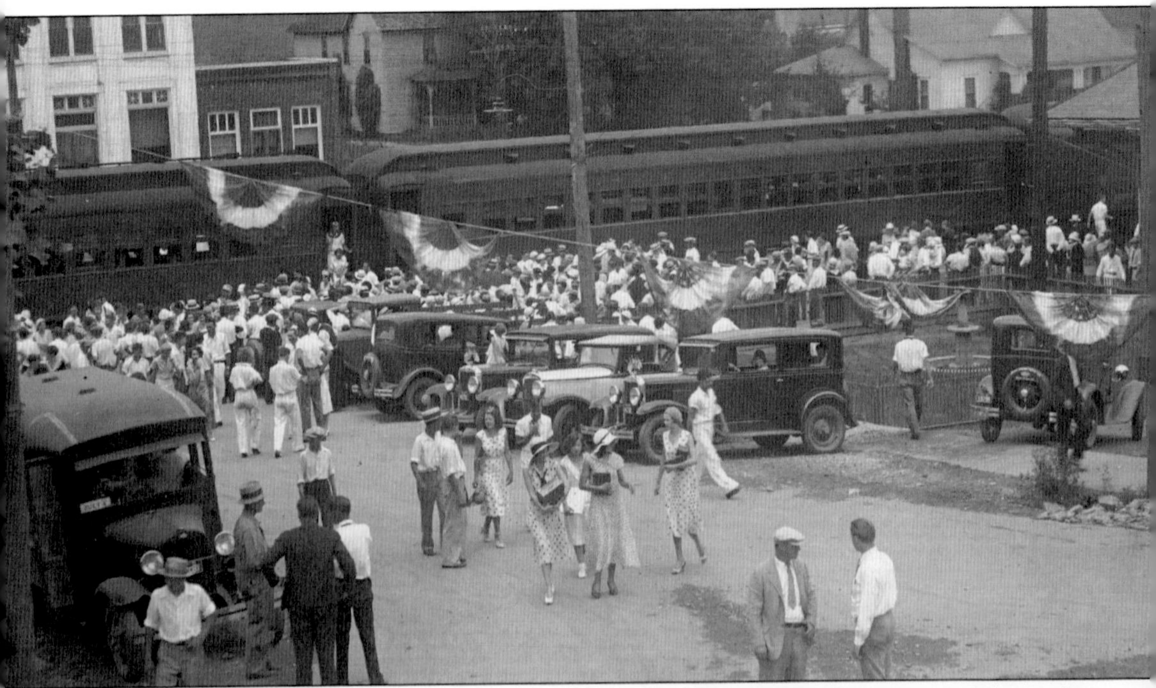

A large crowd gathers on July 4, 1930, for a barbecue in Blue Ridge, Georgia, to celebrate the opening of the hydroelectric plant at Toccoa (later Blue Ridge) Dam. The railroad station is at the far right side of the picture. Fannin County Bank is the white building to the left behind the train. (Courtesy Carolyn and Don Hall.)

On the Cover: A barefoot boy and several adults enjoy Mineral Springs near Blue Ridge, Georgia, around 1916. Note the Model-T Ford and the horseback riders, including one couple riding double. These springs have been a gathering place since prehistoric times. Their supposed curative powers fueled steady tourism once the railroad reached Blue Ridge on Christmas Day in 1886. (Courtesy Ethelene Dyer Jones.)

IMAGES
of America

FANNIN COUNTY

Keith Jones

ARCADIA
PUBLISHING

ISBN 978-0-7385-9188-9

Published by Arcadia Publishing
Charleston, South Carolina

Printed in the United States of America

Library of Congress Control Number: 2011944355

For all general information, please contact Arcadia Publishing:
Telephone 843-853-2070
Fax 843-853-0044
E-mail sales@arcadiapublishing.com
For customer service and orders:
Toll-Free 1-888-313-2665

Visit us on the Internet at www.arcadiapublishing.com

To my unforgotten sons Nathan and Matthew, their wives Kayla and LaTasha; grandchildren Brenna, Samuel, and Joshua; to my son BJ, and always, to Debbie.

Contents

Acknowledgments

It is impossible to fully acknowledge everyone who contributes to any book. I thank my mother, Ethelene Dyer Jones, and my late father, Rev. Grover D. Jones, for fostering a love of history, local lore, and the stories that do not make their way into the history books. Dale Dyer also made rich contributions to preserving the history and heritage of Fannin County.

Fannin County High School students (led by media director Ethelene Jones) produced *Fannin Folio* through the 1980s, a yearly booklet that highlighted local history. From their efforts, joined by many local contributors of family histories, came the 1989 book *Facets of Fannin*. Soon after, members of the Fannin County Historical Foundation came together to preserve the historic Baugh House, which serves as the Fannin County Historical Museum in Blue Ridge. The Foundation also published a book listing burials in all known cemeteries and will soon publish *Facing Forward: A History of Schools in Fannin County*.

I feel a deep gratitude to the photographers—itinerant professionals or citizens wielding simple cameras—for the images included herein. Some of their names are listed in the credits, but others remain unidentified. Ron Henry is perhaps the best-known local photographer. His career was cut short by his early death, but he will be remembered for his beautiful work, his civic-mindedness, and for his pioneering efforts that began at the park along the Toccoa River, which he loved so well. I especially appreciate his family granting me permission to use his photographs a few years ago in *Altitude* magazine and in this book. I also wish to thank the number of other folks who gave me leave to use images they possess.

Brinkley Taliaferro was serving as acquisitions editor when I began the process of producing this work. Elizabeth Bray, senior editor at Arcadia Publishing, provided very helpful guidance, encouragement, and assistance. Of course, any errors that remain in the book are exclusively my own.

The members of Morganton Baptist Church have been gracious in allowing me to continue freelance writing while serving as their pastor. My wife, Debbie, sons, daughters-in-law, and grandchildren have graciously put up with the sprawl of my research during this production.

INTRODUCTION

Fannin County, Georgia, is situated near the southern terminus of the Appalachian Mountain Chain, which extends north-northeast through numerous states, passing through Maine and the eastern provinces of Canada. Mountains with similar geologic characteristics are even found in the Celtic regions of the British Isles. Geologists claim that the Appalachians are the oldest mountains on earth.

The first characteristic of the region that visitors note is the beautiful mountain scenery. In the fall, tens of thousands of tourists come to see the living flame on display as the deciduous trees clothe themselves in brilliant yellow, gold, orange, vermilion, and rust. In winter, the gray branches of these trees contrast with the dark greens of the pines and hemlocks. Snow and frozen fog occasionally blanket the ridges and valleys, transforming their aspect. Spring brings another brilliant display—first the scattered whites (and a few pinks) of the blooming dogwoods, the bright purples of the redbuds, then as many shades of vibrant green as there were reds in the fall. Only the very elderly locals can remember the days before the blight when the mighty American chestnut was the dominant tree and clothed all the hills with blooms that rivaled the snows of winter. Summer, too, provides its visual pleasures, but perhaps visitors appreciate more the almost-constant breezes, which palliate the heat from late spring to early fall.

Of course, without water there would be no beautiful mountain vistas. Sixty-five inches of precipitation fall in an average year in Fannin County. This is well over a foot above the average for Georgia. Fannin County is located west of the eastern Continental Divide, so this abundant water eventually flows to the Gulf of Mexico. How it does so, however, is an interesting saga. Three main rivers drain the hills and valleys of the county—the Toccoa, the Jacks River/Conasauga system, and the Cherry Log Creek/Ellijay River. The city of Blue Ridge sits in a saddle of land, a geographical oddity that is defined as the lowest point between two higher areas of land, which is simultaneously the highest point between two lower areas of land. Thus, rain that falls on the railroad tracks in front of the Blue Ridge Mountains Arts Association divides east and west. The west-flowing water drains past Davenport's wood yard, joining Cherry Log Creek, which flows into the Ellijay River. The Ellijay joins the Cartecay and becomes the Coosawattee.

Meanwhile, just northwest of Blue Ridge, in an area that today is mostly within the Cherokee National Forest, the Jacks River/Conasauga River system drains a far-reaching wilderness area. When the Coosawattee and Conasauga Rivers join, the Oostanaula is formed and makes its way southwestward, where it joins the Etowah in the city of Rome to form the Coosa River. Flowing into Alabama, the Coosa joins the Tallapoosa River near Selma, forming the Alabama River, which joins the Tombigbee River in the swamps north of Mobile, finally discharging into the Gulf of Mexico via the Mobile and Tensaw Rivers, which feed Mobile Bay.

Meanwhile, back at the saddle in Blue Ridge, the rain that falls on the eastern side flows down past the railroad station, eventually forming a creek that winds parallel to Ada Street until is empties into the Toccoa River near the vicinity of the fish trap rocks. The Toccoa originates far to the south (yes, south generally is uphill in Fannin County) near Suches in Union County. Gathering the waters of numerous creeks and minor streams, it is impounded by Blue Ridge Dam to form one of the highest-elevation lakes in the Tennessee Valley Authority system. Below the dam, the Toccoa tumbles rapidly toward Tennessee, joined by the Hemptown and Hot House Creeks.

As the waters pass under the iron bridge in McCaysville, Georgia (only a small corner of the bridge is in Copperhill, Tennessee), the river's name changes from Toccoa to Ocoee. The change in name probably derives from how the Cherokee word sounded to European ears.

The Toccoa/Ocoee is one of the hardest-working rivers one is likely to encounter, generating power repeatedly while also serving as a premier whitewater adventure destination. It was the site of the whitewater events in the 1996 Olympic Games. Joining the Hiawassee River for a few miles, the combined waters enter the Tennessee system, draining past Chattanooga, dipping far south into Alabama at Muscle Shoals, touching the northeast corner of Mississippi at the Shiloh Civil War battlefield, and traversing the states of Tennessee and Kentucky to enter the Ohio River. The Ohio (of course) drains into the Mississippi, which finally discharges its mighty flow into the Gulf roughly 100 miles south of New Orleans. So the Blue Ridge storyteller who says "New Orleans gets its drinking water from here" is spinning no tall tale.

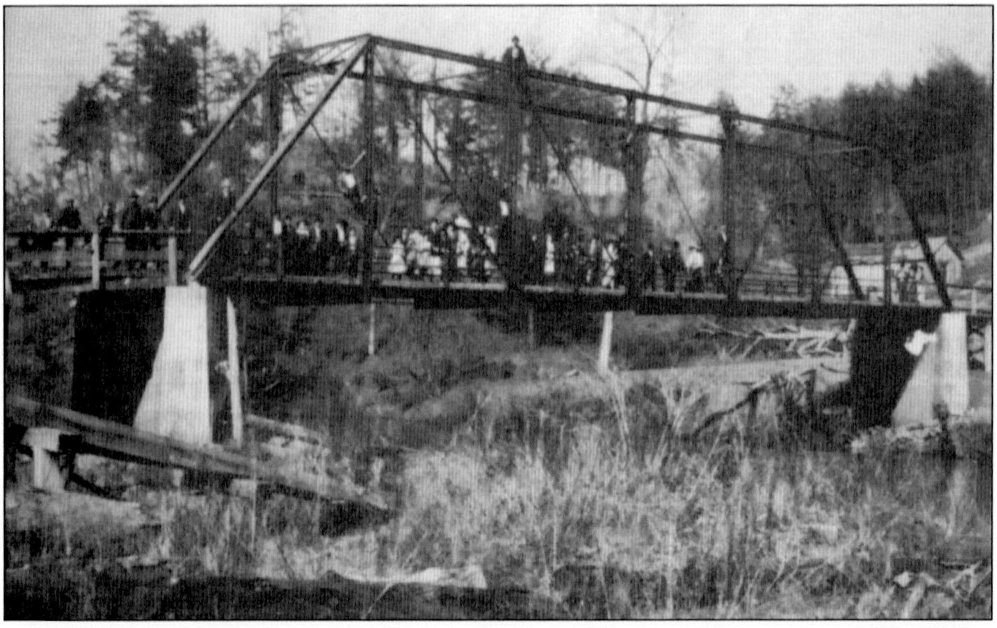

In 1922, this steel bridge was erected across the Toccoa between Morganton and Blue Ridge, approximately halfway from the present Morganton Point and the Blue Ridge Marina. Only a few years later, it was either demolished due to impending flooding by the Toccoa Lake project, or, more likely, it was taken apart and moved to McCaysville-Copperhill (see page 92), where it still carries traffic over the Toccoa/Ocoee. (Courtesy Ethelene Dyer Jones.)

One

Before Fannin County

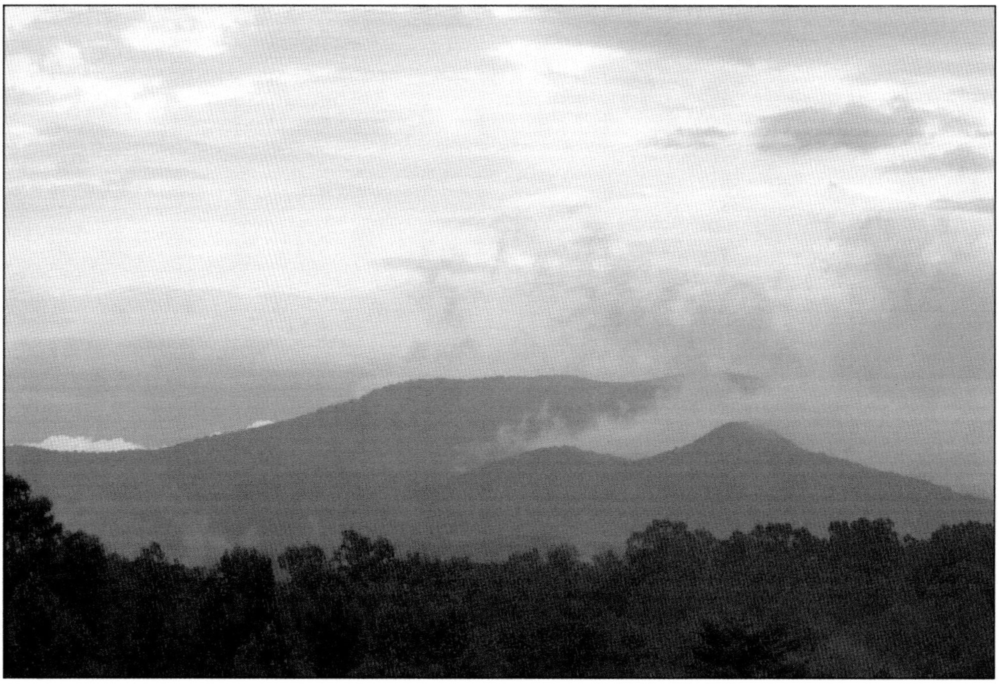

Before Fannin County was established, most Cherokee in the area were driven westward from these coves and valleys on the Trail of Tears. Many in later generations lost their homes to national forests and hydroelectric power plants. Over a generation ago, blight killed the massive American chestnut trees that once dominated the landscape. Yet the mountains remain, serene in beauty. (Courtesy Henry family; photograph by Ron Henry.)

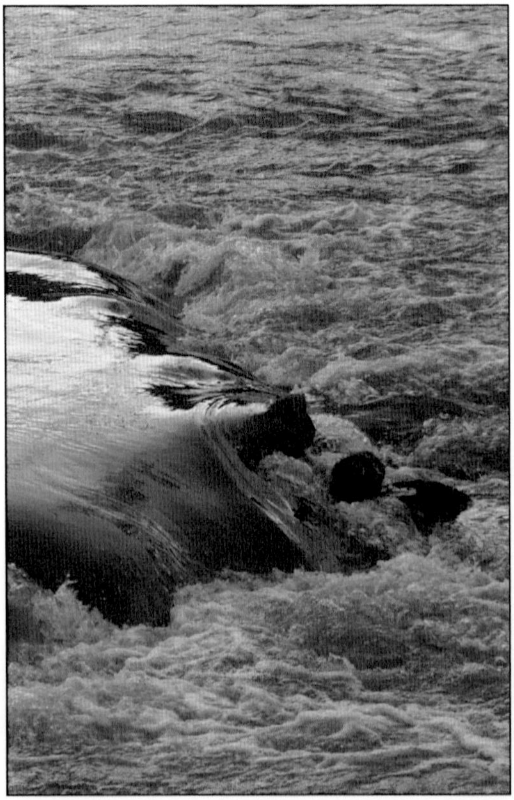

This Native American fish trap is located in the Toccoa River between Curtis Switch and McCaysville. A line of rocks forms a *V* with its point facing downriver. Baskets or nets, placed at the point of the trap, harvested fish. Historians speculate about ancient European or Middle Eastern contacts with North America, and the Cherokees have legends about a people with light skin, hair, and blue eyes associated with Fort Mountain, just west of Fannin County. The first documented European contact occurred during the 1540 Hernando de Soto expedition. A 1567 expedition led by Juan Pardo followed de Soto's route and provides the first written accounts of the Cherokee. At the time of European contact, Cherokee were well established in various towns and villages in the region that now comprises Fannin County. The principal towns were Fighting Town (translated from *Unulsti* meaning "it fights"), Hemp Town, Noontootla, and—far up in the mountains to the south, near the present southern tip of Fannin—Tickanetly. (Courtesy Ron Henry family; photograph by Ron Henry.)

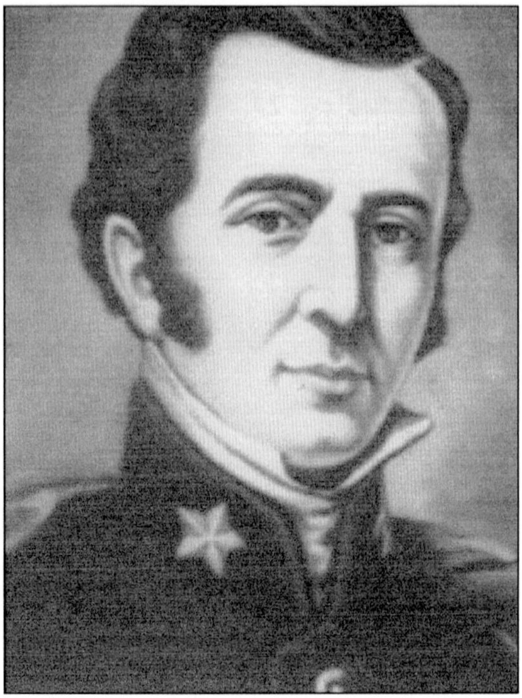

Col. James Walker Fannin was the first of two military men closely related to Fannin County's formation. Fannin was born either in what is now his namesake county, or just over the North Carolina line, probably on January 1, 1804. He attended West Point before becoming a cotton and slave broker in Columbus, Georgia. Immigrating to Texas in 1834, he was involved in the early stages of the Texas Revolution. Commanding an expedition to relieve the Alamo, he was defeated by Gen. José de Urrea at the battle of Coleto, and his command was massacred on orders of Gen. Santa Anna on March 27, 1836. (Courtesy the *New Georgia Encyclopedia*.)

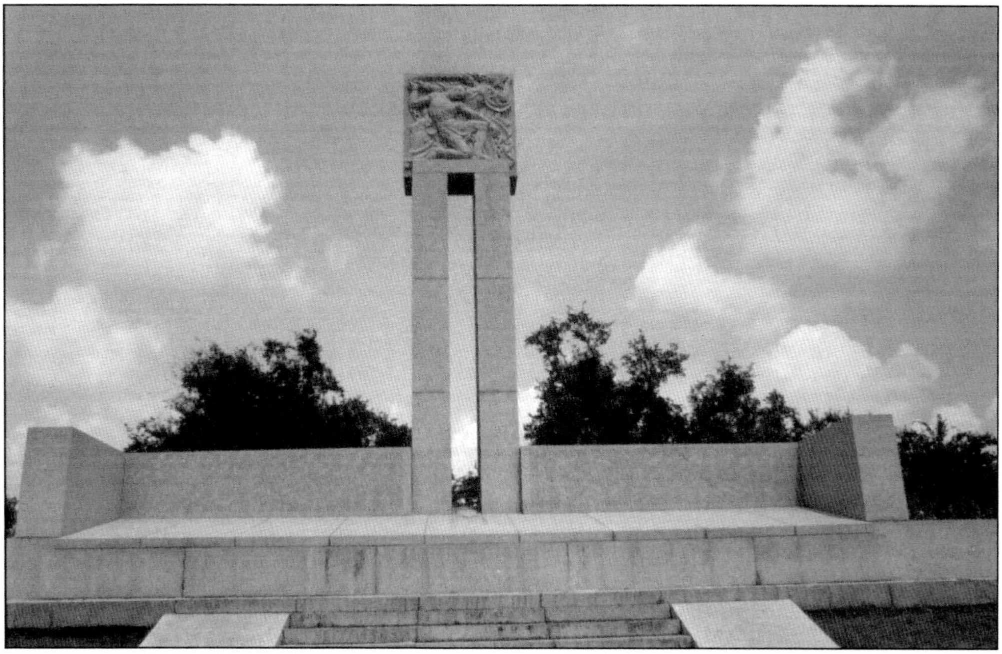

Texas erected this memorial to Fannin and his command near Goliad, Texas. As a guest historian during the Texas Sesquicentennial, Ethelene Dyer Jones took this photograph. The memorial stands at the approximate site where the bodies of Fannin and his men were burned. (Courtesy Ethelene Dyer Jones.)

The mission church is part of the Bahia fortifications near Goliad. A wounded James Walker Fannin was tied to a chair and executed on the parade grounds near this church. Members of his captured command were marched out of the fort in three groups and shot in the fields around the fort. The wife of a Mexican officer rescued a few members of the command, and a few others escaped into the brush or swam the San Antonio River. (Courtesy Ethelene Dyer Jones.)

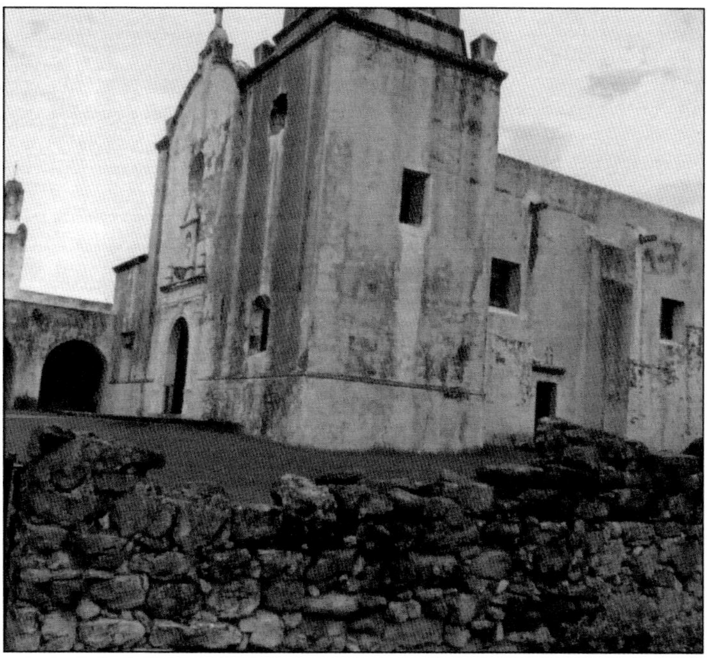

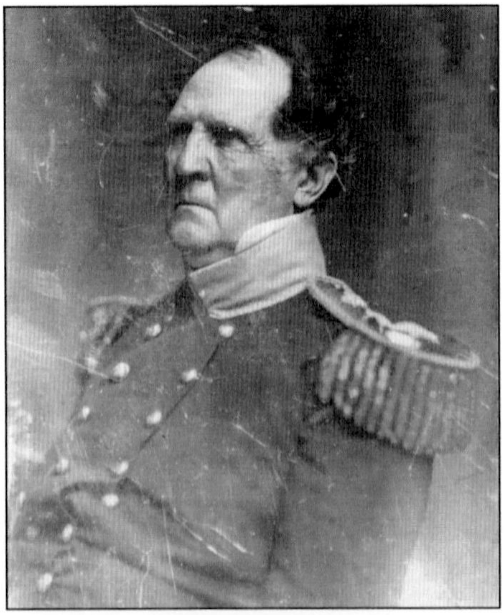

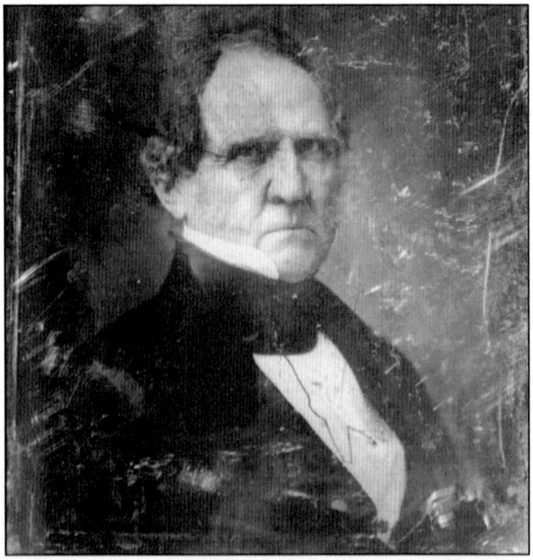

At left, Gen. Winfield Scott (1786–1866) is pictured in uniform during or shortly after the Mexican-American War. More than a decade before, Scott was the commander of Army regulars and volunteers who, in 1838, helped force the Cherokee to relocate to the West, a process that became known as the Trail of Tears. At right, Scott is in civilian clothes. Camp Chastain, a major stockade used in holding captured Cherokees, was located at the junction of Star Creek and the Toccoa River. The road leading from Morganton Point recreation area through Morganton, along Old Highway 76, and up Loving Road to the Nottely River in Union County, is one of the strands of the Trail of Tears. (Both, courtesy Ishah Roads, allphotosmaps.com.)

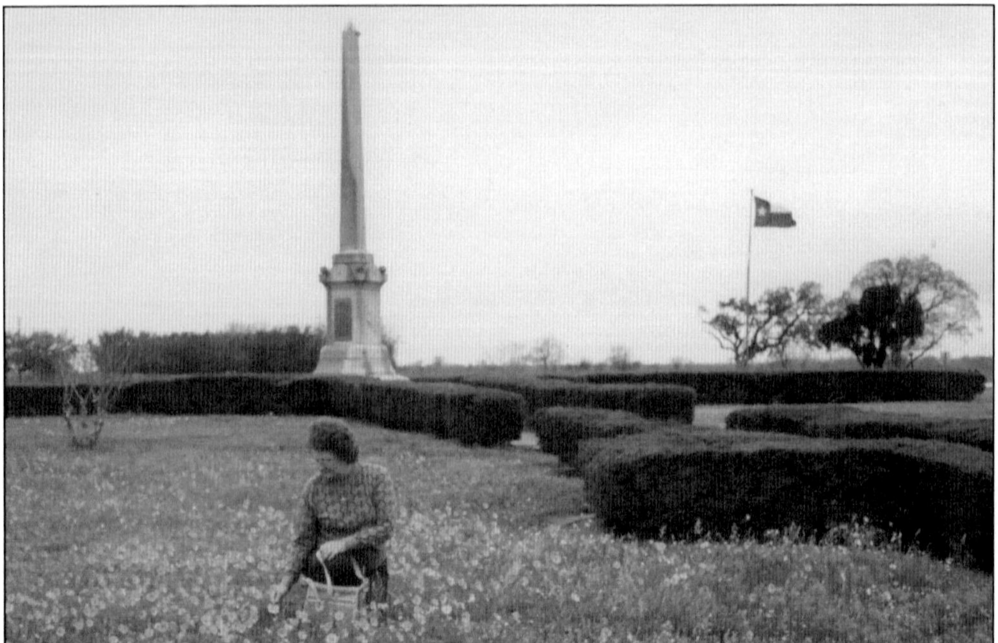

An unidentified woman picks bluebonnets in front of a monument on the site of the battle of Coleto, where James Walker Fannin and his men were surrounded and forced to surrender. (Courtesy Commissioner Bill Simonds, Fannin County Courthouse collection.)

Two

EARLY STRUGGLES

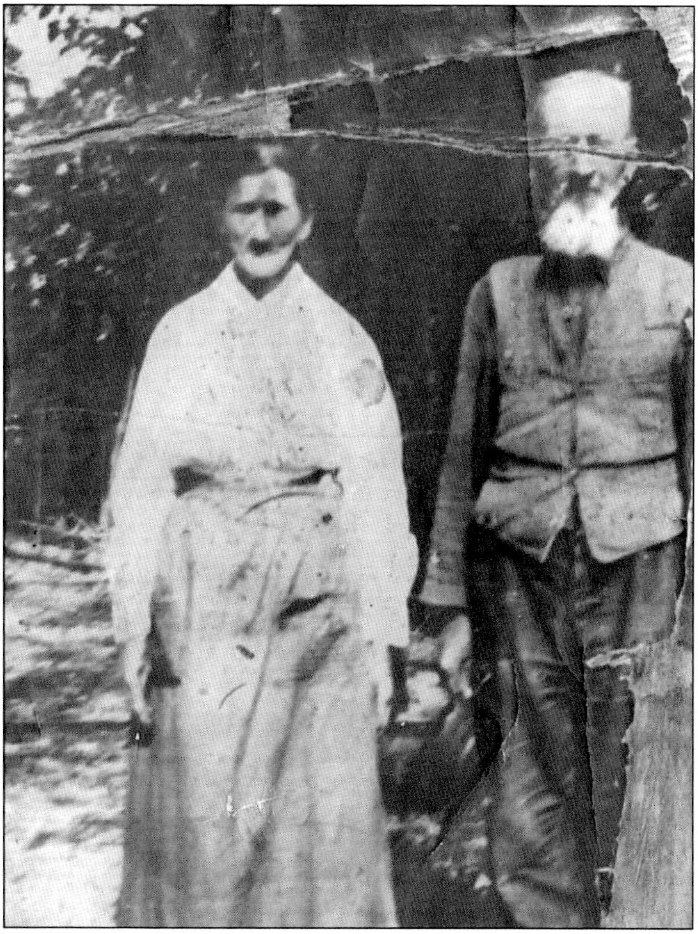

Martin Jefferson Dilbeck and his wife, Nancy Adeline Dyer, were early settlers. Born June 21, 1840, in Lumpkin County, he was listed in the 1850 Gilmer County census. Due to the formation of Fannin County (January 1, 1854, from parts of Union and Gilmer) and probably without moving, he was in Fannin Militia District 980 at the time of his marriage in 1860. He survived until 1923 and is buried in Colwell Cemetery. (Courtesy Danny Mashburn.)

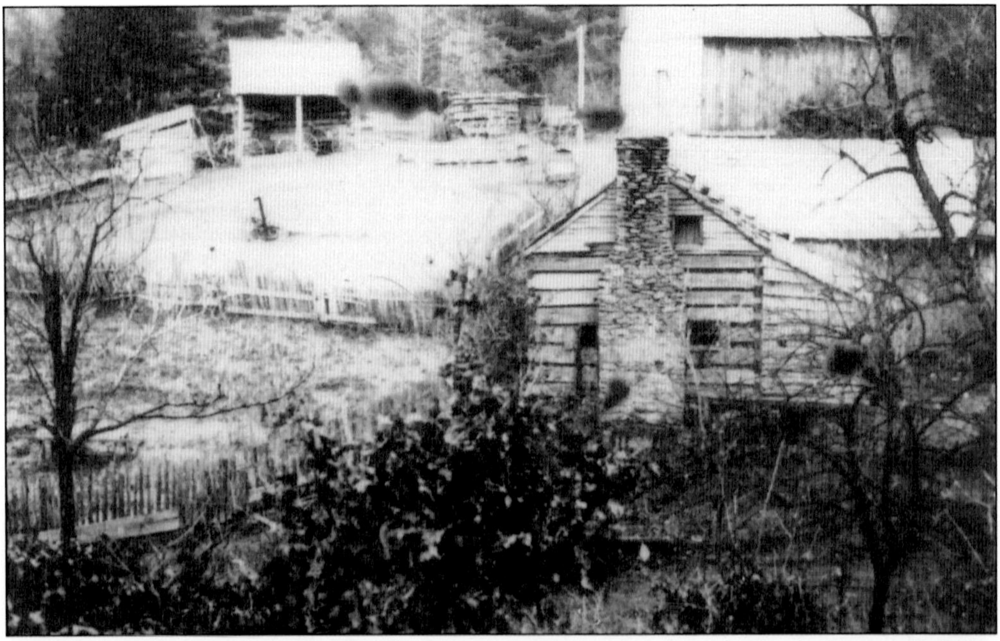

The home of Joseph Edmondson in the Margret community is typical of early farmsteads. Note the main house's notched log construction, supplemented by a board-sided addition, probably made as the family grew and as sawmills began to operate. Various barns and outbuildings were constructed to serve agricultural needs. This photograph was taken before the advent of range enclosures, so the garden plots have paling fences to prevent incursions of free-ranging hogs and cattle. (Courtesy Betty Parker.)

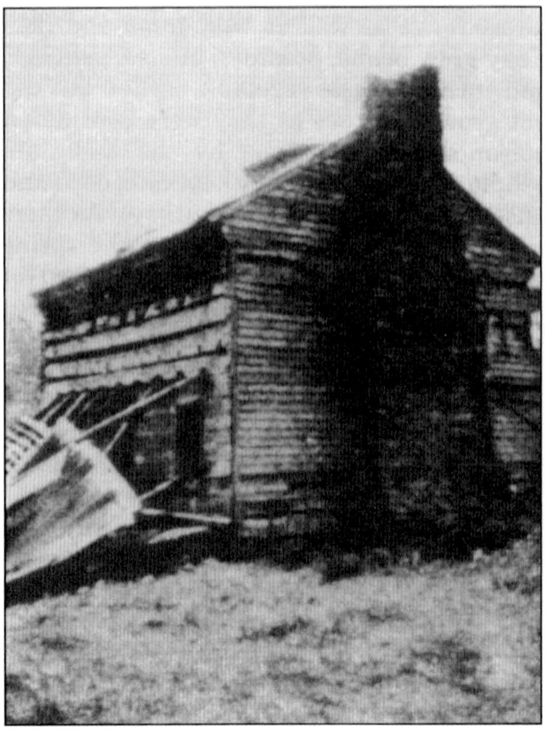

The Holden cabin, built prior to the 1838 removal, may well have built by Cherokees. The neglect evident in this picture shows the fate that befell many early structures, whose historic importance was not realized until too late. (Courtesy Holden family via Ethelene Dyer Jones.)

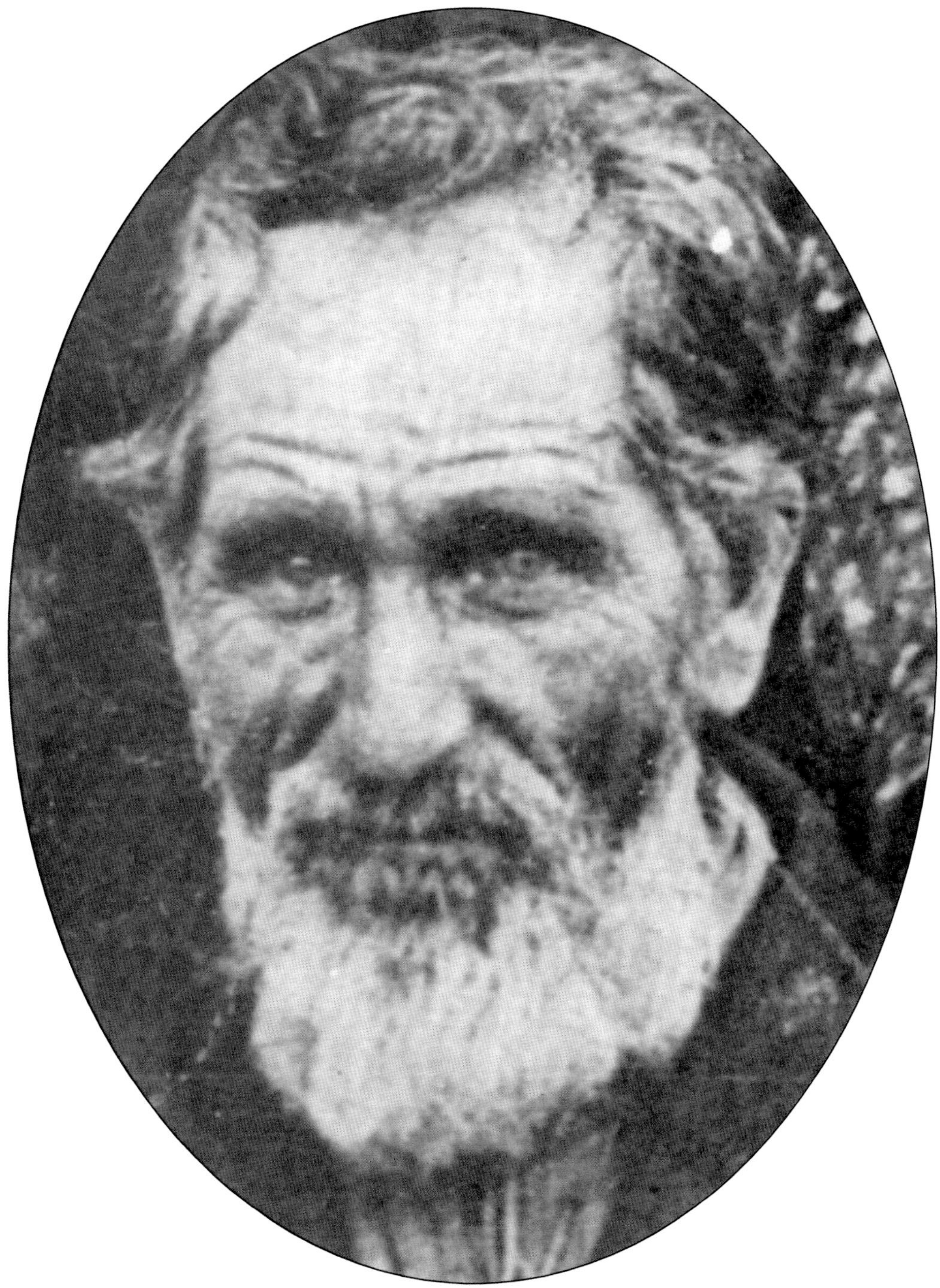

Uriah Holden served two years in the Confederate Home Guard and two years in the Confederate States Army. Fannin County provided soldiers to each side during the Civil War, and those who stayed at home suffered depredation from various official and freelance raiders. Memorialized on a 2011 historical marker in McCaysville, several Fannin County men were killed near Ducktown, Tennessee, caught by a Confederate contingent as they were leaving the area to enlist in the Union army. (Courtesy Holden family via Ethelene Dyer Jones.)

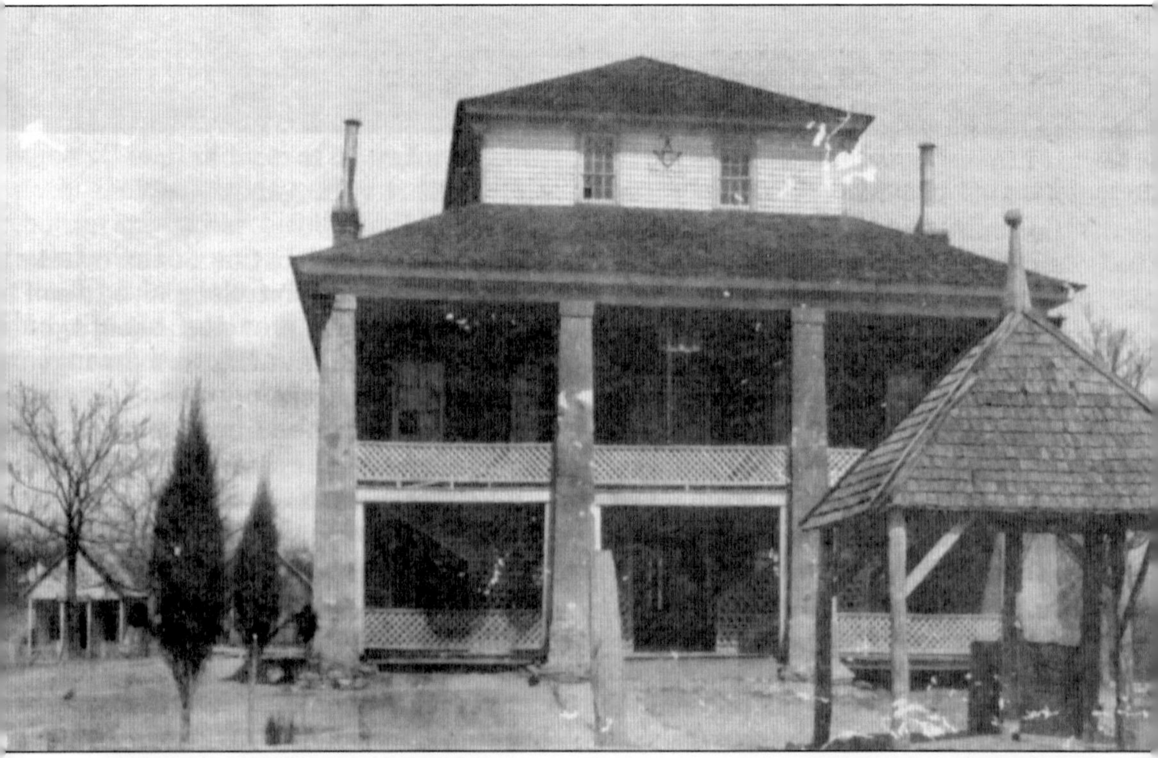

Within a couple of years of its establishment, Fannin County boasted this fine courthouse at the first seat of government, Morganton. Two attorneys who practiced before court sessions in this building attended the convention that voted for Georgia's secession from the Union. After the county seat moved to Blue Ridge, this building was used by North Georgia Baptist College. (Courtesy Ethelene Dyer Jones.)

Three

Reconstruction, Rails, and Religion

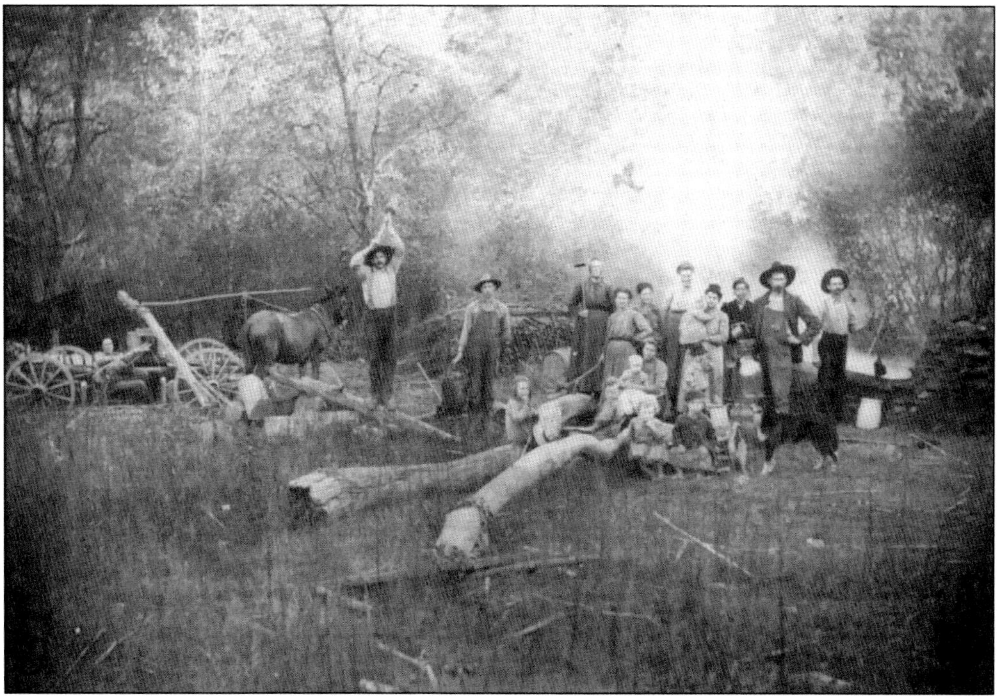

The Woody family made sweet sorghum syrup. Dallas M. Woody is on the far right, holding a skimming shovel that was used to remove the foam that formed as the sorghum juice was boiled down. This image from the very early 1900s would have been typical from the 1860s onward. Sorghum syrup was the main sweetener in the diet of most Fannin residents. (Courtesy Louise Woody Wilson and Kimberly Wright.)

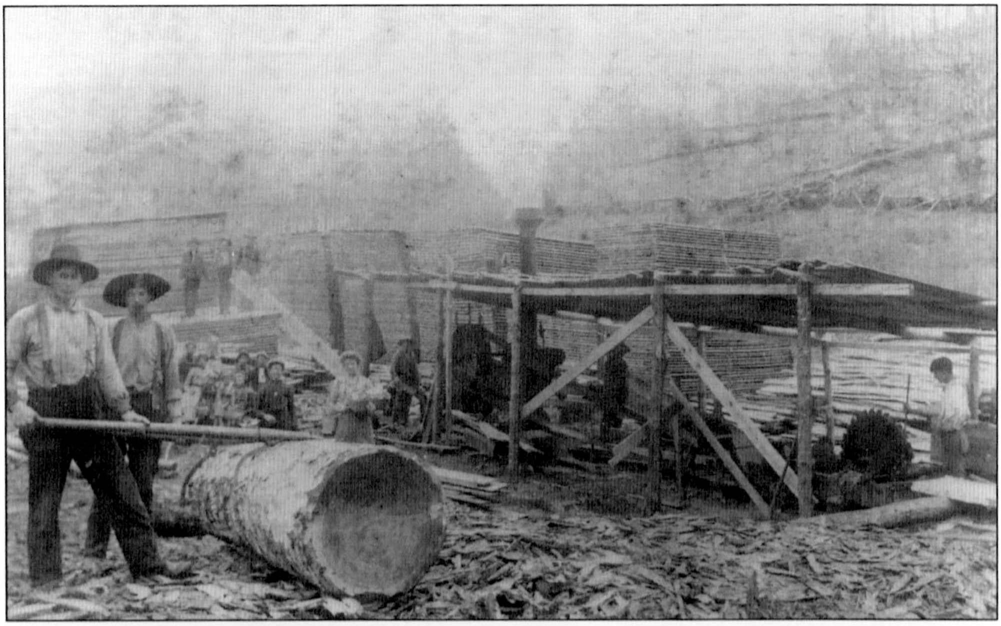

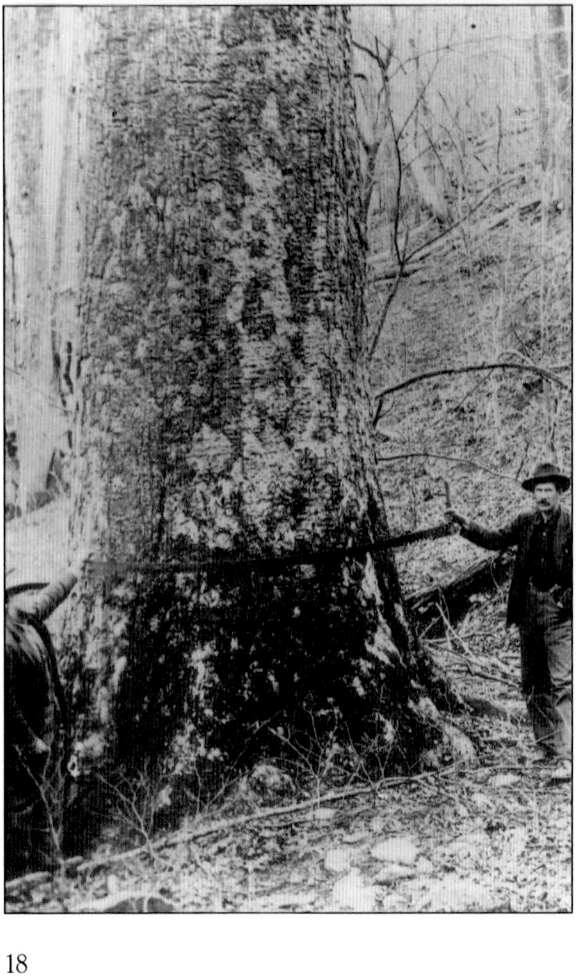

At the far right, in the sawpit, William L. Edmondson works at a steam-powered sawmill in Margret in the late 1800s. The other workers are unidentified. Many such mills operated, powered first by waterwheels and later by steam engines. After about 1925, electricity became available to run saws. Timbering was a major industry. Southern Appalachia was denuded of its virgin forests to feed the building boom "up north," following the Civil War. (Courtesy William "Bill" and Lucille Wenger via Betty Parker.)

Polk "Pokie" Edmondson and William L. Edmondson wield a crosscut saw to fell what appears to be a large American chestnut tree. These trees were prized for timber and for the bark that was used in the tanning industry. The dominant tree of Appalachian forests until the chestnut blight, this tree also provided abundant nuts that fed wildlife, free-range cattle and hogs, and people. (Courtesy Betty Parker.)

The advertisement for the patent medicine Vita-Ore recommended its purchase at a business run by local merchant George L. Godfrey. At far right, Godfrey's family poses for a formal portrait. In the center are G.L. and his wife, Martha German Godfrey. In back is their elder daughter, Rosa Lee Godfrey, who would later marry Samuel McKinney. In front is their younger daughter, Lillie. (Both courtesy Baugh House collection.)

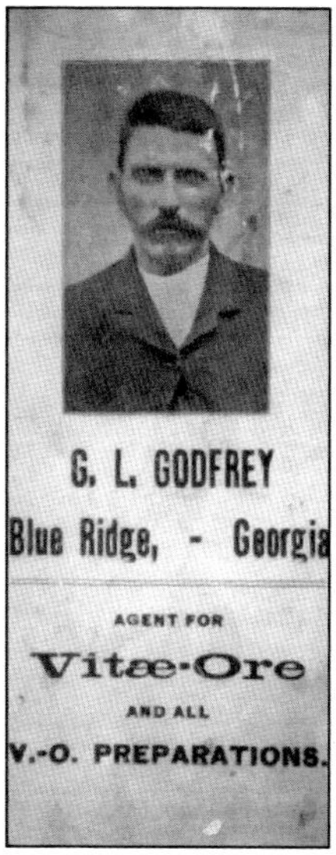

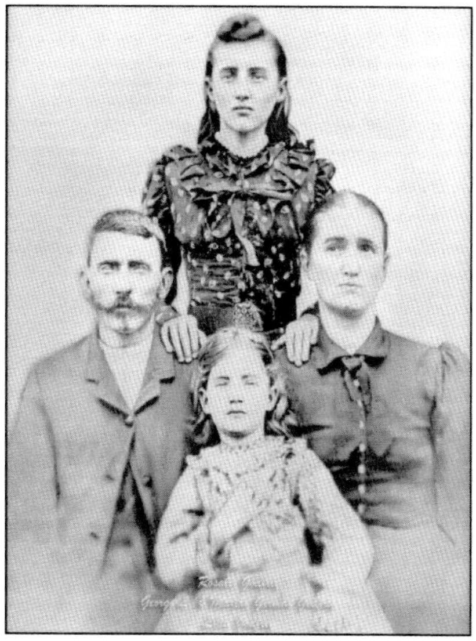

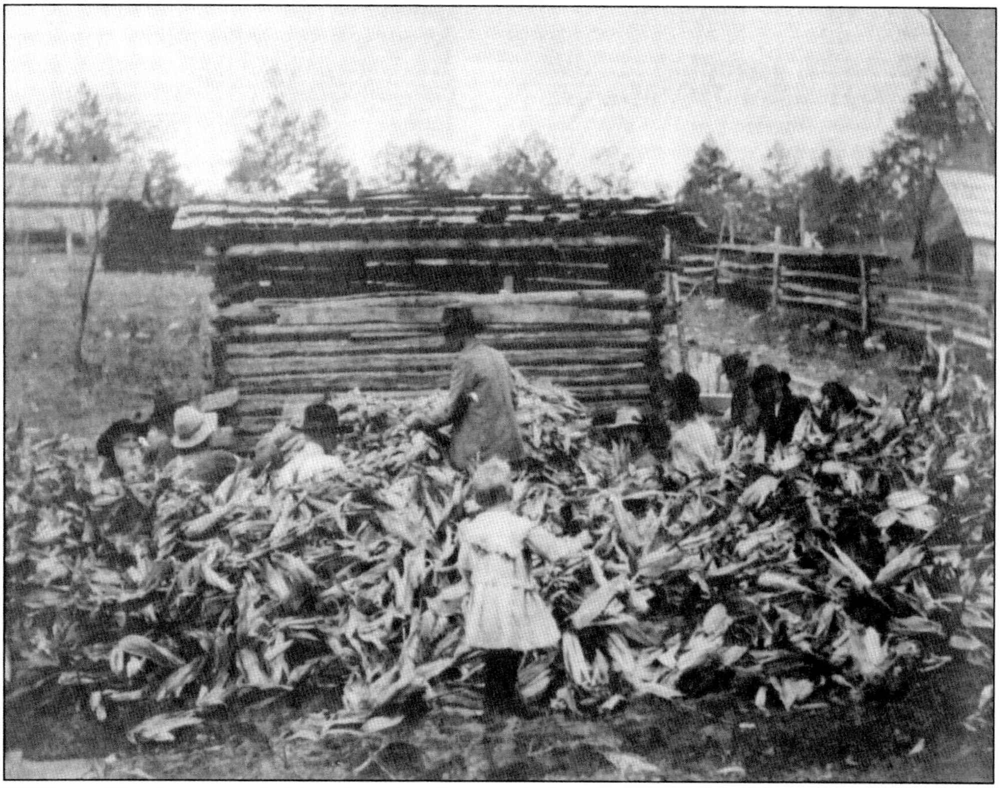

William Woody's extended family is hard at work shucking corn in this c. 1908 photograph. Similar scenes would have been enacted from the time of original settlement until the advent of mechanical harvesting combines in the last third of the 20th century. The only people known in this photograph are the following: William Woody (left) with a beard, Dallas M. Woody (fourth from the right) in the light hat, and Dallas's Ernest Woody (in the center with his back to the camera) wearing a dress. It was common for young children of both sexes to wear dresses until about age five. (Courtesy Louise Woody Wilson.)

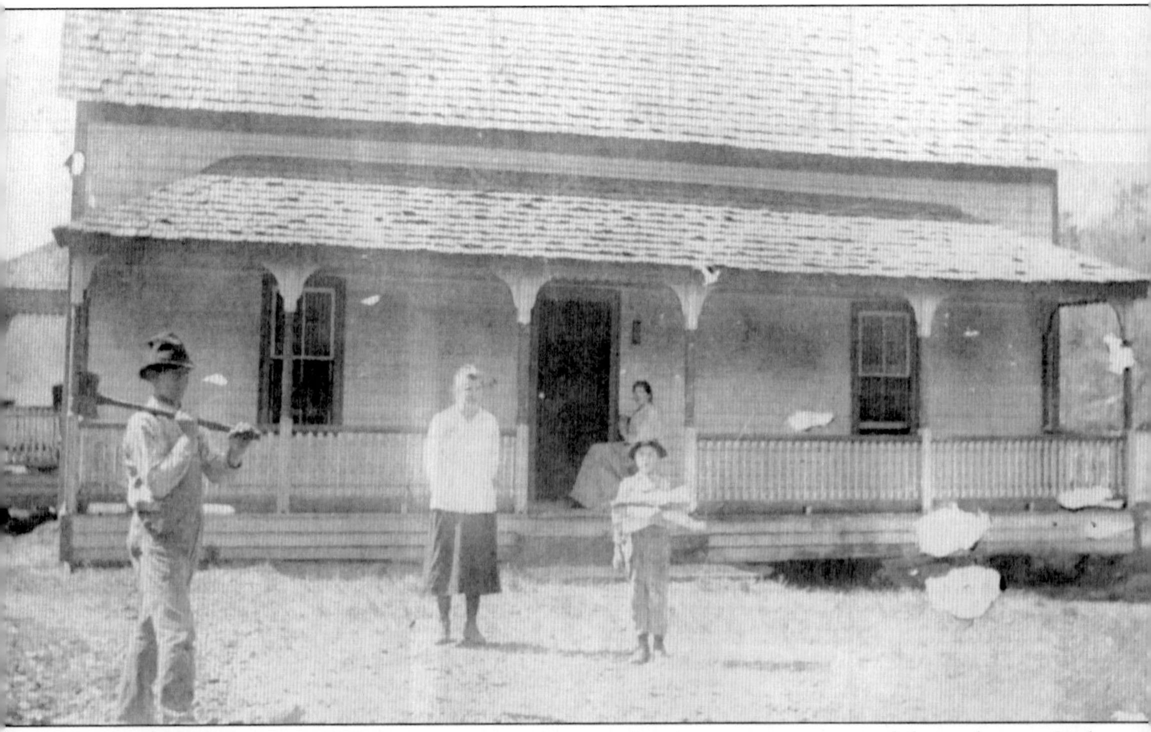

At their home near Hidgon's store, the Thomas family engages in typical farm chores. Carl Thomas (left) shoulders an axe. He may have just finished cutting firewood or chopping kindling. Essie Thomas is next to him in the white shirt. Fred Thomas (front right) carries an armload of firewood, while Callie Thomas sits on the porch. George and Lori Woodall later restored this house. (Courtesy George and Lori Woodall via the Baugh House collection.)

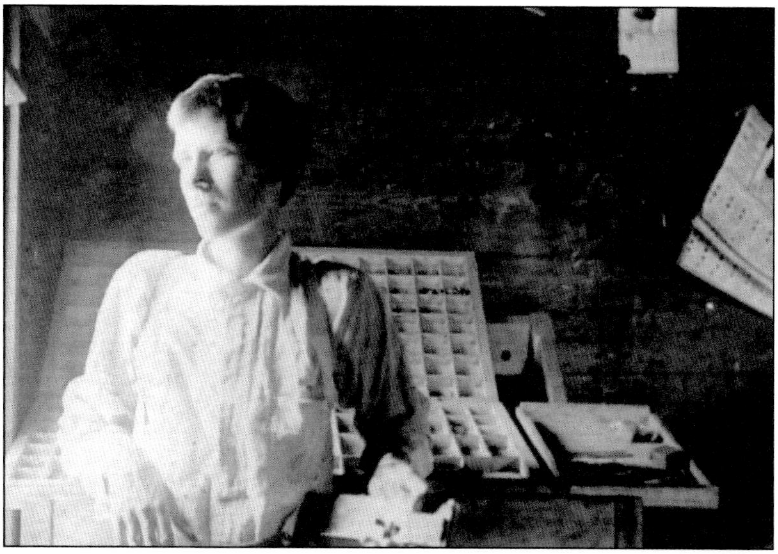

In his mother's kitchen, 12-year-old Luther Cobb takes a brief break from setting type at their home in Dooley, Union County, around 1903. He later moved a short distance to Fannin County and had a long career as a publisher and printer. (Courtesy Wilson and LaVerne Cobb.)

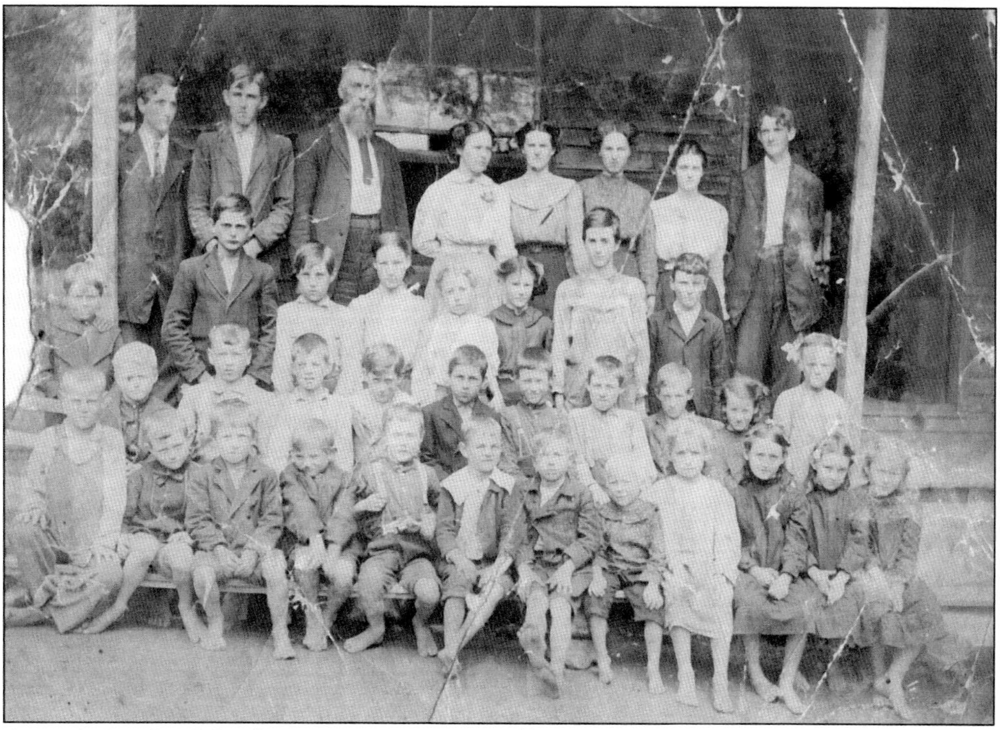

An early Sunday School group poses at Sugar Hill Baptist (also known as Salem No. 1) in the early 1900s. From left to right are (first row) Jim Wright, Ernest Shelton, Lester Shelton, Avery Walker, Tate Woody, Ernest Woody, Nelson Sisson, Boone Sisson, Stella Sisson, Ora Walker, Nellie Walker, and Mary Butt; (second row) Roscoe Woody, Ralph Wright, unidentified, Cliff Daves, Carl Shelton, Hunt Woody, Marvin Woody, Harrison Brawley, ? Brawley, and Ada Woody; (third row) Reed Woody, Milford Ricketts, Walt Shelton, ? Ricketts, Lizzie Sisson, Laurel Woody, Brian Hunt, and Clarence Gilreath; (fourth row) Ralph Daves, Ed Shelton, Adam Davenport, Myrtle Woody, Dovie Walker, Minnie Hunt, Arlene Walker, and Reed Daves. (Courtesy Louise Woody Wilson.)

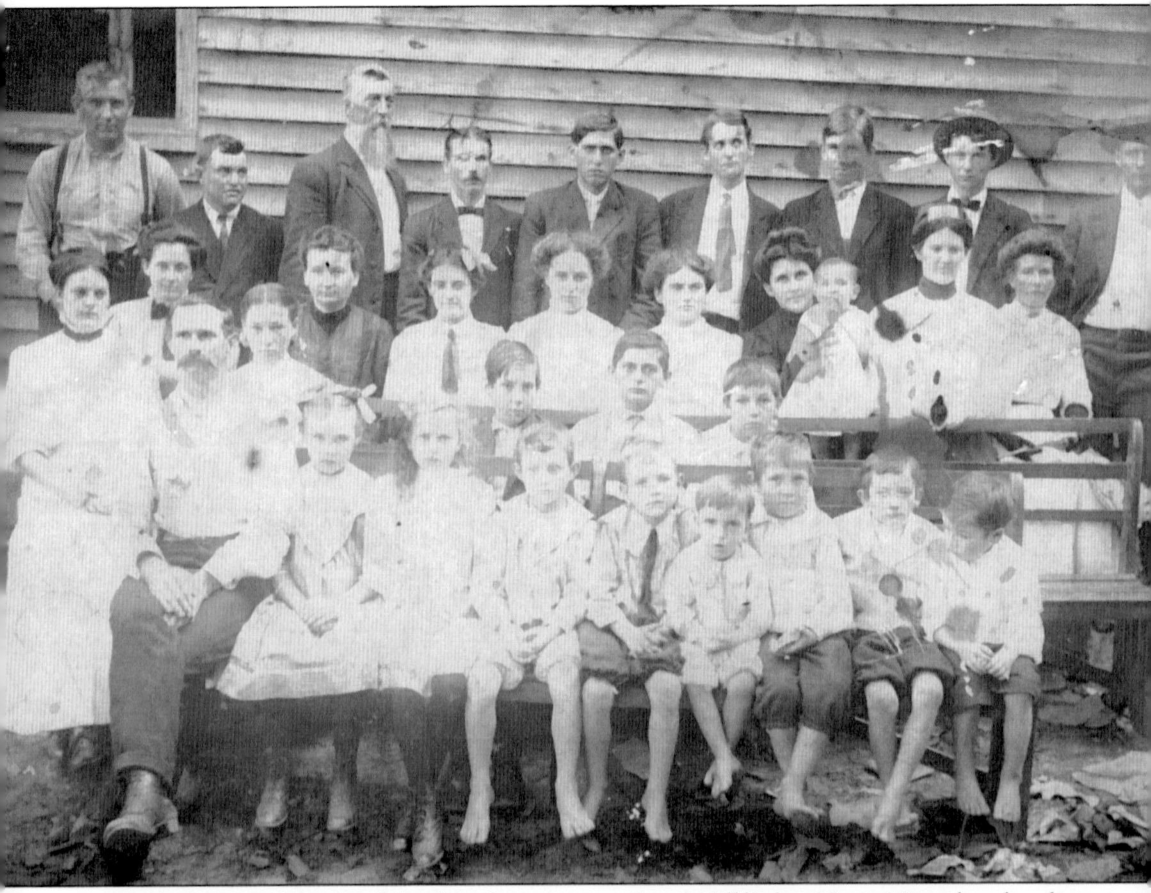

Another group of Sunday School students poses at Sugar Hill/Salem No. 1. Most churches from the mid-1800s through the mid-1920s housed community-based schools. With multiple grades in the same room, Pres. Abraham Lincoln termed this type of school a "blab school," since the students often recited different lessons at the same time. From left to right are (first row) D.M. Woody, Ada Woody, Velma Hunt, Cliff Daves, Ernest Woody, Carl Woody, Carl Shelton, Willie Olivet, and Ernest Olivet; (second row) unidentified, Walt Shelton, Milford Ricketts, and Marvin Woody; (third Row) Della Walker, Louanna Walker, Denie Woody, Irlene Walker, Minnie Hunt, Deshia Woody Seabolt, Mamie Woody Ellis, Dodie Walker, and Sara Ann Sisson; (fourth row) George Shelton, ? Rogers, Adam Davenport, John Olivet, Esburn Seabolt, Reed Daves, Edd Shelton, ? Bramlett, and unidentified. (Courtesy Louise Woody Wilson.)

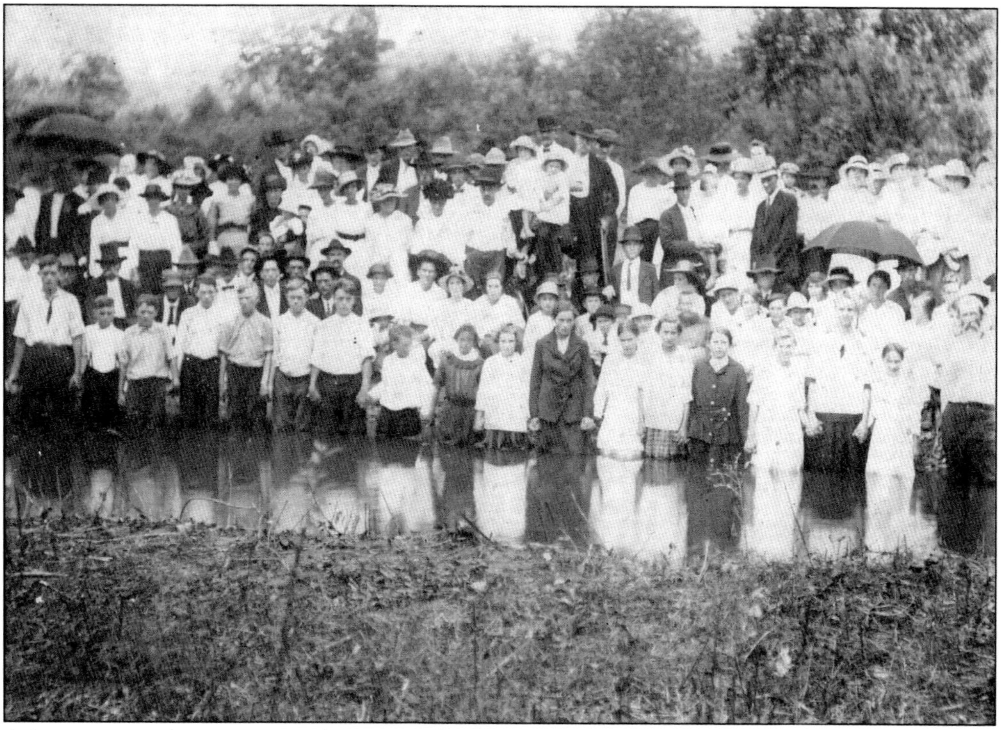

A large group of new converts has stepped into the baptismal waters of Skeenah Mill pond between 1900 and 1905. This pond, located across Skeenah Gap road from Sugar Hill/Salem No. 1 Baptist Church, was convenient to summer revivals, when many new church members were acquired. This mill is one of the oldest in the county and still survives as a tourist campground in the second decade of the 21st century. (Courtesy Louise Woody Wilson.)

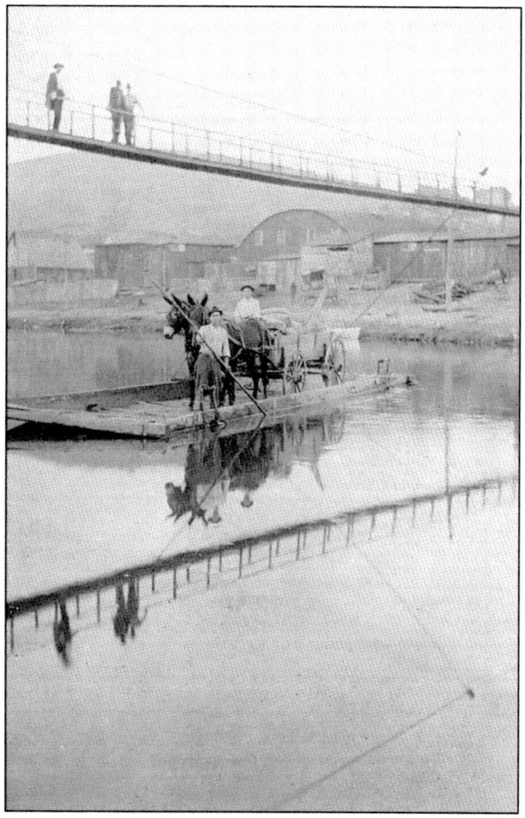

While on the high, narrow footbridge, men walk to work from McCaysville, Georgia, to the smelting and mining operations in Copperhill, Tennessee, the ferry crosses in the opposite direction carrying a team, driver, and wagon. To the right in this image, the end point of the ferry crossing was located at the end of Ferry Street in Copperhill, where, in 2011, the Copperhill Police Department offices were one block behind the New York Restaurant. (Courtesy Ron Henry family.)

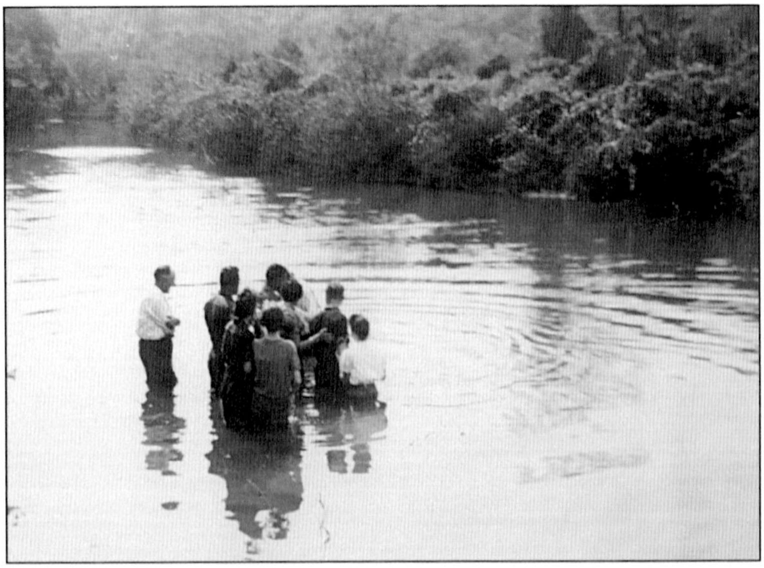

Another group of converts gather at the river for a baptism service. This is probably in the Toccoa River near McCaysville or perhaps in either Hemptown Creek or Hothouse Creek. (Courtesy Ron Henry family.)

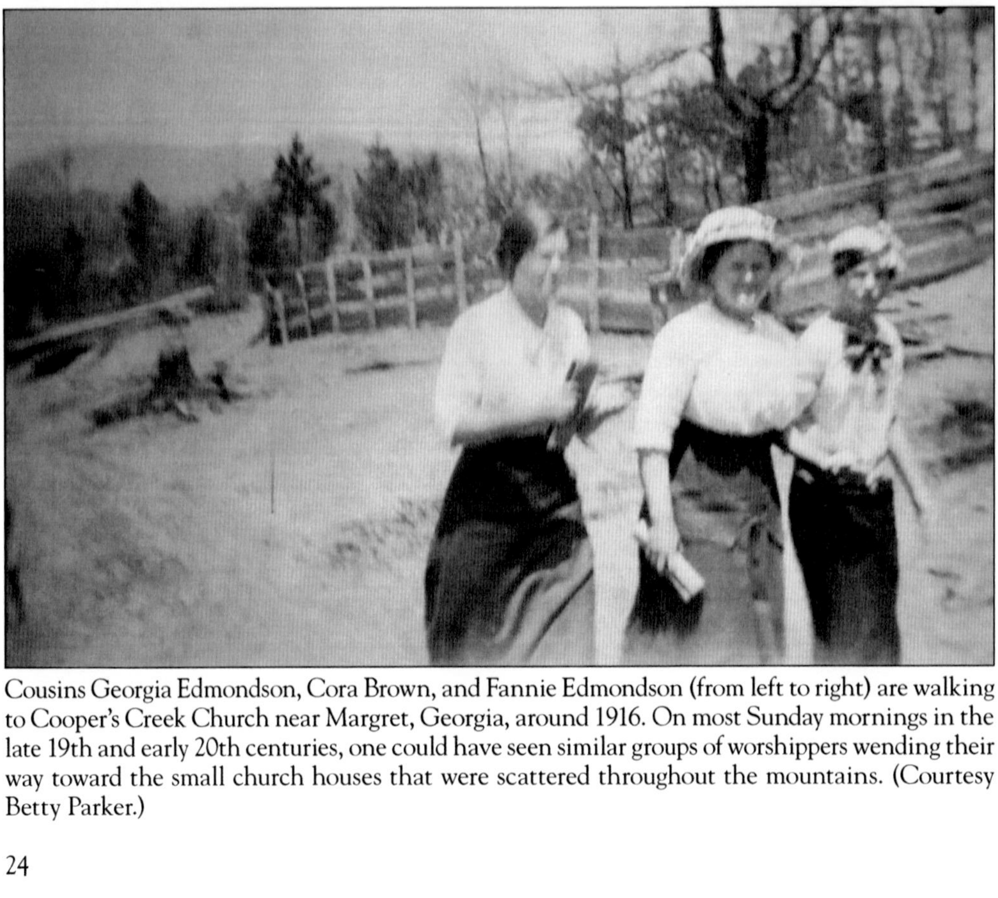

Cousins Georgia Edmondson, Cora Brown, and Fannie Edmondson (from left to right) are walking to Cooper's Creek Church near Margret, Georgia, around 1916. On most Sunday mornings in the late 19th and early 20th centuries, one could have seen similar groups of worshippers wending their way toward the small church houses that were scattered throughout the mountains. (Courtesy Betty Parker.)

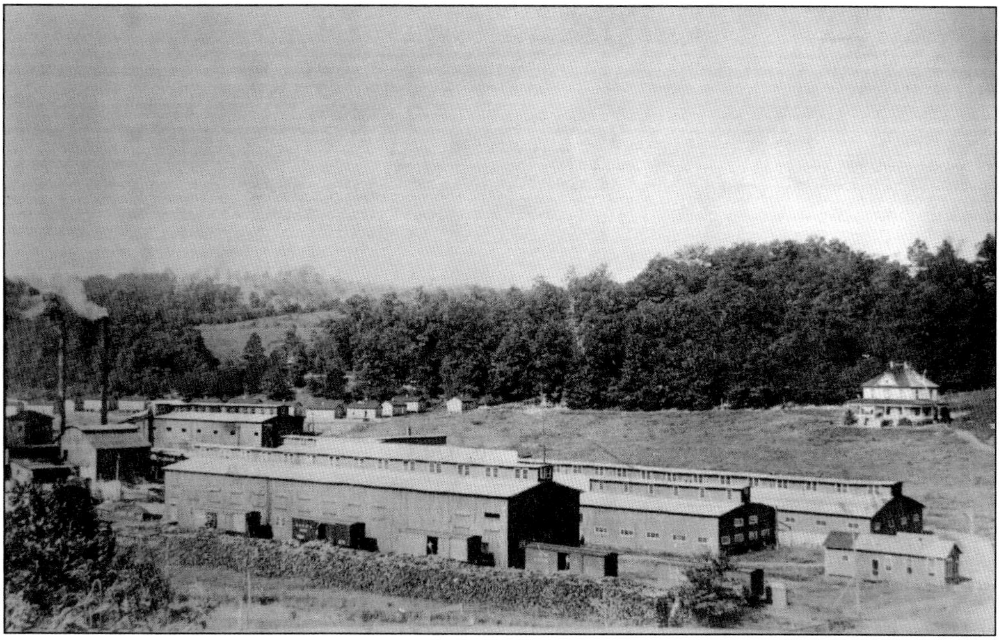

The Mineral Bluff Tannery, which operated before World War I, was one of several industries in the town. The Baugh family operated brickworks, while mica and other minerals were mined nearby. A large apple tree nursery was the first commercial application of apple-related agriculture in the county. Note that boxcars (center) are on the siding adjacent to the main building, and cordwood is stacked near the same siding. (Courtesy Georgia Archives, Vanishing Georgia Collection, image fan011-83.)

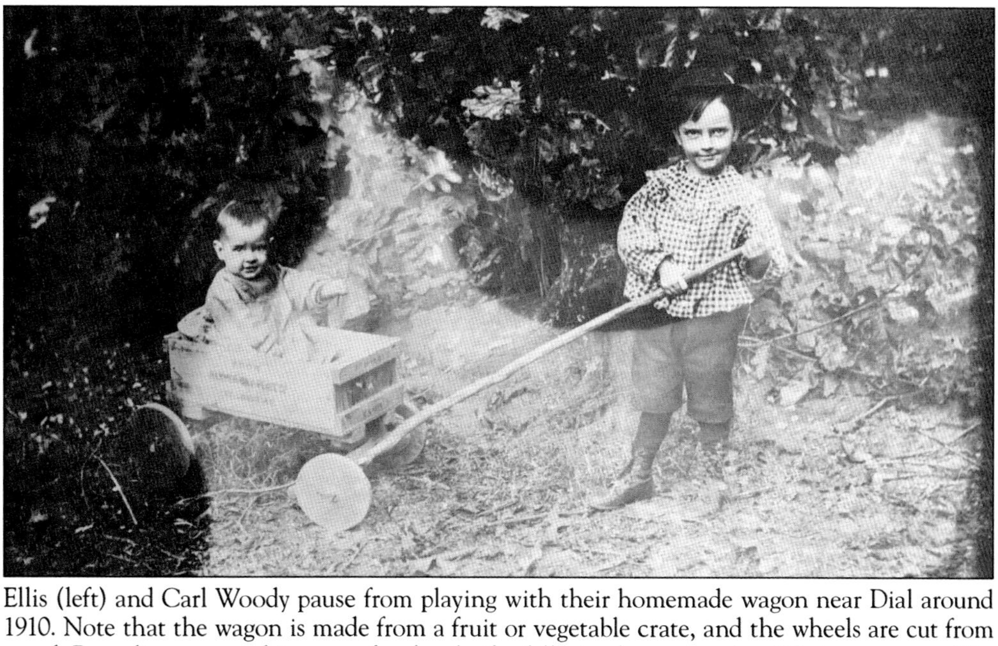

Ellis (left) and Carl Woody pause from playing with their homemade wagon near Dial around 1910. Note that the wagon is made from a fruit or vegetable crate, and the wheels are cut from wood. Recycling was nothing new for the thrifty folks in the mountains. Their motto was "fix it up, wear it out, make do or do without." (Courtesy Georgia Archives, Vanishing Georgia Collection, image fan-005.)

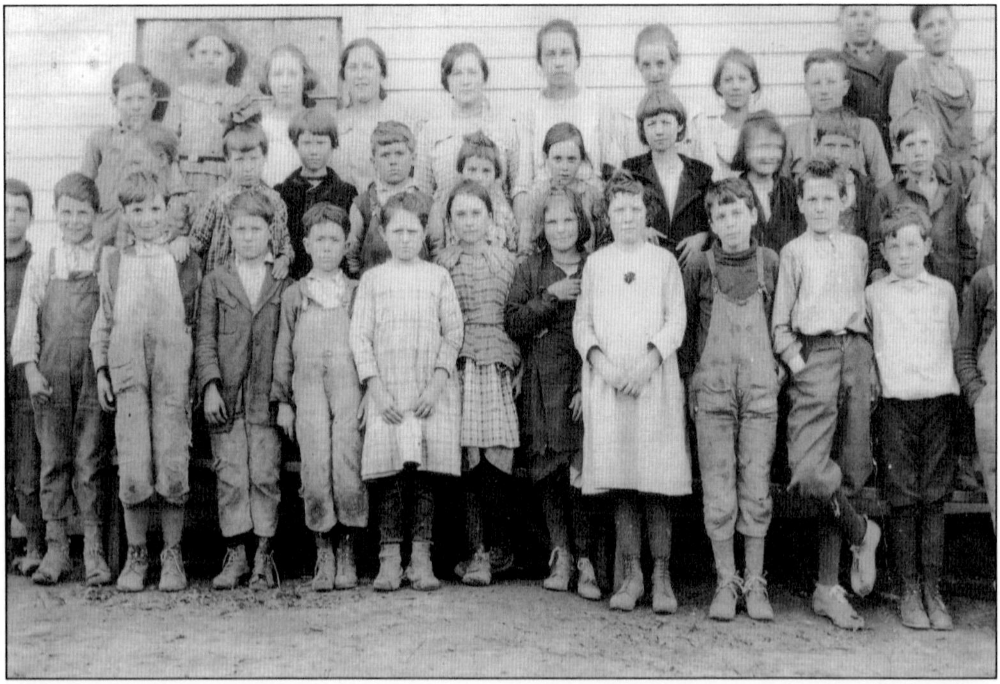

Students line up outside Lebanon School. From left to right are (first row) unidentified, Grady Housley, Otis Patterson, four unidentified, Elvie Russell, Vinnie Campbell, unidentified, Lester Housley, unidentified, and Jessie Campbell; (second row) unidentified, Juanita Davis, ? Dunn, two unidentified, Annie Patterson, Elvana Rose, Vinnie Russell, and three unidentified; (third row) two unidentified, Laura Abernathy, Janie Abernathy, Jennie Abernathy, Nellie Hayes, Edith Patterson, Ina Patterson, Luther Patterson, Claude Patterson, and Vernie Patterson. (Courtesy Baugh House collection.)

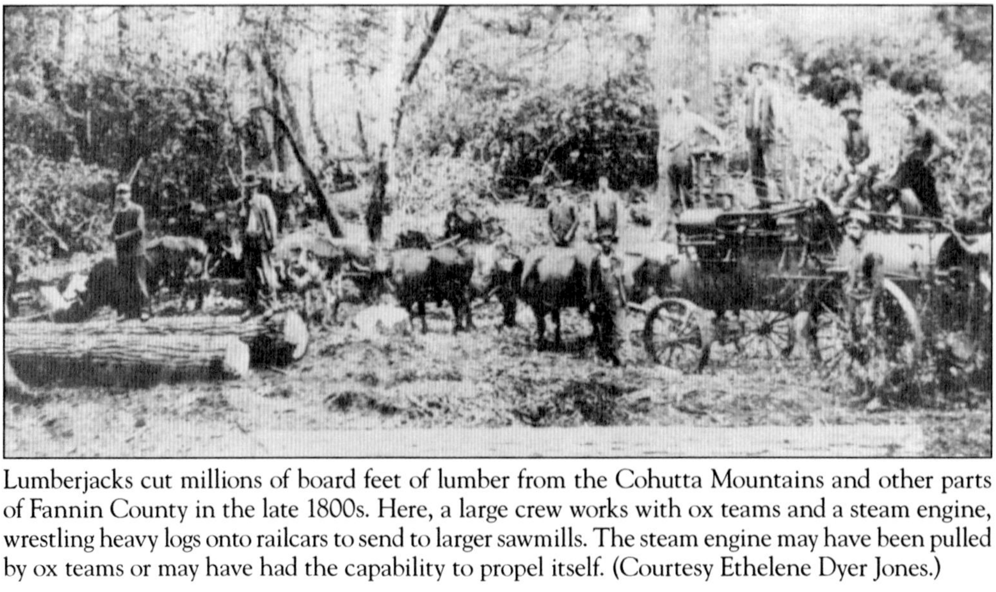

Lumberjacks cut millions of board feet of lumber from the Cohutta Mountains and other parts of Fannin County in the late 1800s. Here, a large crew works with ox teams and a steam engine, wrestling heavy logs onto railcars to send to larger sawmills. The steam engine may have been pulled by ox teams or may have had the capability to propel itself. (Courtesy Ethelene Dyer Jones.)

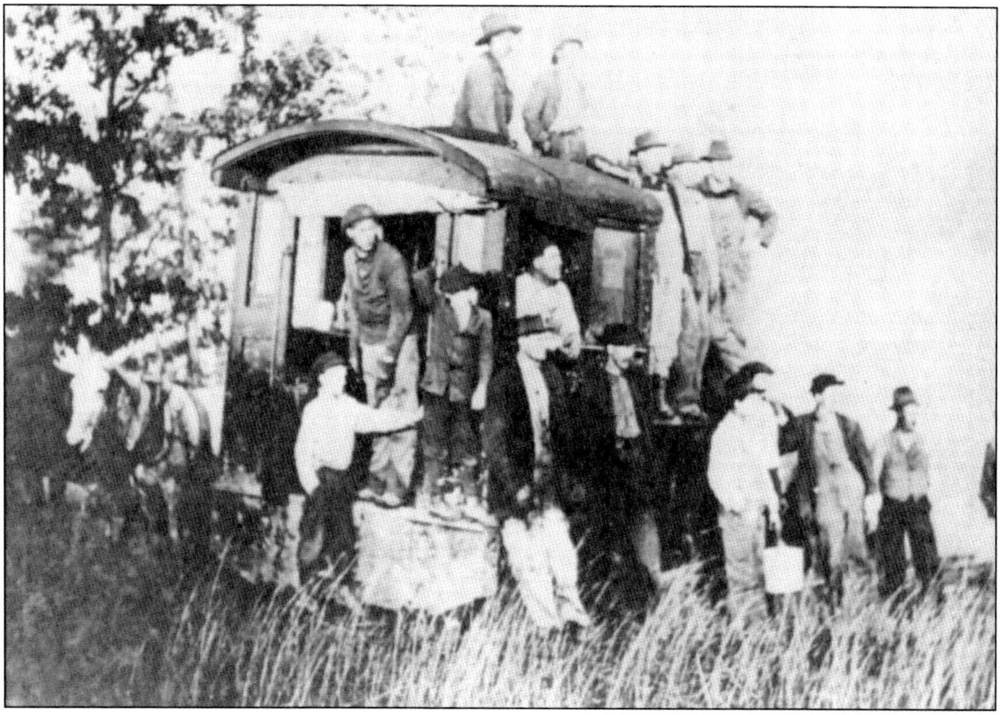

This engine worked the temporary rail lines that snaked into the Cohuttas to bring out logs from timber operations. Once the large trees had been topped, felled, and stripped of their limbs, ox teams would drag them along temporary "skid roads" to where they could be loaded onto flatcars. (Courtesy Ethelene Dyer Jones.)

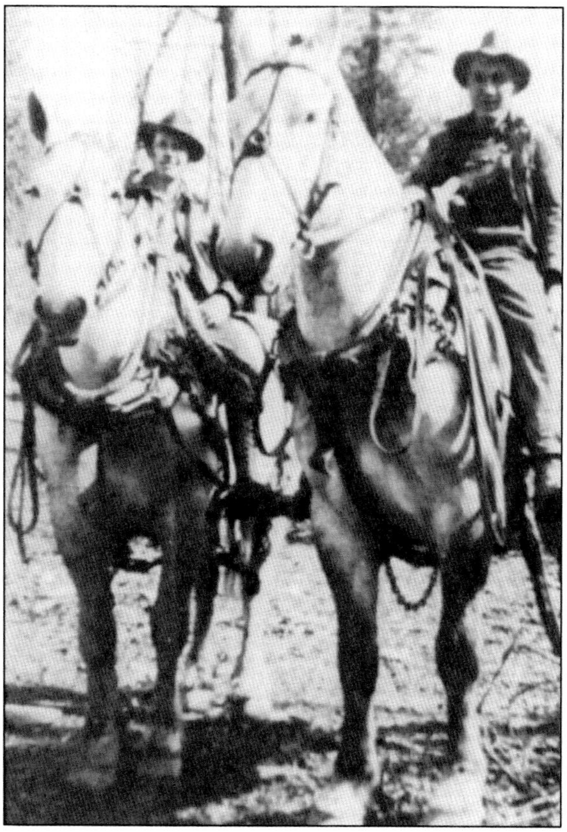

Heavy draft horses were also used extensively in lumber operations in western Fannin County. After timber operations ceased, very little virgin forest remained in Fannin County. The ecology changed drastically as species such as the Eastern timber wolf and whitetail deer were wiped out. (Courtesy Ethelene Dyer Jones.)

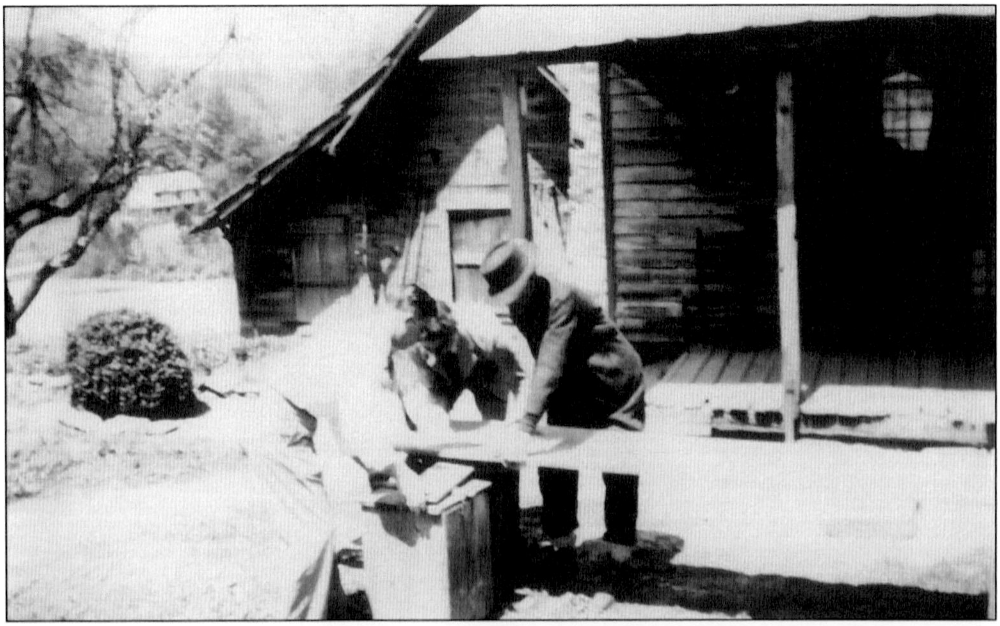

Don Edmondson (left) in the white shirt and Allen Edmondson (right), wearing a hat, seem to be either laying out plans or preparing to saw some boards. The person in the center of the trio is unidentified. (Courtesy Betty Parker.)

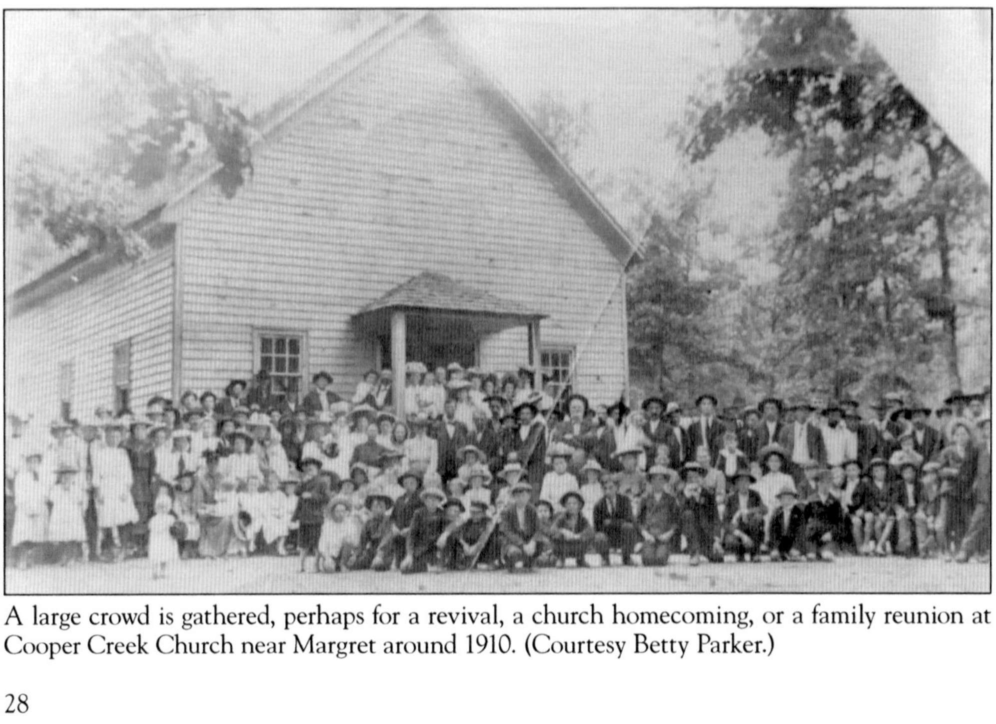

A large crowd is gathered, perhaps for a revival, a church homecoming, or a family reunion at Cooper Creek Church near Margret around 1910. (Courtesy Betty Parker.)

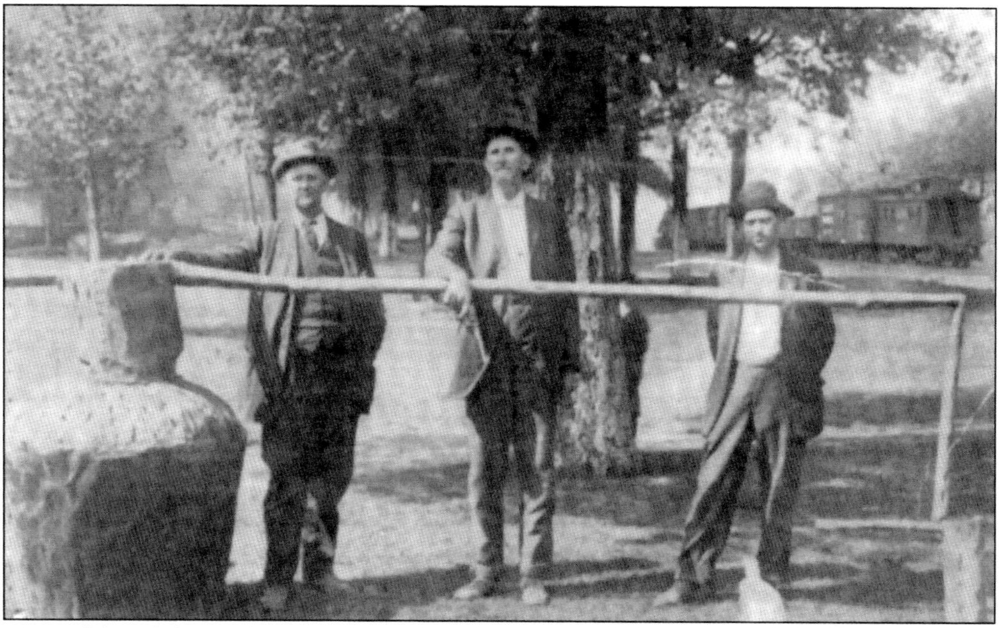

Pictured from left to right, in 1910, Charlie Stewart, Sheriff Bill Lovingood, and Joe Brown Kincaid display a captured whiskey still in the city park in front of the courthouse. Note that railcars are visible in the background. During reconstruction, farmers made whiskey as a cash crop, since the distilled spirits were much more easily transported than bulk corn. This brought them into conflict with the federal tax authorities and local law enforcement. (Courtesy Baugh House collection.)

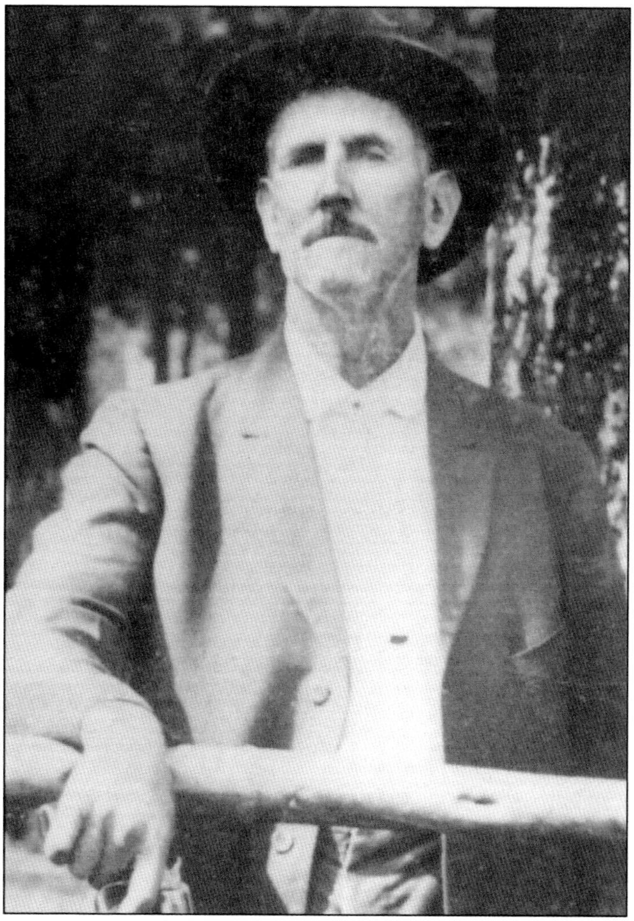

This image shows Sheriff Lovingood casually holding his pistol. He was called "the last Democrat sheriff" of Fannin County. A legend holds that he once rode his horse into the main courtroom to make a point. No record remains as to whether the judge or jury was duly impressed. (Courtesy Baugh House collection.)

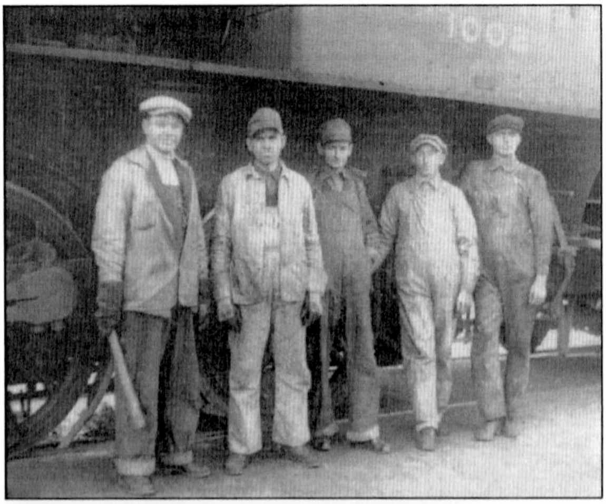

In this photograph, from left to right, flagman Jack Walker, brakeman ? Jenkins, conductor Jule Adams, engineer John Kellar, and fireman Sam Nix get ready for work on a train in front of the Blue Ridge depot in 1926 or 1927. Such sights would have been common in Blue Ridge for the previous 40 years. (Courtesy Baugh House collection.)

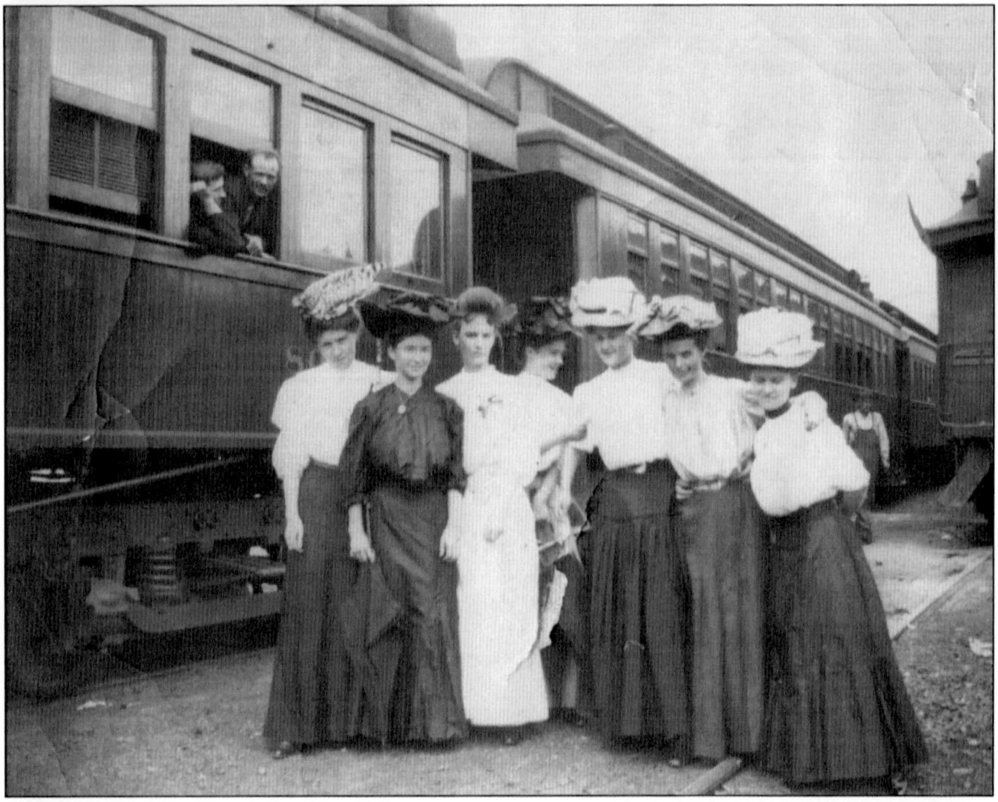

While admirers look on from the passenger car window, a group of women pose at Blue Ridge depot around 1910. The railroad came to Fannin County in the mid-1880s, largely at the instigation of "Colonel" Mike McKinney. Grade was prepared from Ellijay in 1885. The tracks reached the present site of Blue Ridge by 1886. Temporarily blocked in a plan to proceed through Mineral Bluff to Murphy, North Carolina, rising copper prices caused the railroad planners to extend the line down the valley of the Toccoa through Copperhill and eventually on to Knoxville. The city of Blue Ridge was founded and boomed in the 1890s during the "decade of the railroad." Machine shops and a roundhouse maintained the equipment on what was the shortest rail route from Atlanta to Knoxville at the time. (Courtesy Michael Eaton.)

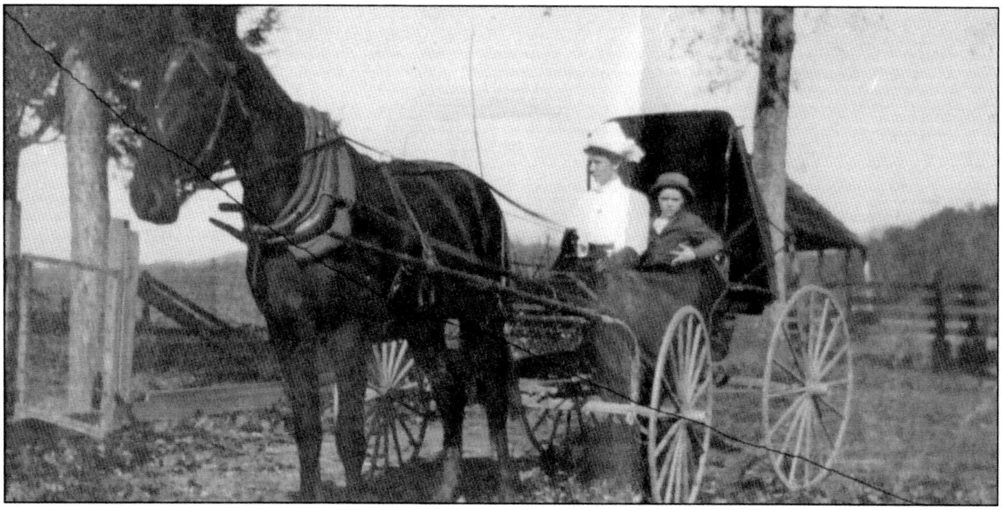

Pictured here around 1910, Ella Lloyd, wearing a flowered hat, and an unidentified passenger look very fashionable as they drive around Blue Ridge in a buggy with a retractable roof. (Courtesy Michael Eaton.)

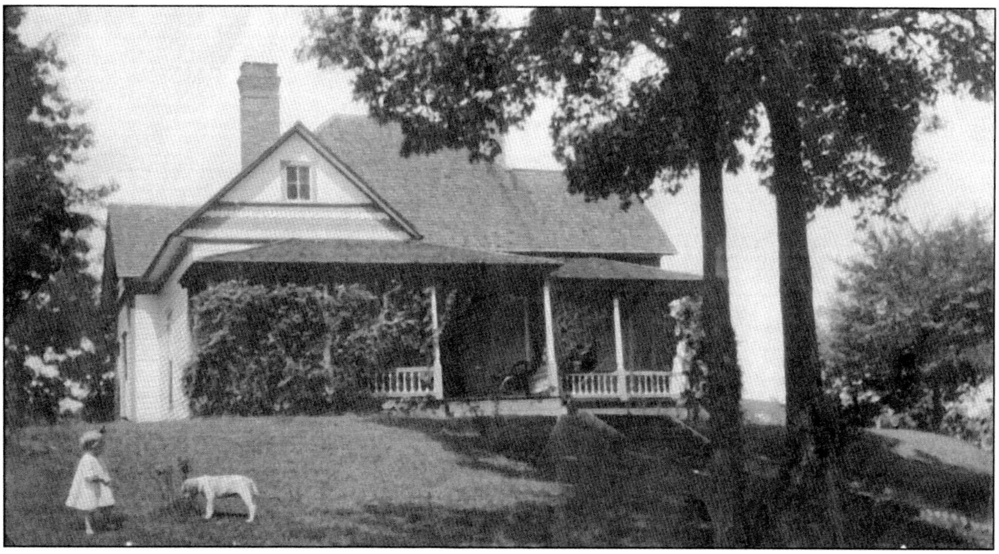

A child plays with a dog in the yard of the Lloyd house, located on the hill behind the courthouse around 1909. (Courtesy Michael Eaton.)

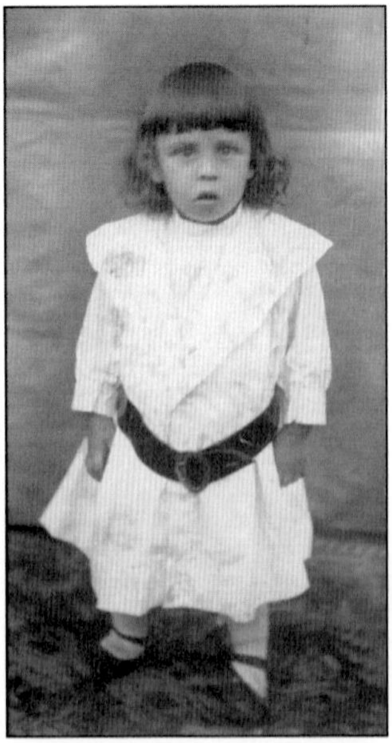

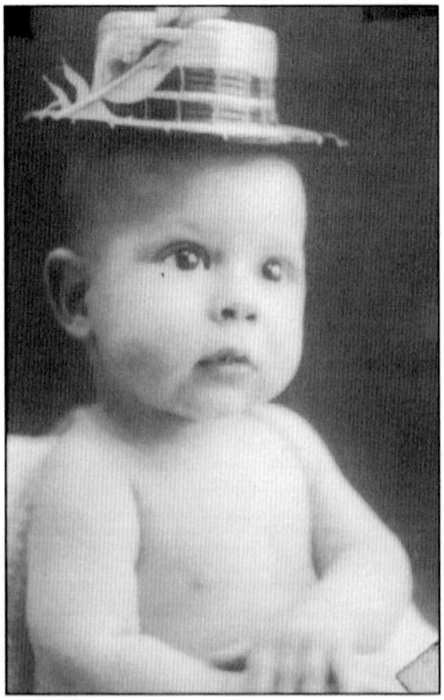

Pictured at far left around 1914, Joseph Milton Eaton Jr. (later known as J.M.) is still wearing petticoats at about age four. According to the custom of the time, he would not get his first long pants until about age five. Apparently, parents in every era delight in taking pictures that will embarrass their children. In the 1912 image at left, the baby is possibly Jack Lloyd or Eva Mae Lloyd. (Both courtesy Michael Eaton.)

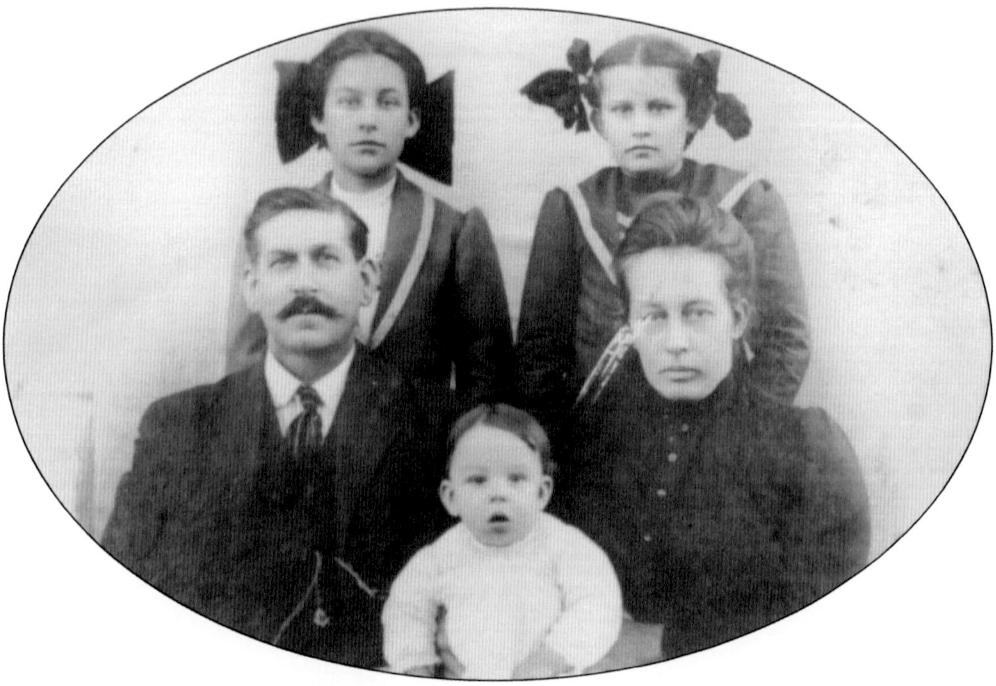

Baby J.M. Eaton Jr. is front and center in this c. 1910 family portrait. His father, Joseph Milton Sr., founded the Fannin County Bank in 1916, and J.M. Jr. later served as its president until 1986. On the right is Mattie Leigh Eaton. Her two older daughters (unidentified) stand in back. (Courtesy Michael Eaton.)

Cassius Gudger "C.G." Lloyd had this portrait made in 1903. He earned his pharmacist's license the following year and soon became proprietor of the Blue Ridge Pharmacy. (Courtesy Michael Eaton.)

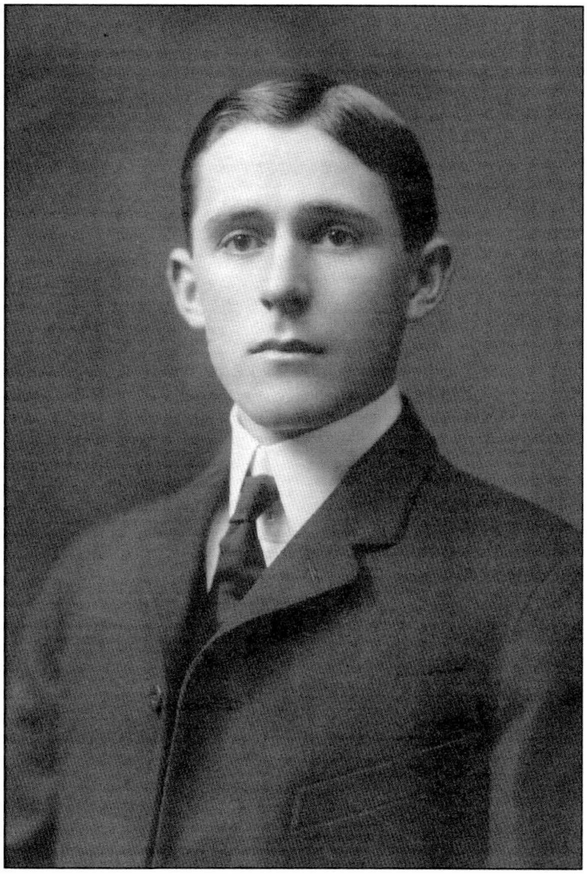

C.G. Lloyd stands at the left in this interior view of Blue Ridge Pharmacy. Eva Mae Lloyd Mashburn stands by a glass display case; the gentlemen are unidentified. (Courtesy Michael Eaton.)

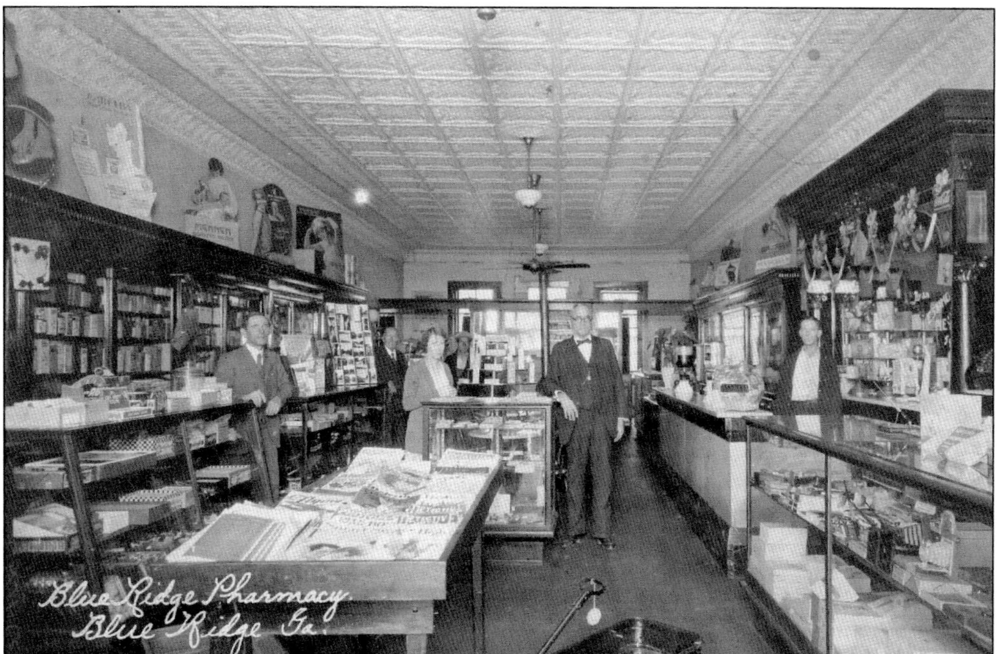

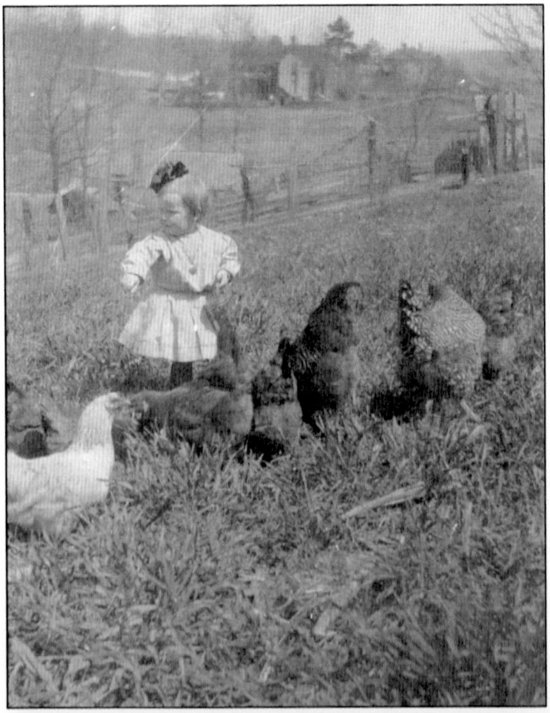

Eva Mae Lloyd tends the family chickens around 1911. (Courtesy Michael Eaton.)

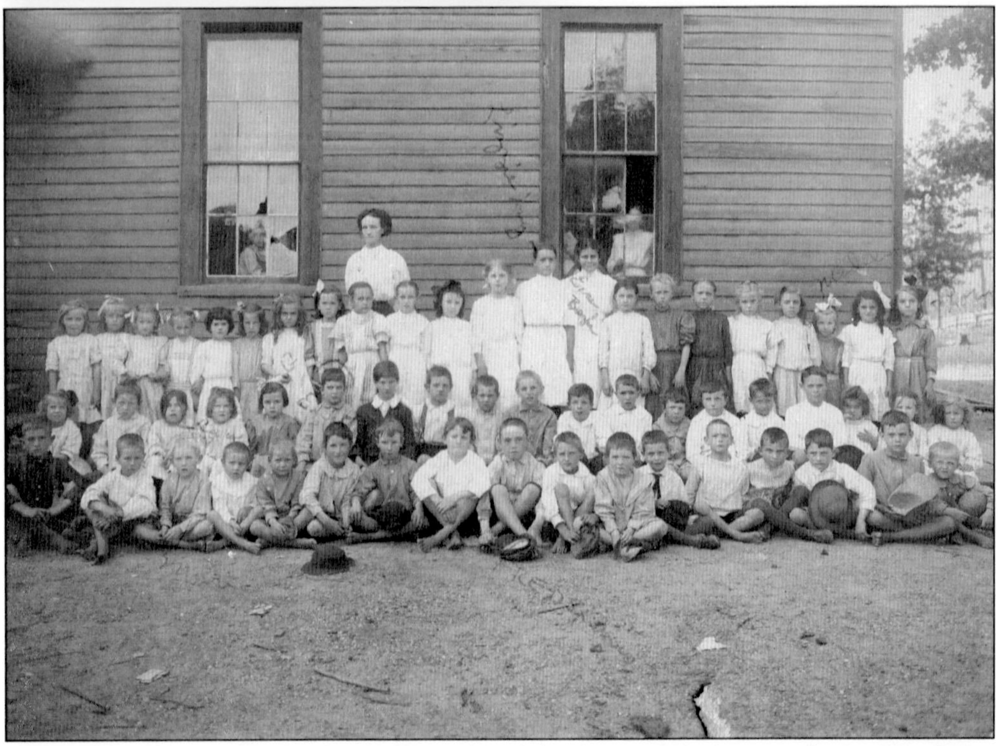

By the time these teachers and students gathered for this c. 1919 photograph, the Blue Ridge school building was showing some signs of wear. Note the broken pane in the right window. (Courtesy Michael Eaton.)

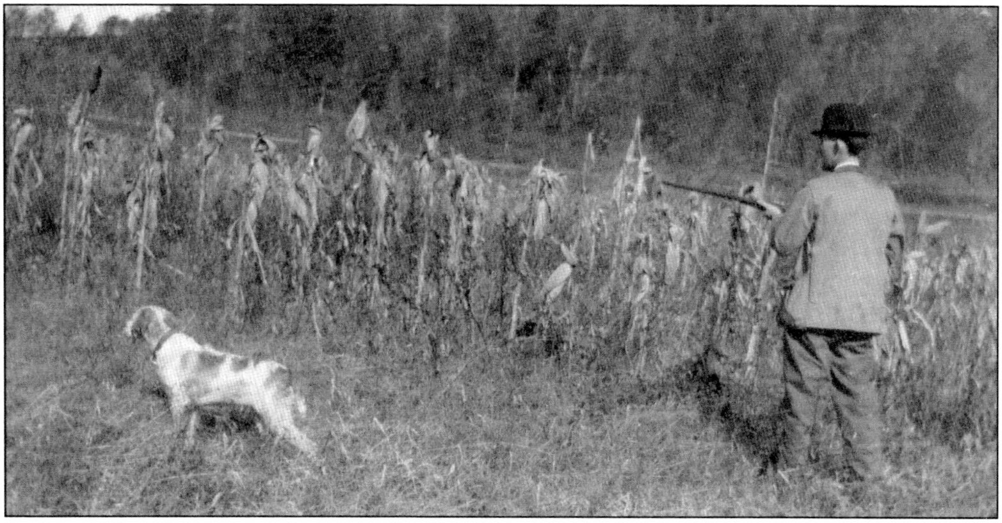

In this early 1900s image, C.G. Lloyd and his dog pose a clear and present danger to any game in the corn patch along the railroad tracks. (Courtesy Michael Eaton.)

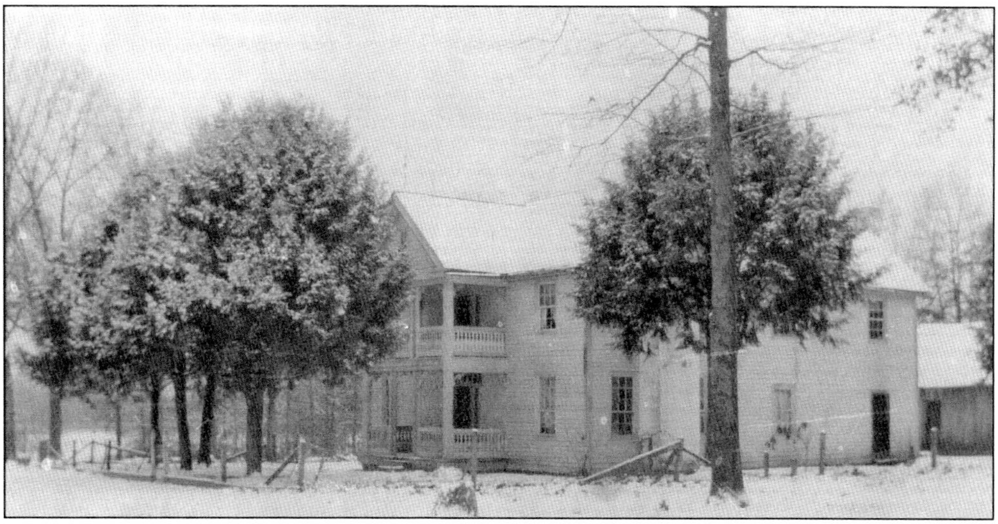

In the early 1900s, C.G. Lloyd's home presented a beautiful facade, especially when the evergreens were dressed with snow. (Courtesy Michael Eaton.)

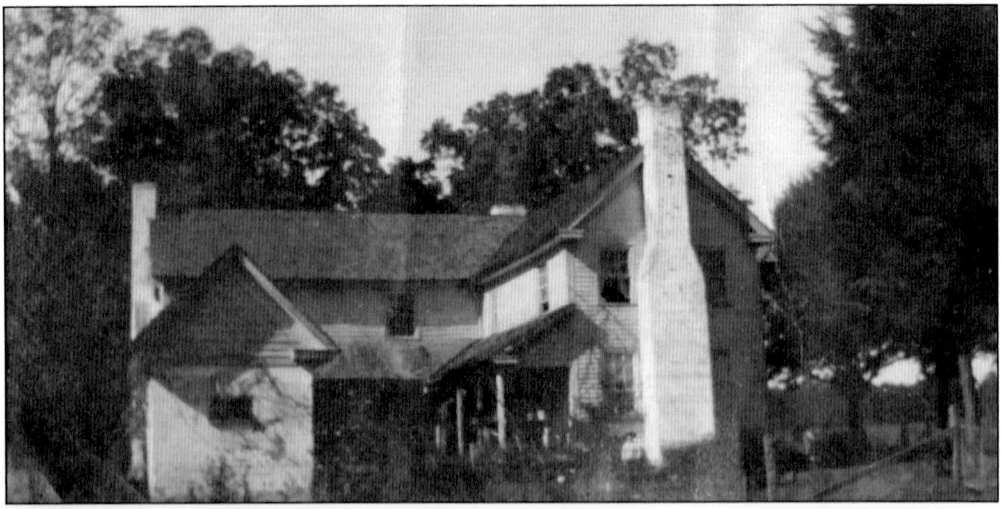

Even the back of C.G. Lloyd's home was impressive. The home stood on the current location of St. Anthony's Catholic Church. (Courtesy Michael Eaton.)

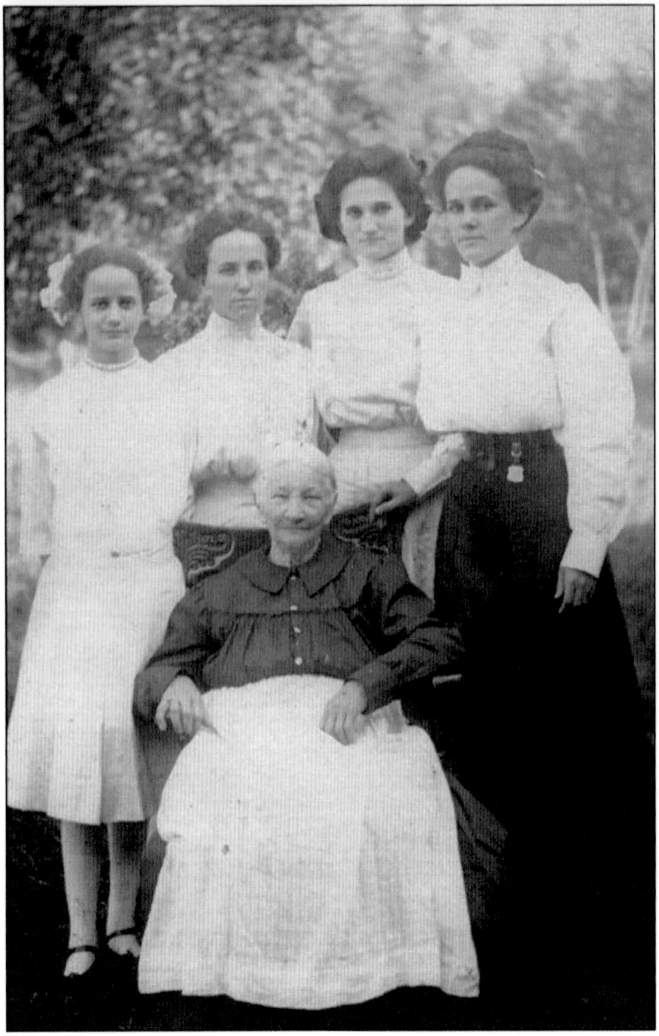

Nancy Woody Daves, born in 1828, is flanked in this 1910 photograph by her granddaughters (from left to right) Winnie, Nannie, Elizabeth, and Minnie Lee. (Courtesy Louise Woody Wilson.)

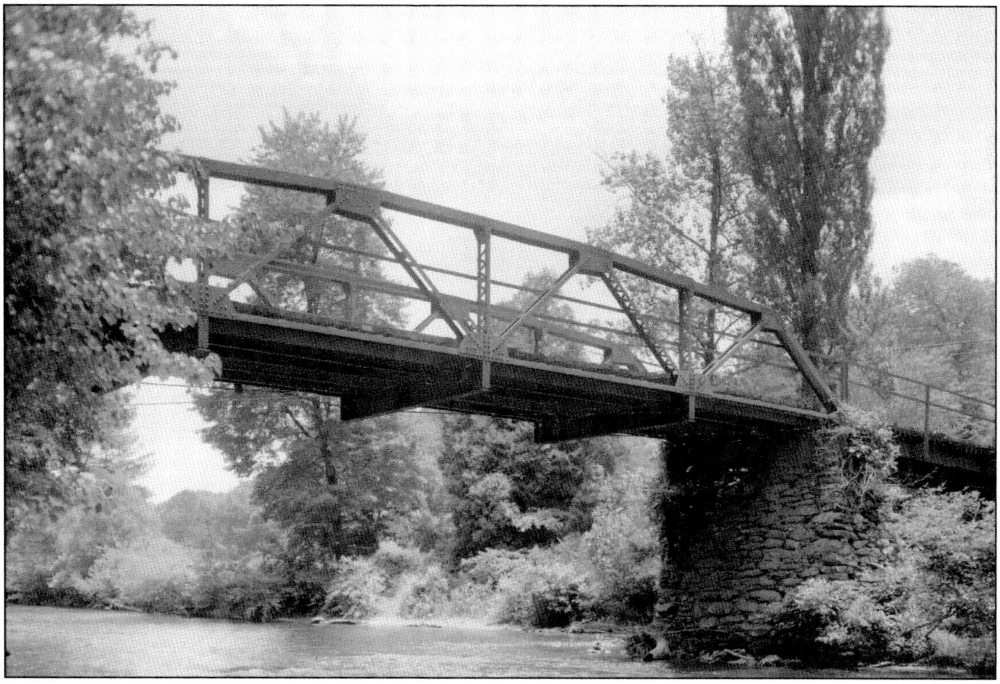

In the early 20th century, Fannin County began to replace wooden bridges with steel structures. This bridge crossed the Toccoa River in Dial near Van Zandt's store. (Courtesy Library of Congress.)

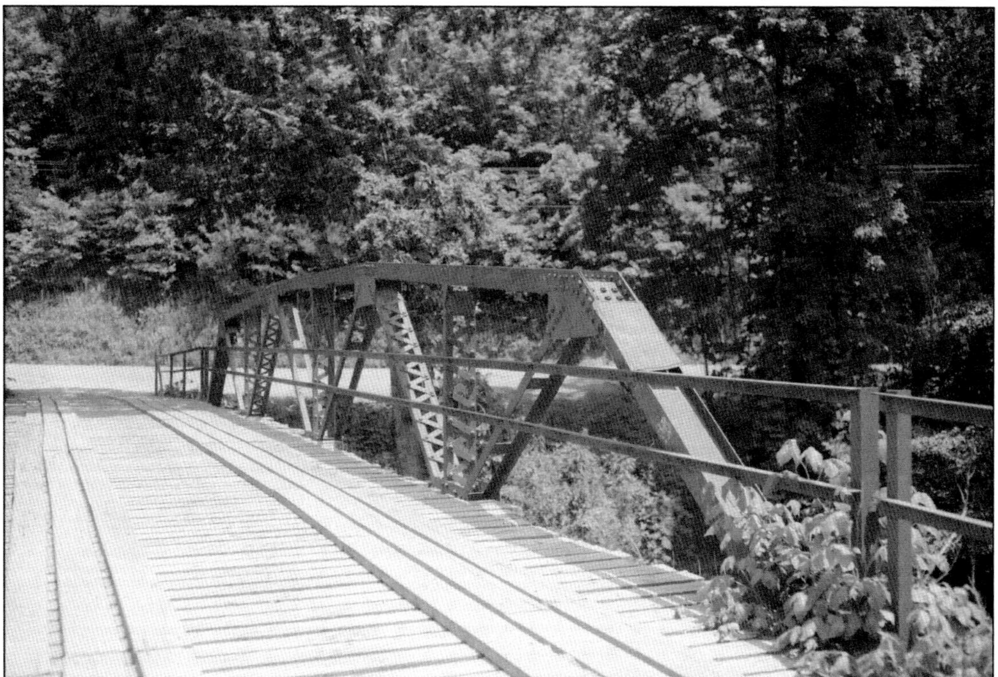

Here is another view of the Toccoa River Bridge in Dial. Twisted metal and a few rotting boards are all that remain of this structure in 2011. Similar ruins stand downstream of the concrete bridge over the Toccoa at Curtis Switch Road. (Courtesy Library of Congress.)

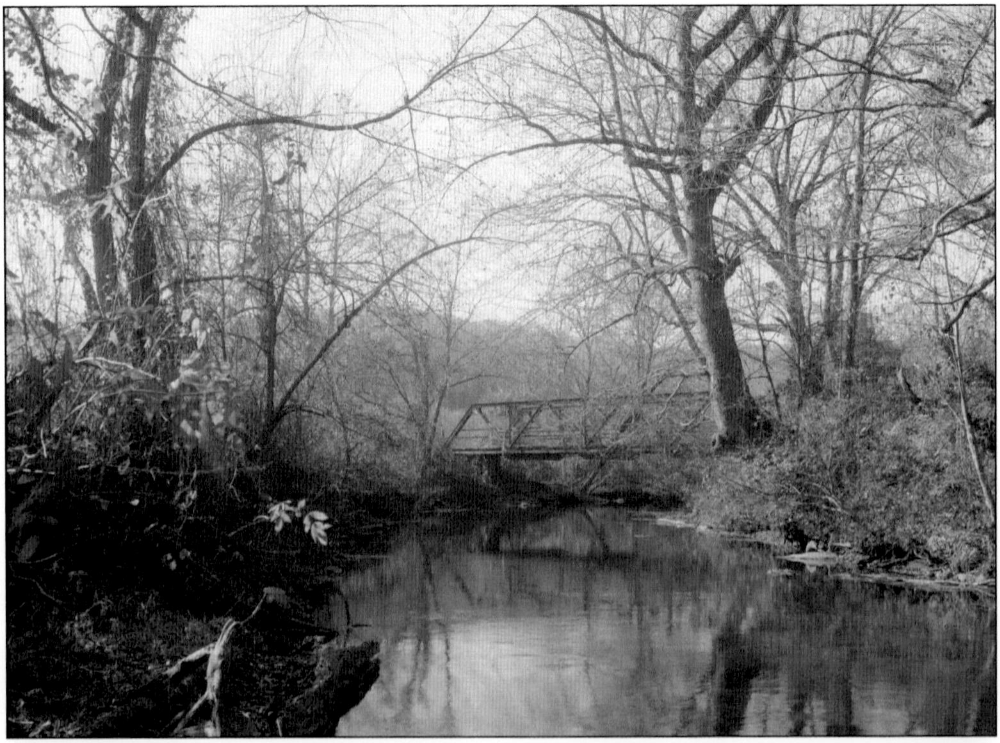

County Road 218 crossed Noontootla Creek via this bridge. (Courtesy of Library of Congress.)

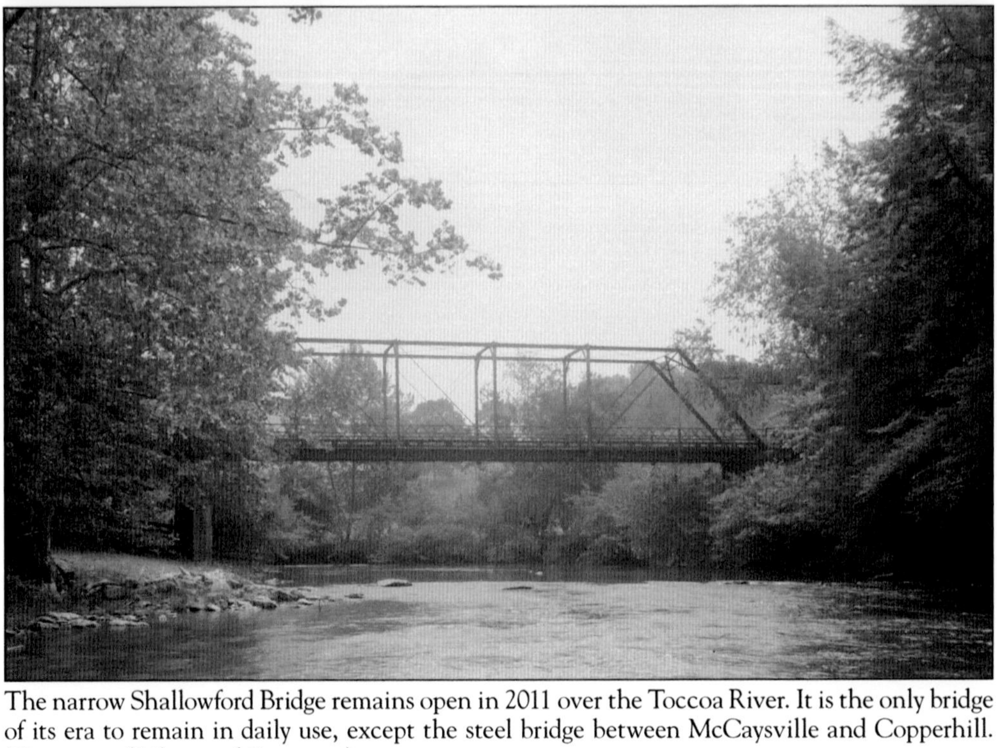

The narrow Shallowford Bridge remains open in 2011 over the Toccoa River. It is the only bridge of its era to remain in daily use, except the steel bridge between McCaysville and Copperhill. (Courtesy of Library of Congress.)

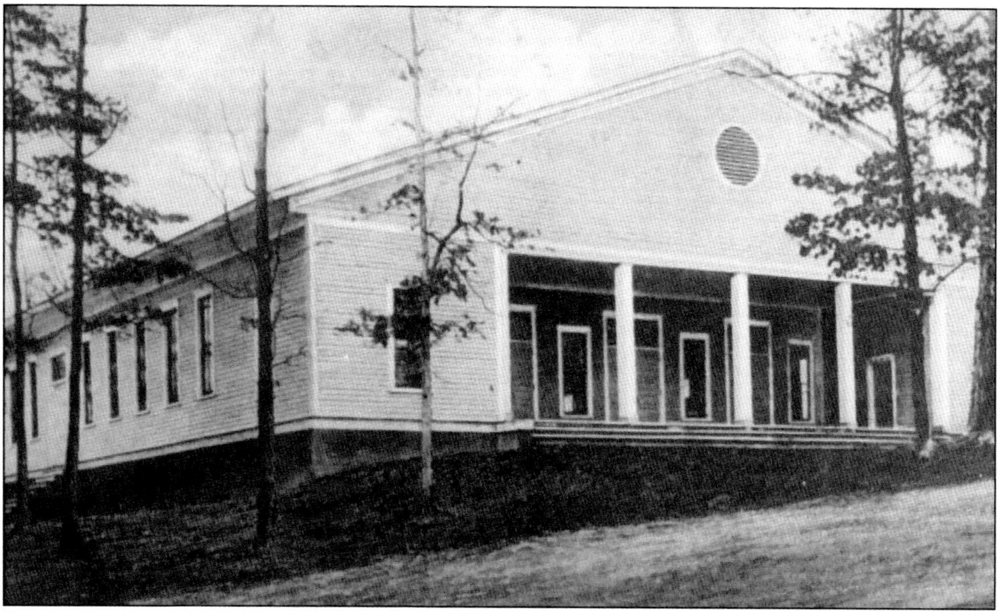

By 1910, Georgia Baptists erected this assembly building near the Mineral Springs in Blue Ridge. It was used, especially in the summer, for conferences, retreats, and similar activities. (Courtesy Don and Carolyn Hall.)

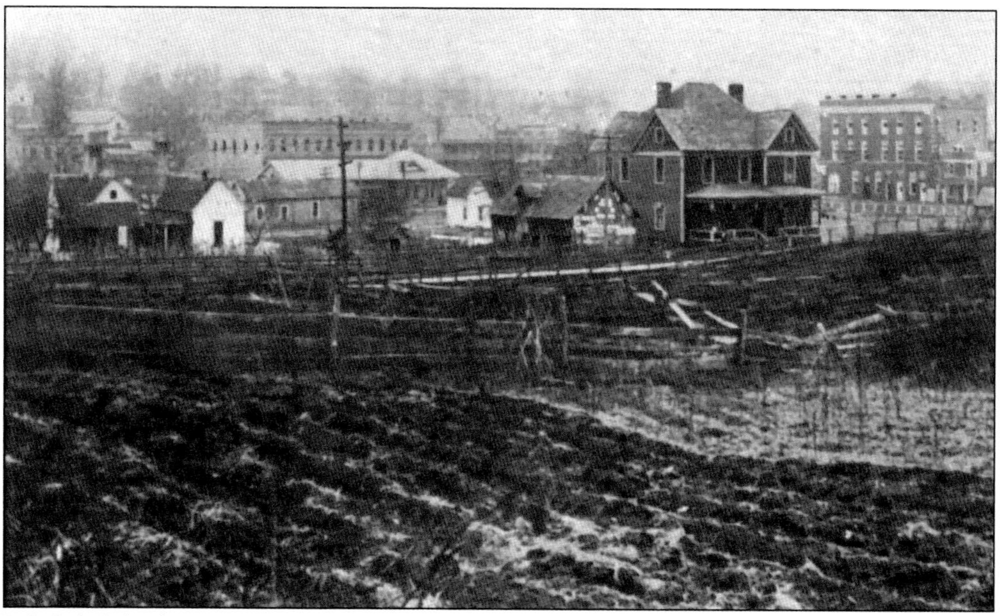

Labeled "A bird's eye view of Blue Ridge, GA," this image shows several interesting features from roughly the first decade of the 20th century. Note that a plowed field (foreground) is still adjacent to the downtown area. In front of the main house (center distance) is the boardwalk that led from downtown to the area of the Georgia Baptist Assembly and later the Mary P. Willingham School for girls. The Gartrell Hotel (right) and the train depot are in place, but neither the L&N building nor Fannin County Bank have yet been built. (Courtesy Don and Carolyn Hall.)

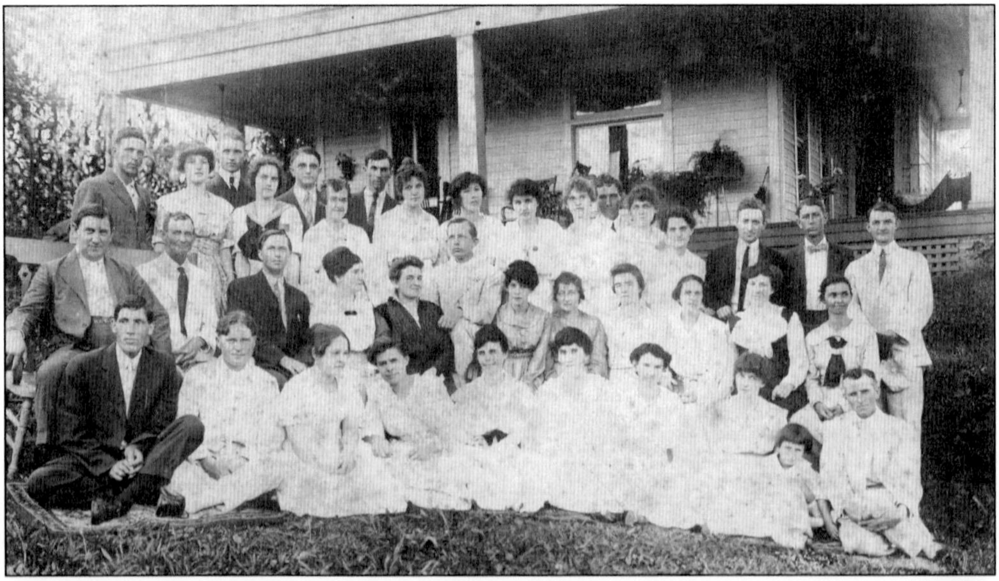

A group gathers for a portrait at the home of Dr. Claud Burton "C.B." Crawford and his wife, Edna Mae Tone Crawford, after a social event in 1916 honoring Dr. George F. Granberry. A native of New York, Dr. Granberry settled in Blue Ridge where he taught piano, led community choirs, and built a substantial house. Pictured here are, from left to right, (first row) Jim Underwood, Dr. C.L. Stocks, Nell Jo Bowers, Myra Bowers, Elizabeth Hackney, Ellen Pruitt, Edna Mae Tone Crawford, Bertha Waldrop, Louise Waldrop, and Claude Griffith; (second row) Dr. C.B. Crawford, Reverend Yourbea, unidentified, Essie Drake ("Aunt Tone"), Ivy Arp, Dr. George F. Granberry (director), Florence Hackney, Clara Gartrell, Grady DuPree, unidentified, Carrie Griffith, and Medlie Holt; (third row) unidentified, Inez McKinney, Frank Daves, unidentified, Hugh Cook, Otis Woody, Wade Carruth, four unidentified, Bill Underwood, unidentified, Mrs. Frank Starkes, Frank Starkes, Kinsey McKinney, and Cecil McKinney. (Courtesy Michael Eaton.)

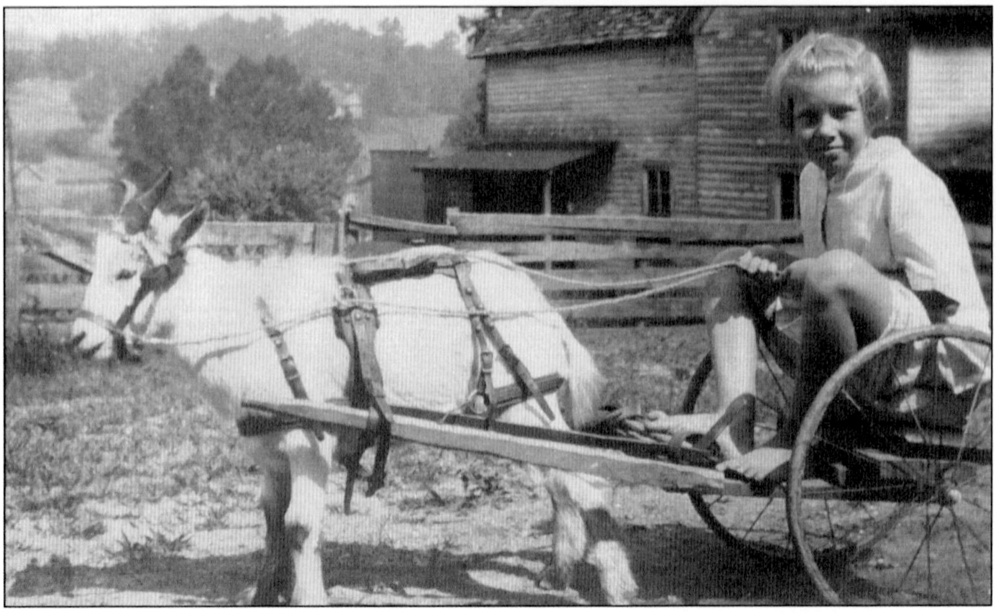

Violet Morrison proudly rides her goat cart through Blue Ridge. (Courtesy Michael Eaton.)

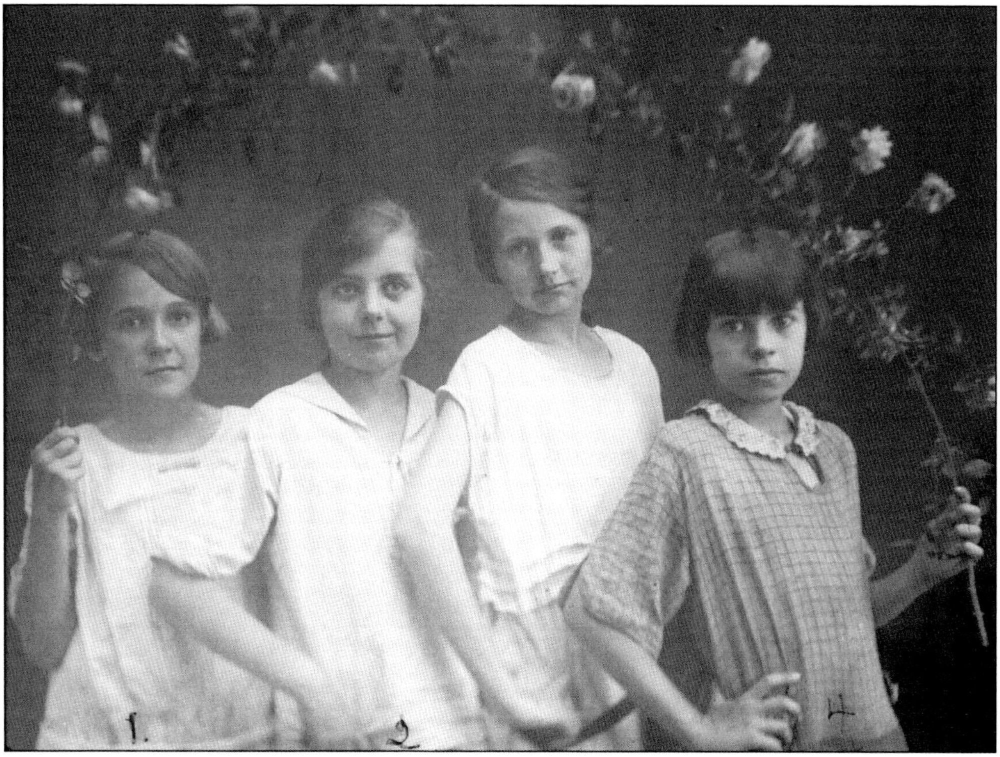

These girls proudly labeled this 1914 image "our club" and listed officers: Pres. Suella Eaton, secretary Sara Mae ?, treasurer Kathleen ?, and Vice Pres. Emma Louise ?. (Courtesy Michael Eaton.)

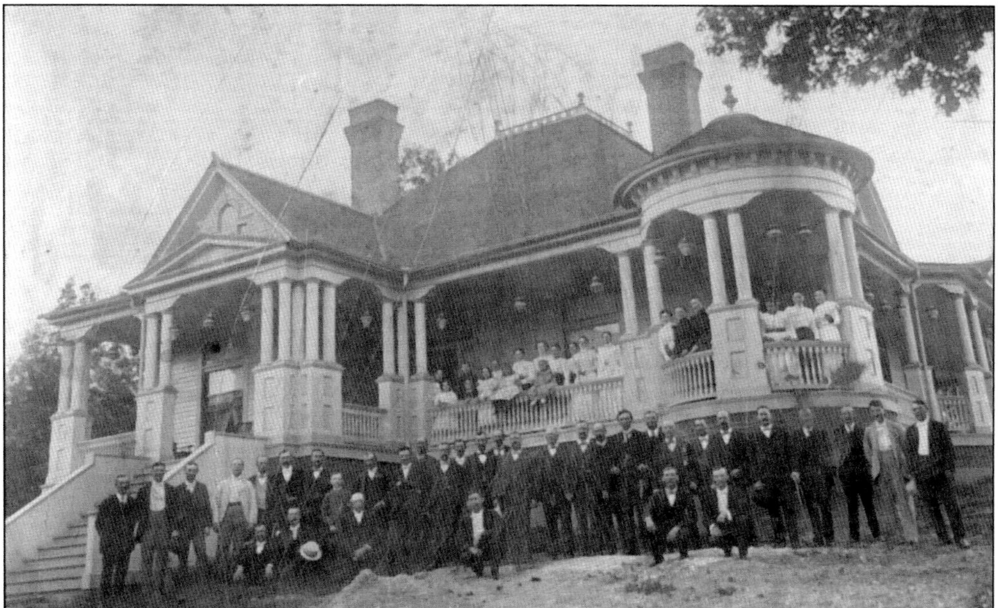

A Sunday School group from Blue Ridge Methodist gathers at the Whitfield house in 1904 or 1905. (Courtesy Lynn Doss.)

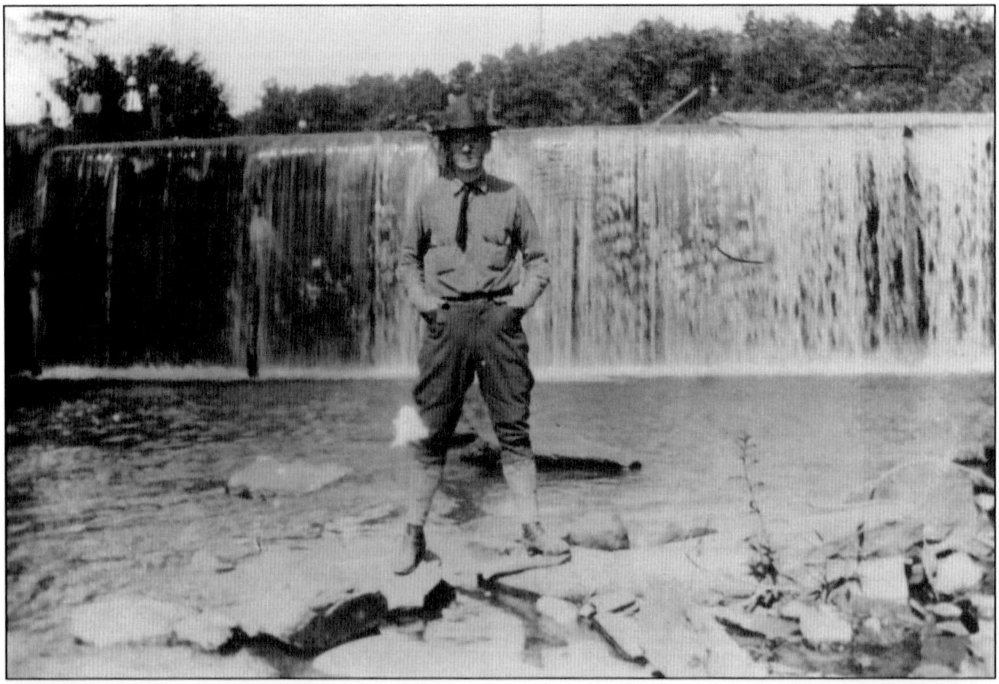

This man standing so stalwartly may be Clinton Cutts, a basketball coach at the Mary P. Willingham school, and later, a Baptist pastor and educator. He is standing below the Purser Dam near Blue Ridge, which after 1909 impounded a small lake near the Georgia Baptist Assembly and provided drinking water for the city's first water system. Note the fearless men standing (top left) on the slippery edge of the 20-foot dam. (Courtesy Ethelene Dyer Jones.)

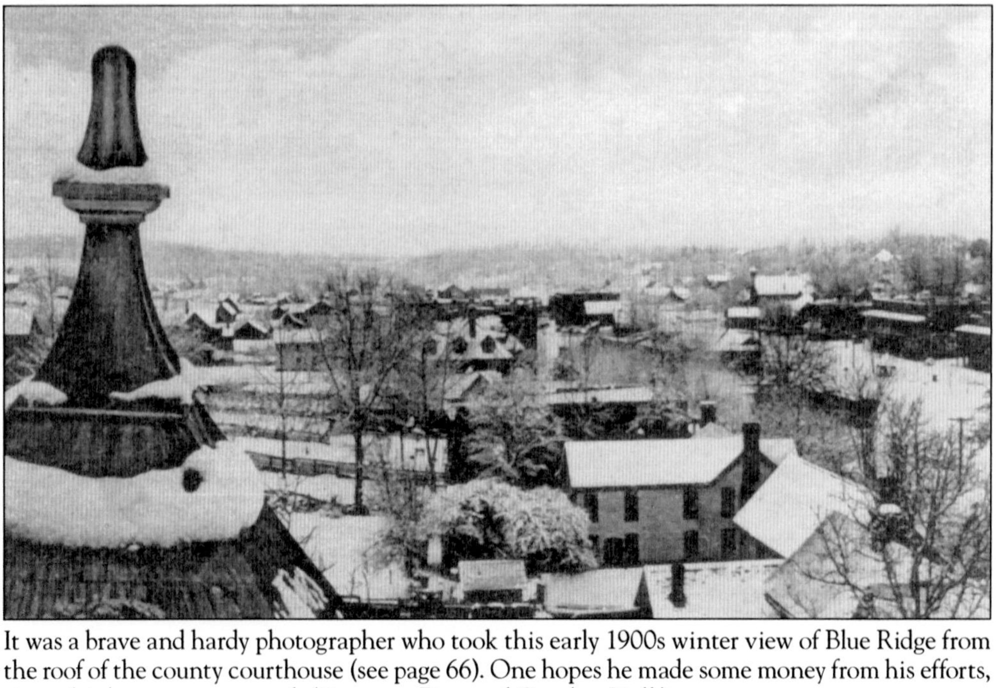

It was a brave and hardy photographer who took this early 1900s winter view of Blue Ridge from the roof of the county courthouse (see page 66). One hopes he made some money from his efforts, since this became a postcard. (Courtesy Don and Carolyn Hall.)

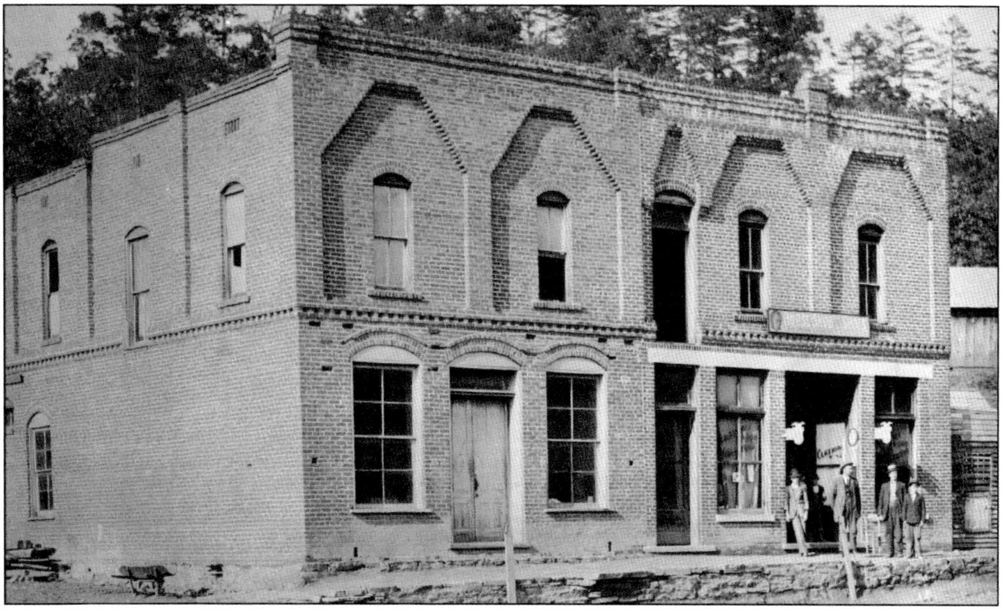

Several men stand in front of George Patton Dickey's general store in Mineral Bluff prior to 1912. In 1909, Robert T. Hampton purchased an interest in this store and in 1912 bought out all of Dickey's remaining ownership. (Courtesy Georgia Archives, Vanishing Georgia Collection, image fan017-83.)

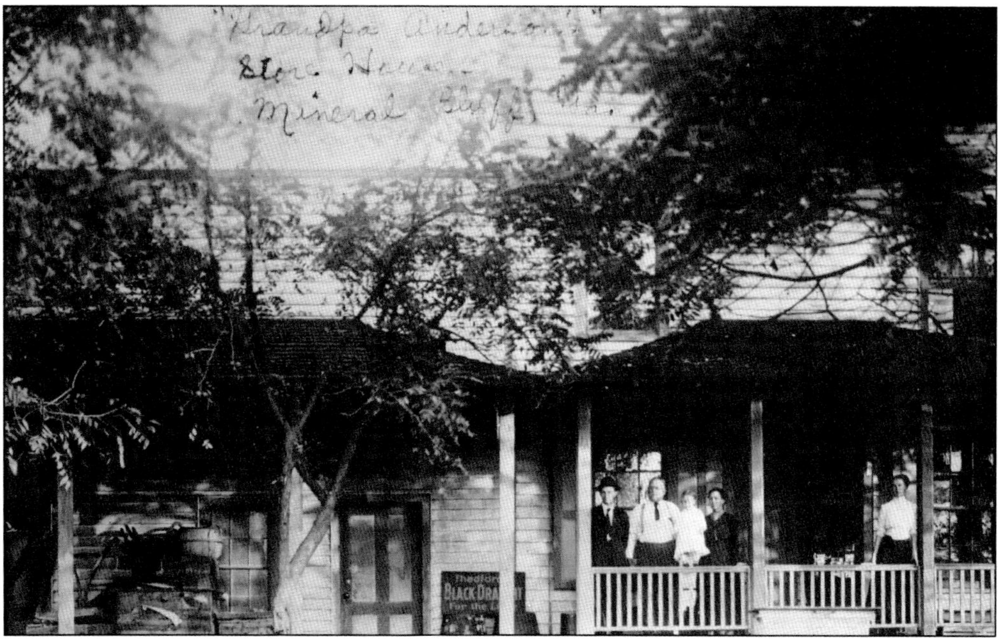

This building housed John Anderson's general store in Mineral Bluff around 1915. A handwritten note identifies it as "Grandpa Anderson's store house." Also note that an advertisement for Black Draught is leaning against the porch. (Courtesy Georgia Archives, Vanishing Georgia Collection, image fan015-83.)

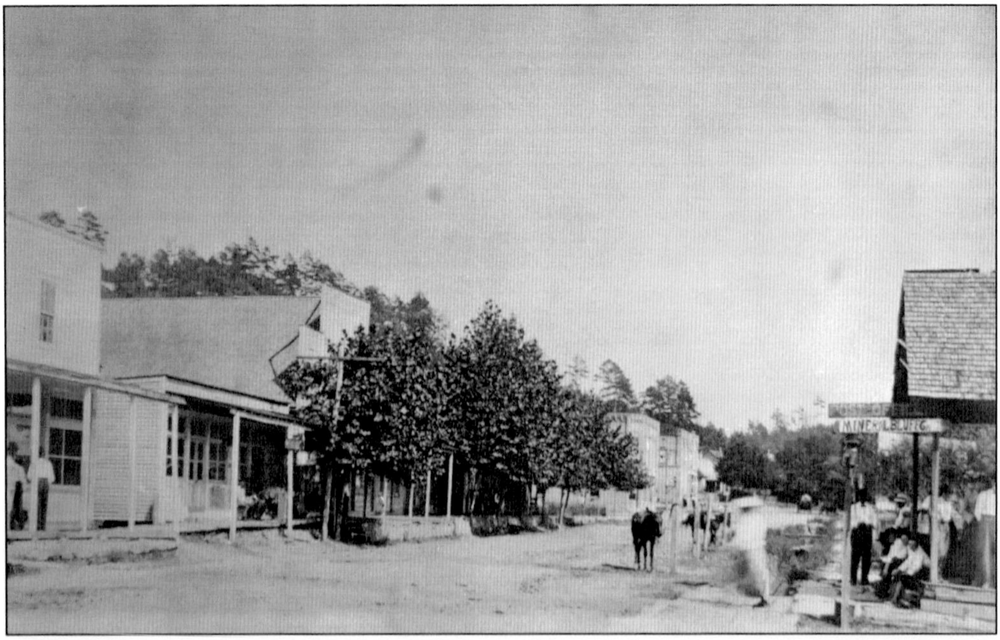

In this 1903 view of downtown Mineral Bluff, the blurred lady in the white hat is Cathryn Cole Baugh, perhaps on her way from the post office on the right. The building on the left side of the street, partially screened by the right edge of the trees, housed the Dickey (later Hampton) General Store (see page 43). (Courtesy John P. Nichols.)

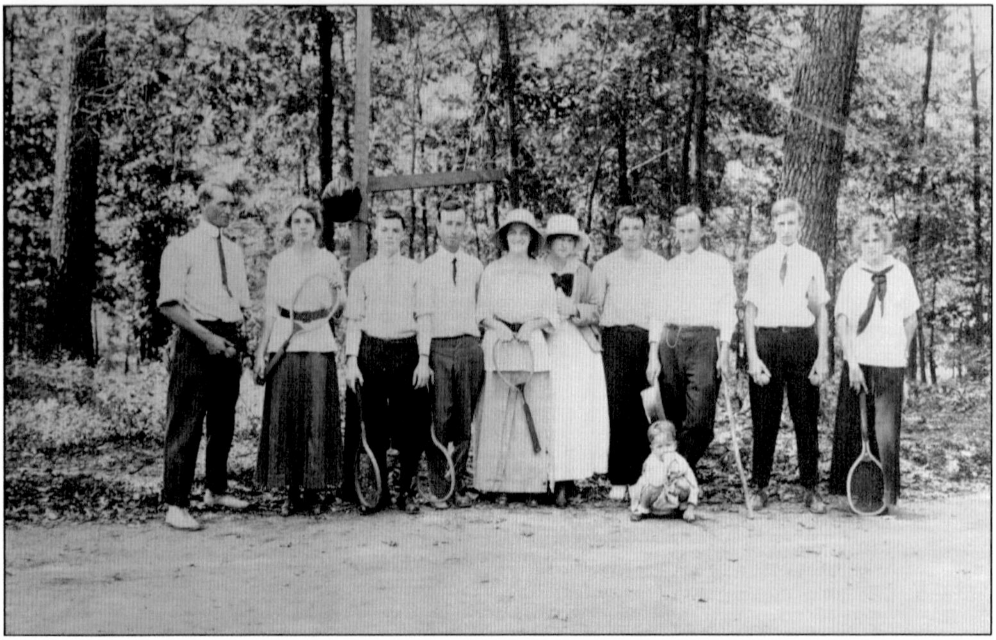

A group of tennis players pause for a group snapshot in Blue Ridge in the early 1900s. The only identified person is Leo T. Barber, who is third from the left. However, the sailor-style tops worn by some of the women are similar to the everyday uniforms worn at the Mary P. Willingham school for girls, so the photograph may have been taken in 1916 or later. (Courtesy Georgia Archives, Vanishing Georgia Collection, image fan001.)

Four

Educational Efforts

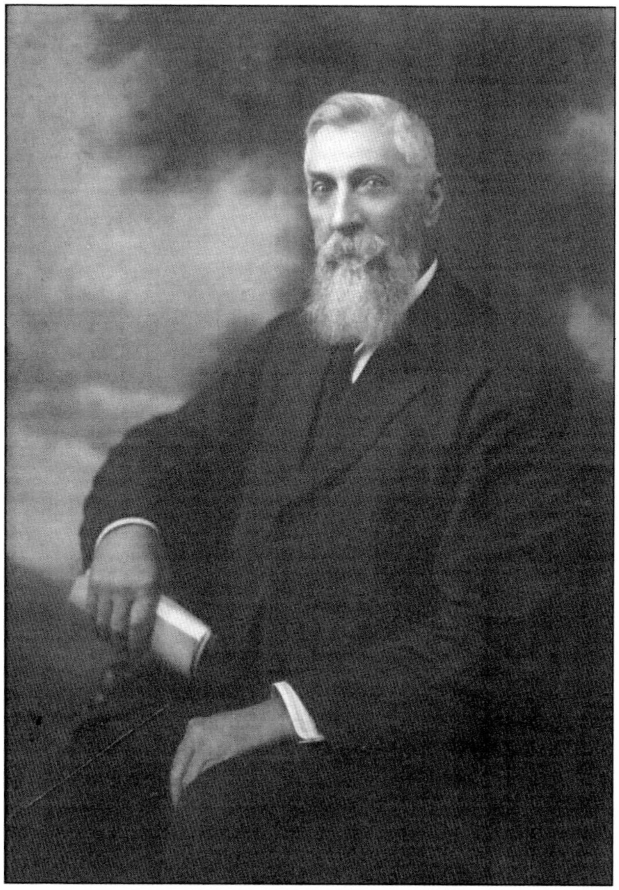

Adam Davenport had a 50-year career as an educator in Fannin County. Born in 1845, he enlisted in Company H, First Line Georgia State Troops in 1863. He fought in the battles of New Hope Church, Kennesaw Mountain, and Sandtown before being wounded in the Battle of Atlanta. First appointed as school commissioner by the board of education in 1879, he was elected school superintendent in 1887 and continued in office for 22 years. He wrote many articles on science, religion, and education that were published nationally and in Canada. Also a musician, he composed several hymns. He and his wife, Mary Ann Ashworth, had 10 surviving children at his death in 1927, when he was eulogized in the state Baptist newspaper, the *Christian Index*. He is buried at Hemptown Church. (Courtesy Ada Reed Davenport via Ethelene Dyer Jones.)

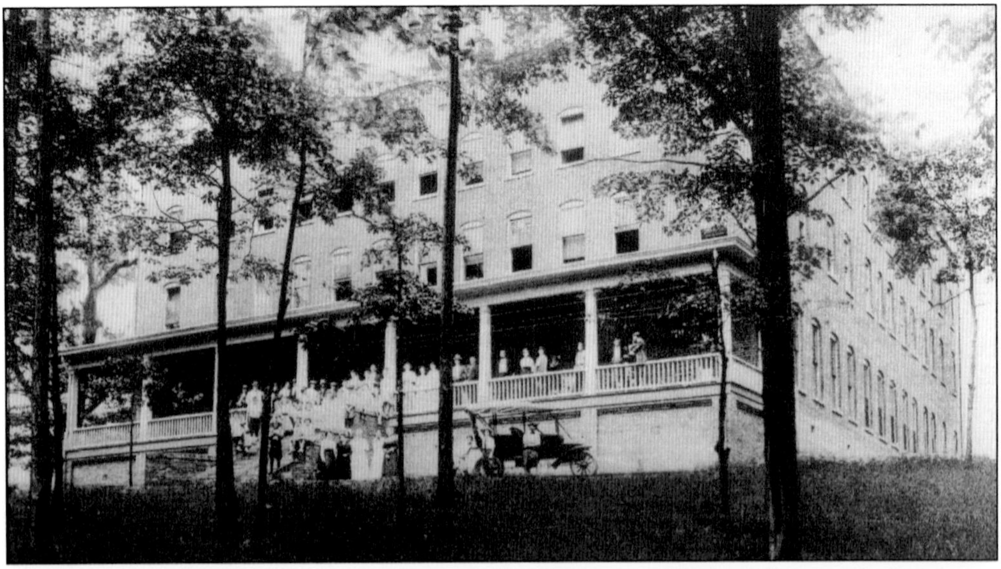

The Mary P. Willingham School for girls was founded by the Woman's Missionary Union, an auxiliary of the Georgia Baptist Convention, to provide education for "poor mountain girls." It operated from September 1916 until the Depression led to its closure in 1931. Girls from the surrounding mountains and some girls from outside the region could attend 7th through 11th grades. Some of the students were orphans. The sturdy brick building, pictured here, served as the administration building, classrooms, dormitory, and hosted visitors to the nearby Georgia Baptist Assembly in the summer months. (Courtesy Don and Carolyn Hall.)

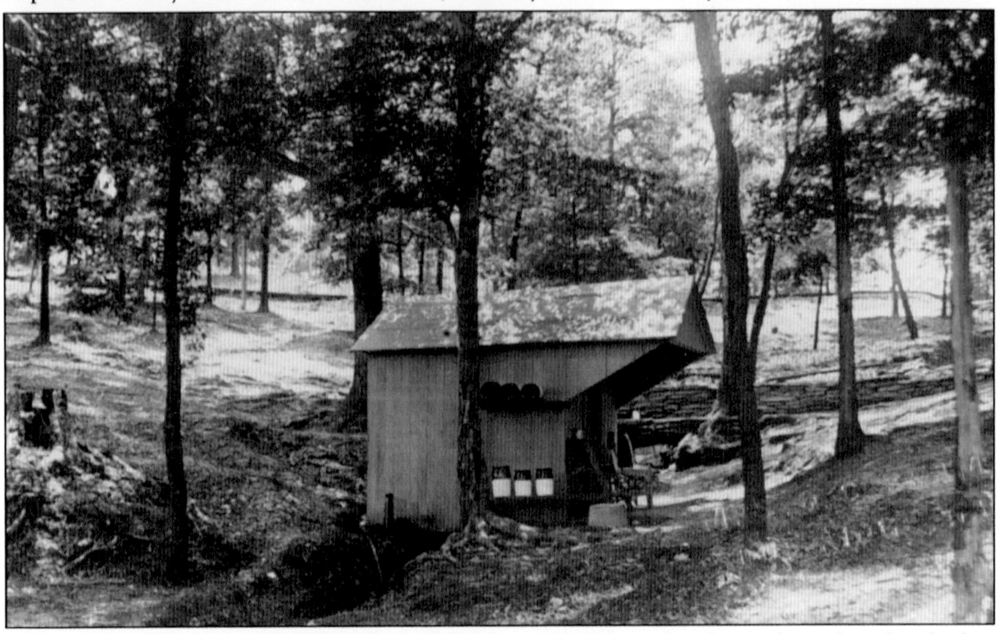

The springhouse at Mary P. Willingham School provided water for the students, but they had to fetch it themselves. Note that pitchers are lined up next to the building, and the rock retaining wall is shown behind the shed. Students who stayed over for the summer could find work serving in the Georgia Baptist Assembly's dining hall or might fetch water in these same pitchers for guests. (Courtesy Ethelene Dyer Jones.)

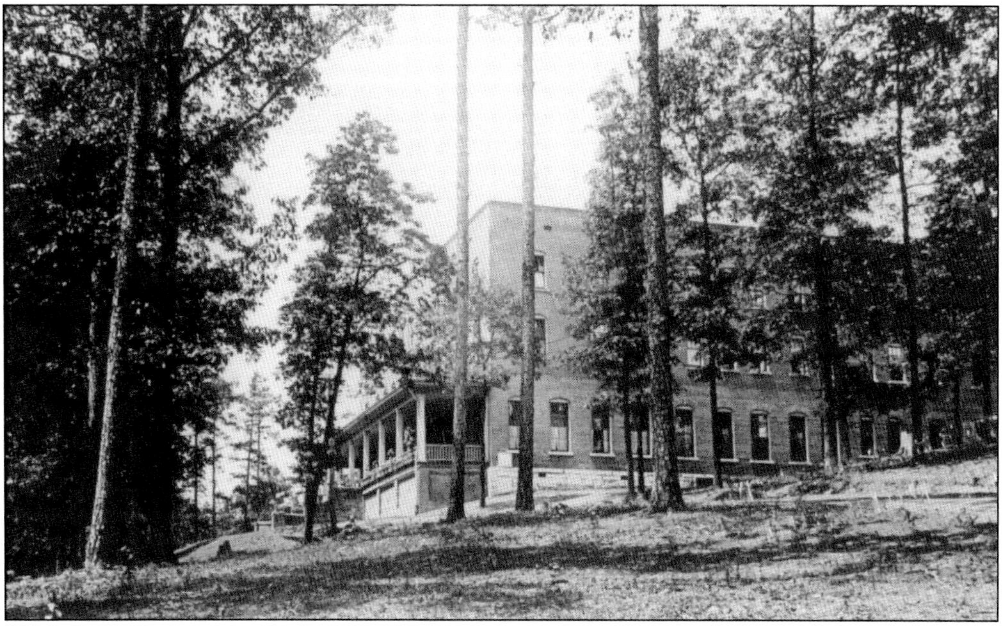

This photograph of the Mary P. Willingham School's main building was taken around 1920. (Courtesy Ethelene Dyer Jones.)

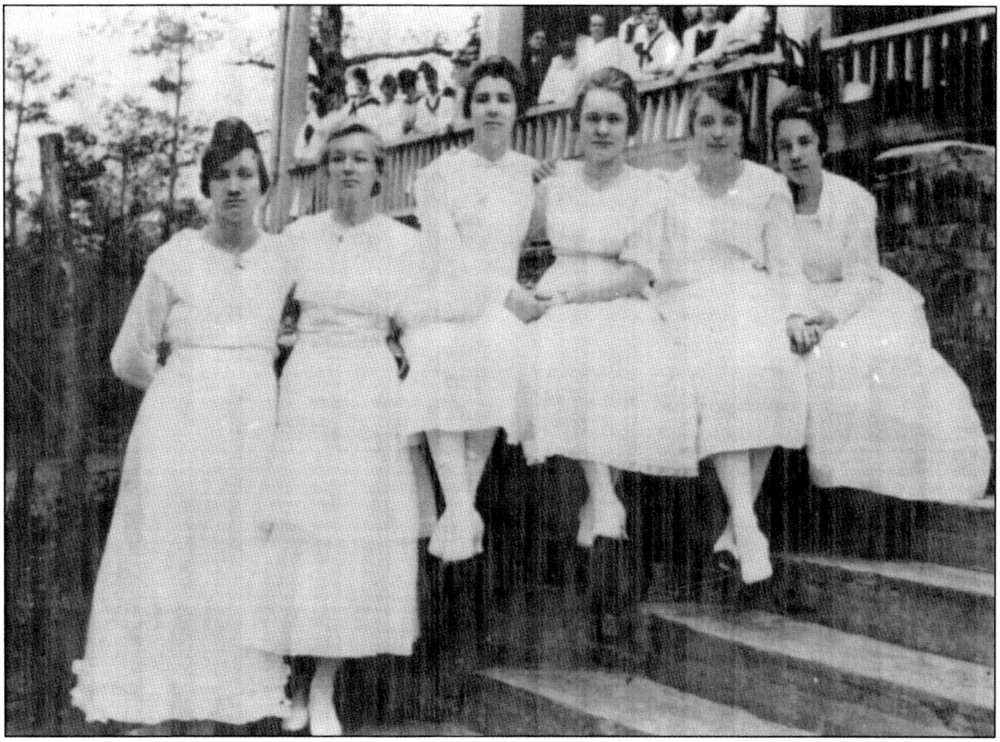

Only two years after it opened, the Mary P. Willingham School had its first graduates, shown here on the front steps of the main building. Pictured are, from left to right, Jane Keeter, Texas Knight, Myrtle Wade, Vera Harrison, Sarah Chandler, and Bonnie Jones. (Courtesy Ethelene Dyer Jones.)

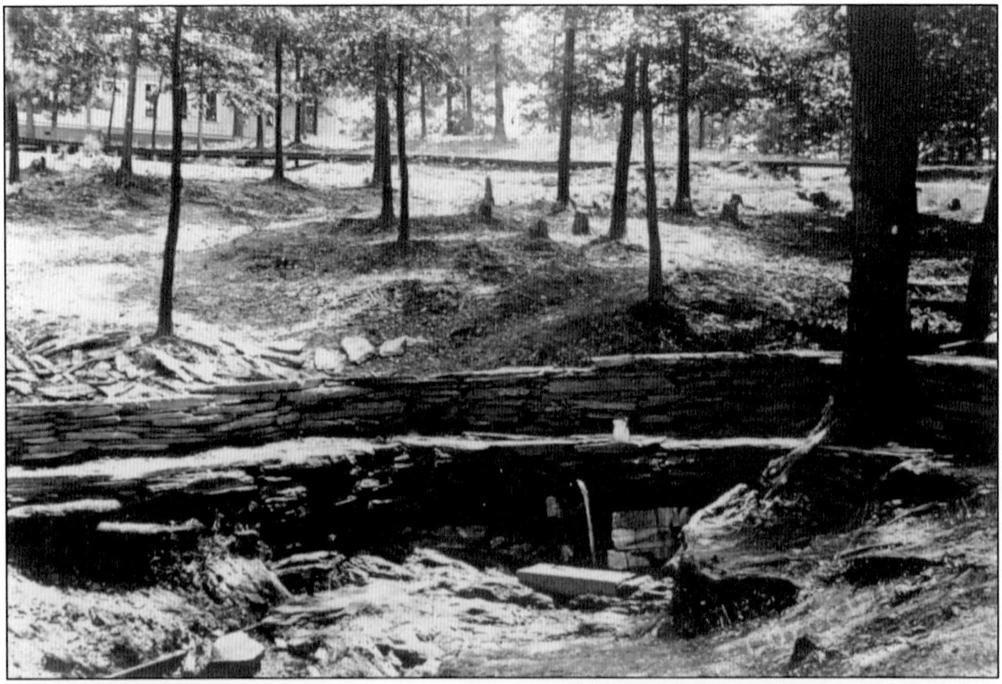

This view of the rock wall near the spring at Mary P. Willingham School shows the tiny trickle of water that made it convenient to refill pitchers. This photograph may have been taken before the construction of the wooden springhouse on the previous page. The house in the background is the school's domestic sciences building. (Courtesy Ethelene Dyer Jones.)

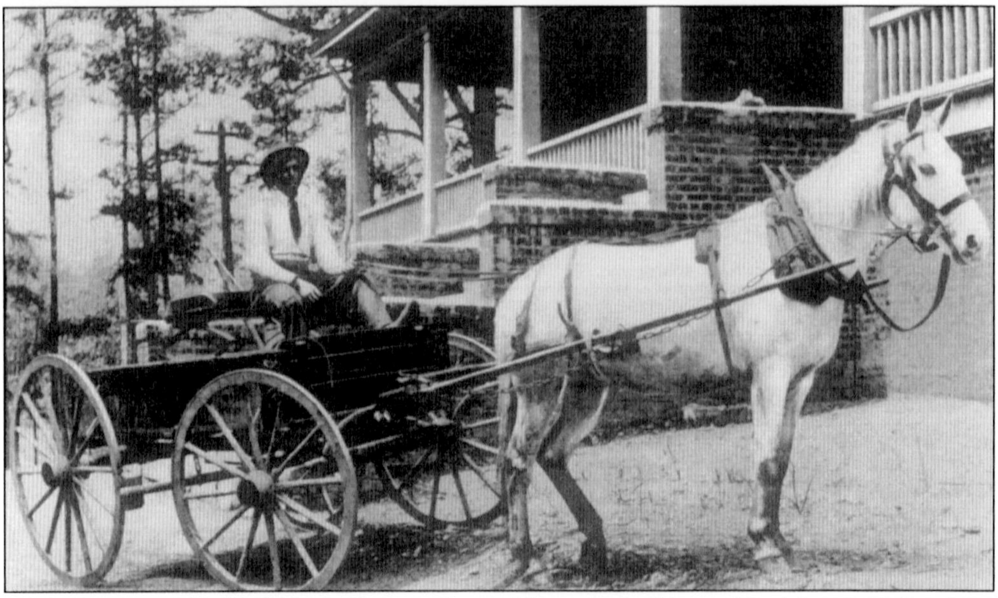

A Mr. Smith and "Bob" the horse pose in front of the main building of the Mary P. Willingham School. They met students at the train station in Blue Ridge to bring them to campus, except that on the first day of school, there was a walking procession as the president led the students to the school. The pole and wires in the background of the photograph show that telephone or electrical service was now available in Blue Ridge. (Courtesy Ethelene Dyer Jones.)

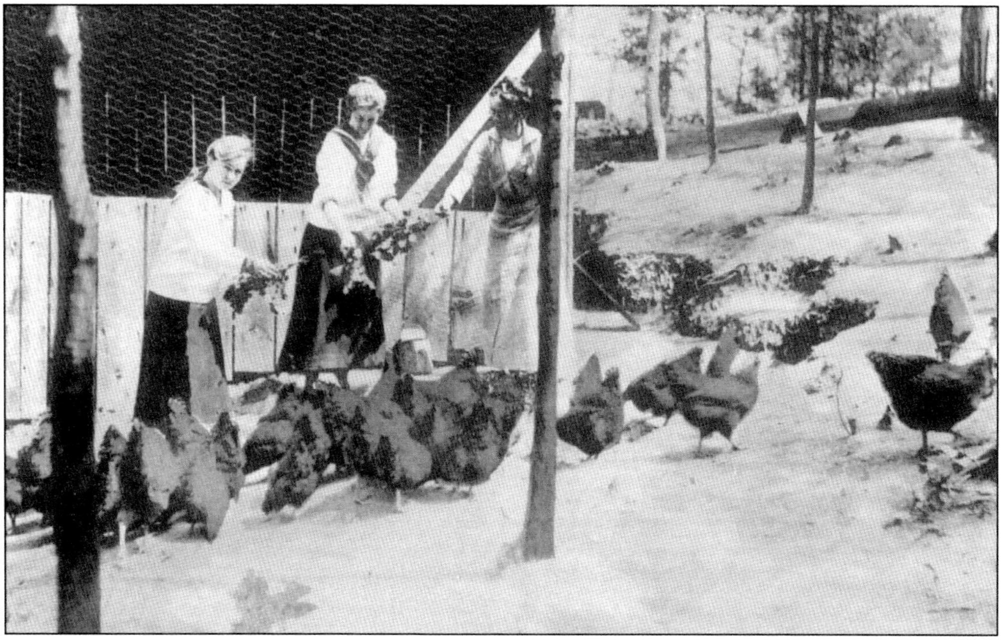

Two students in uniform feed chickens in the "Barred Rock" yard of Mary P. Willingham School in an image from an early postcard. (Barred rock is a breed of chickens.) (Courtesy Ethelene Dyer Jones.)

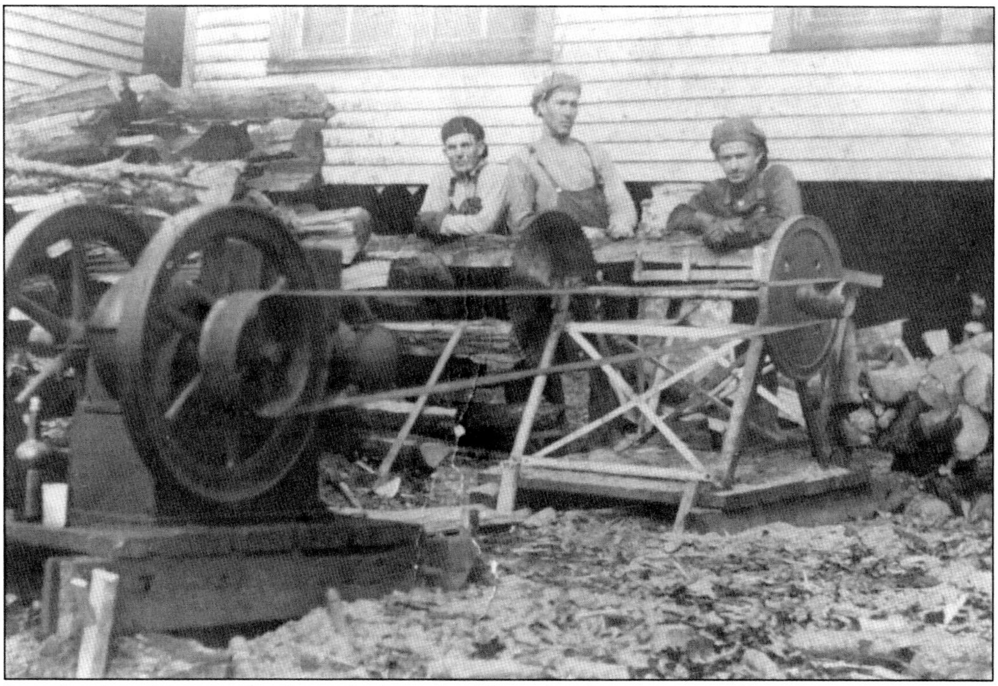

It took a lot of firewood to heat the large buildings for the Mary P. Willingham School. In this image, a team of three men uses a power-driven saw to quickly produce a quantity of fuel. (Courtesy Ethelene Dyer Jones.)

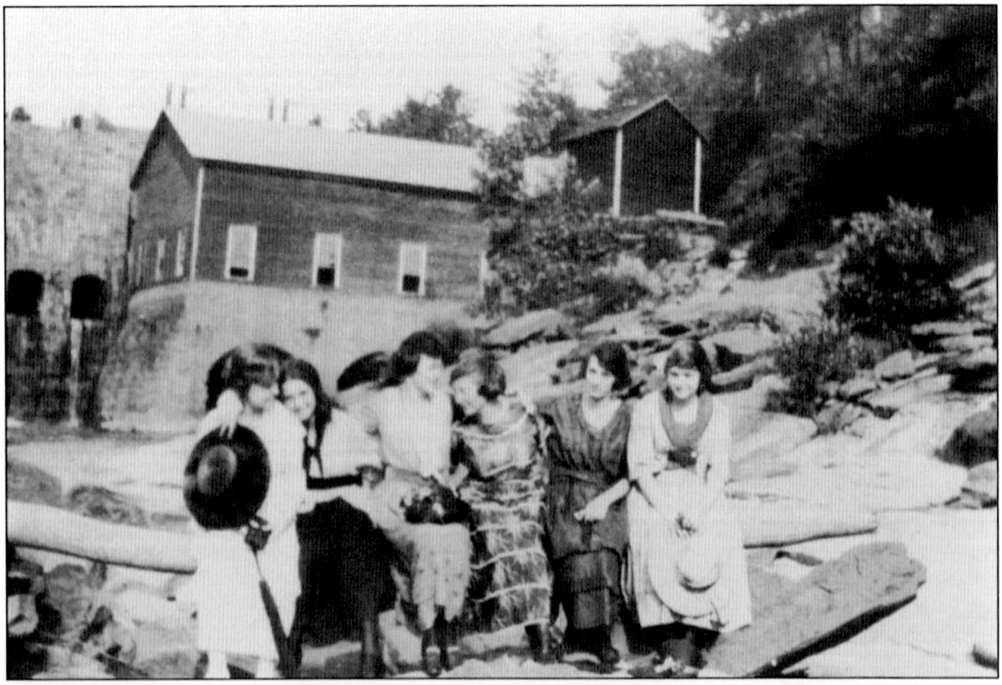

A group of students from the Mary P. Willingham School enjoys an outing below the Purser Dam near Blue Ridge. The mill house is in the background. (Courtesy Ethelene Dyer Jones.)

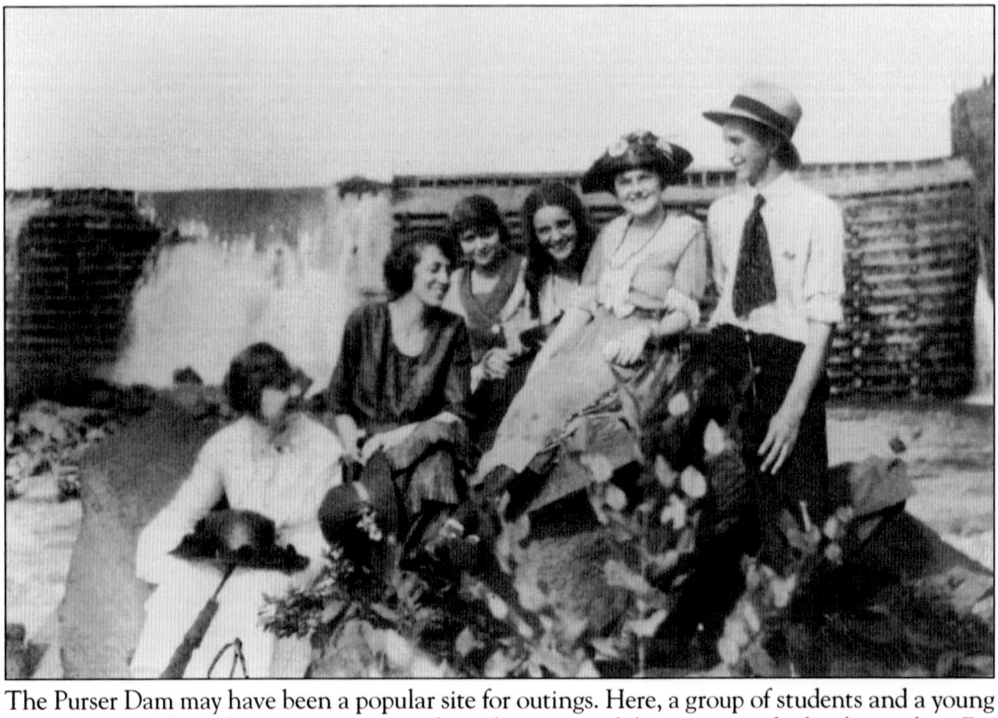

The Purser Dam may have been a popular site for outings. Here, a group of students and a young man enjoy the day. The young man may have been one of the six sons of school president Dr. William L. Cutts. (Courtesy Ethelene Dyer Jones.)

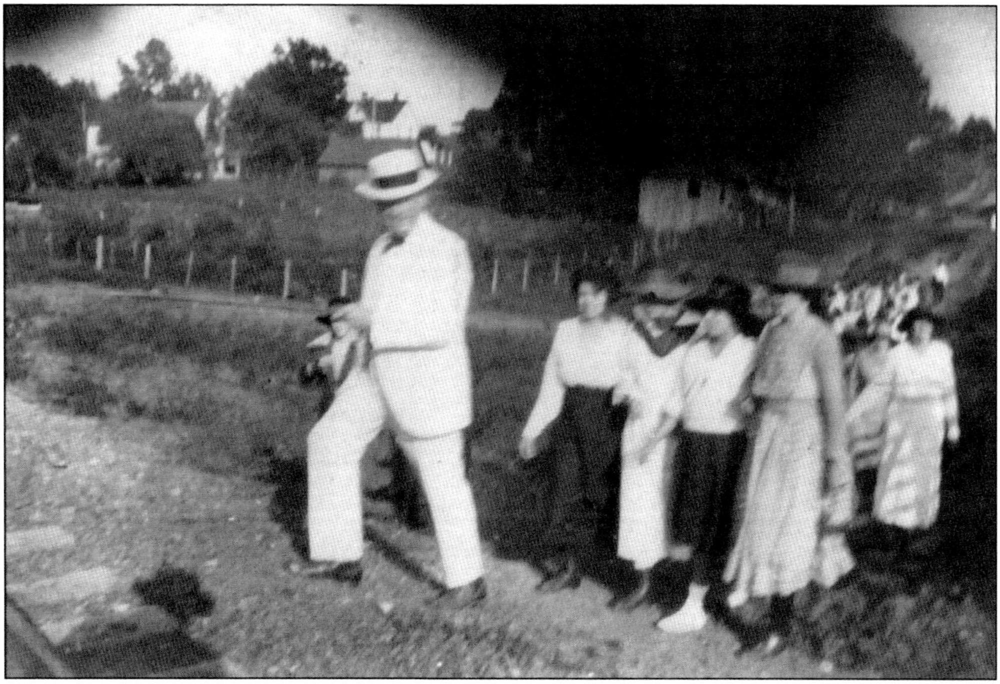

Above, Pres. William Loomis "W.L." Cutts leads a procession of Mary P. Willingham faculty and students near the railroad tracks in Blue Ridge. Below at left, Cutts is shown with his wife, Susan Saphronia Clark Cutts, in front of the school's main building. Below at right is a c. 1919 photograph of Dr. Cutts's pet collie checking out the wagon on campus. (All, courtesy Ethelene Dyer Jones.)

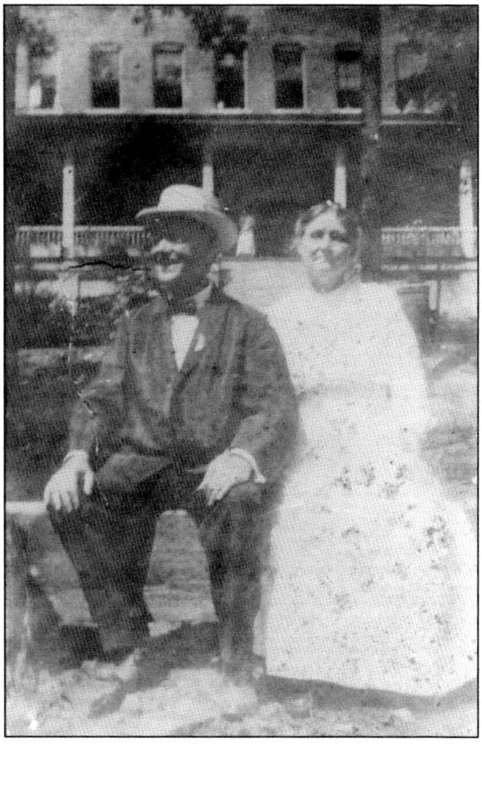

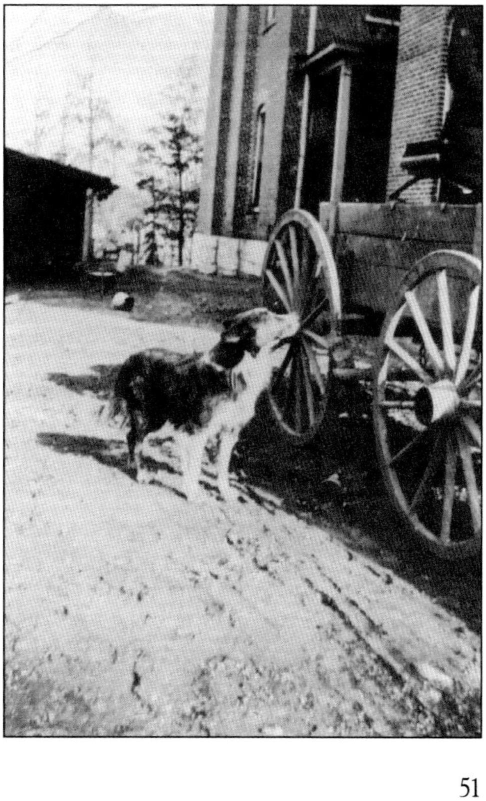

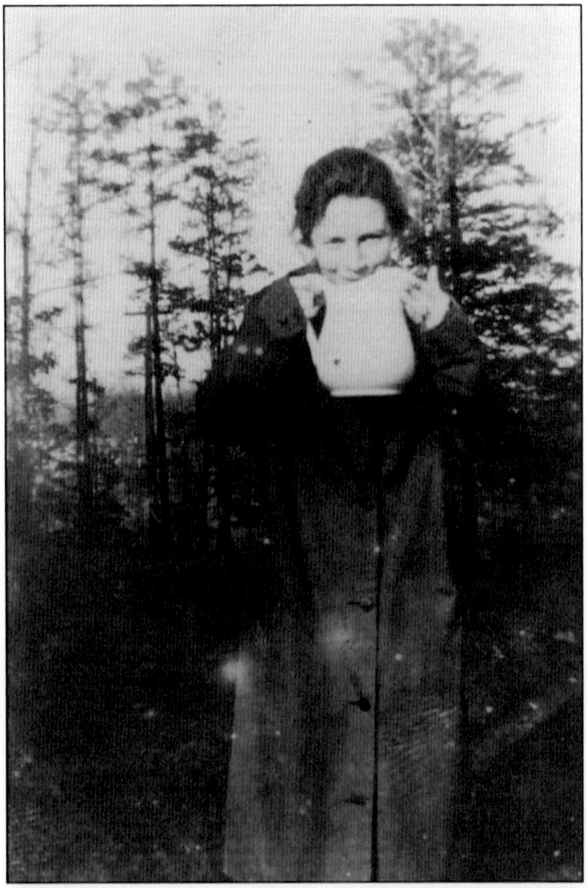

Vera Harrison, who would later become the wife of Dr. L. Clinton Cutts, clowns a bit with her pitcher at the Mary P. Willingham spring. Dr. L.C. Cutts is one of the six sons of Dr. W.L. Cutts. (Courtesy Ethelene Dyer Jones.)

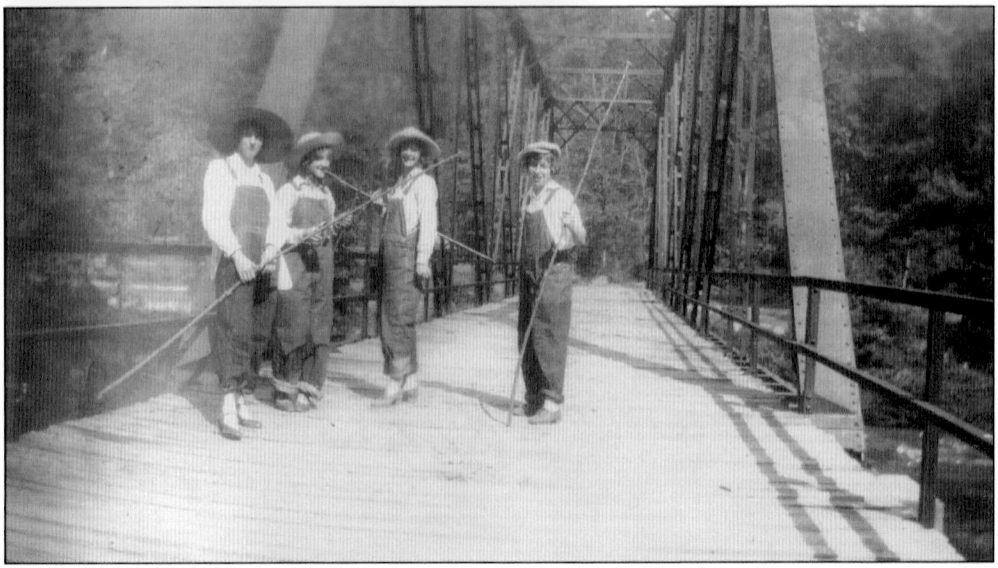

A sprightly group of "Huck Finns" (students at the Mary P. Willingham school), enjoy an outing to the Shallowford Bridge in Hurst on July 4, 1927. Eva Mae Lloyd is on the left. The others are, from left to right, Ruby ?, Mattie ?, and Fenna ?. (Courtesy Michael Eaton.)

Even before the Mary P. Willingham School operated in Blue Ridge, the North Georgia Baptist College operated in Morganton. This photograph shows the former county courthouse, which housed the school until its permanent buildings were constructed at the corner of Loving Road and Blairsville H1ighway. Note the Masonic inscription on the top floor of the building. (Courtesy Baugh House collection.)

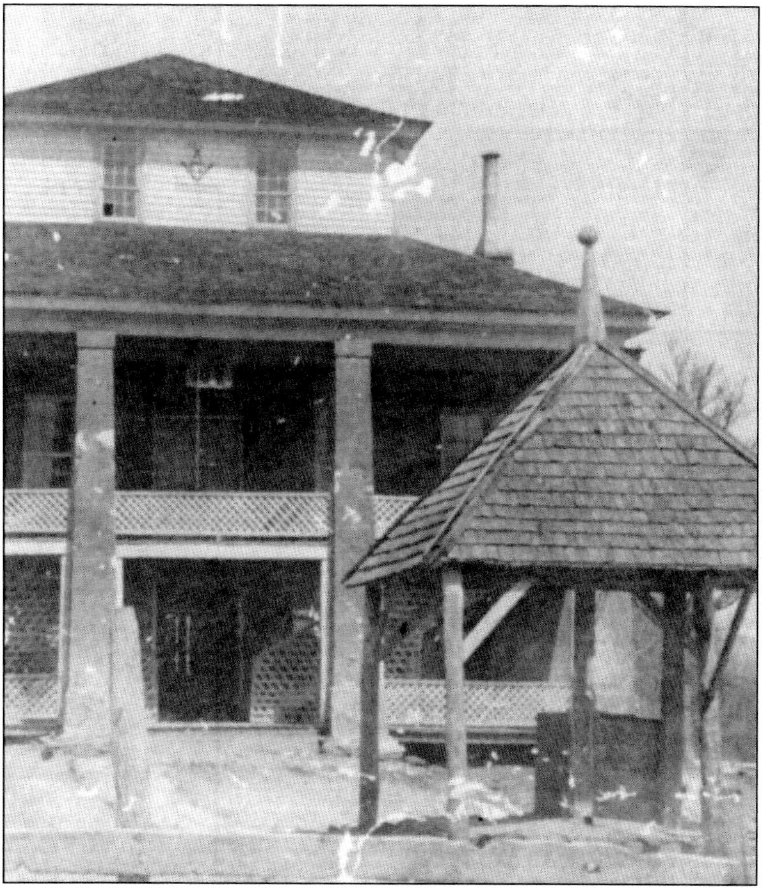

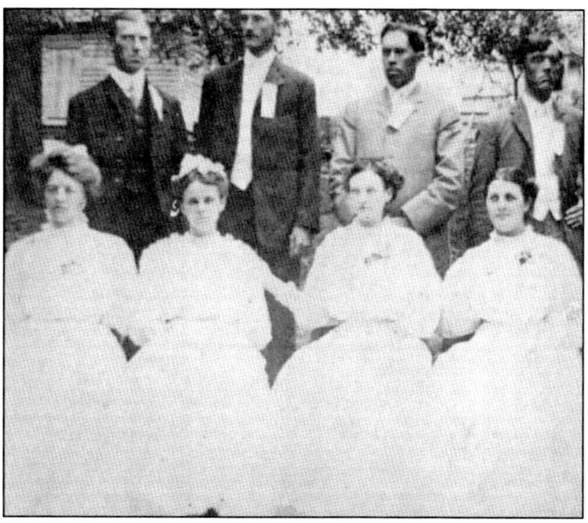

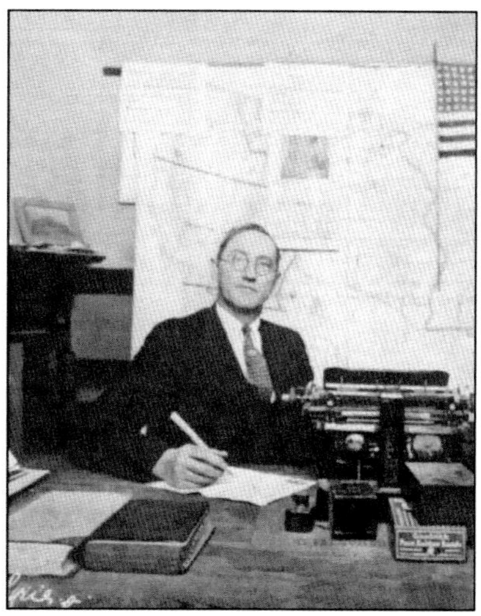

In the image at left, 1907 graduates of North Georgia College pose near the school in Morganton. They are, from left to right, (first row) Minnie Daves Davenport, Ophie Chastain, Ann Lovingood, and Siddie Davis; (second row) M.C. Lunsford, O.R. Guthrie, Pinson Hughes, and Altus Green. In the 1929 photograph at right, Guthrie sits in his office at the courthouse. He served as Fannin County's school superintendent, as did his son. (Both, courtesy Baugh House collection.)

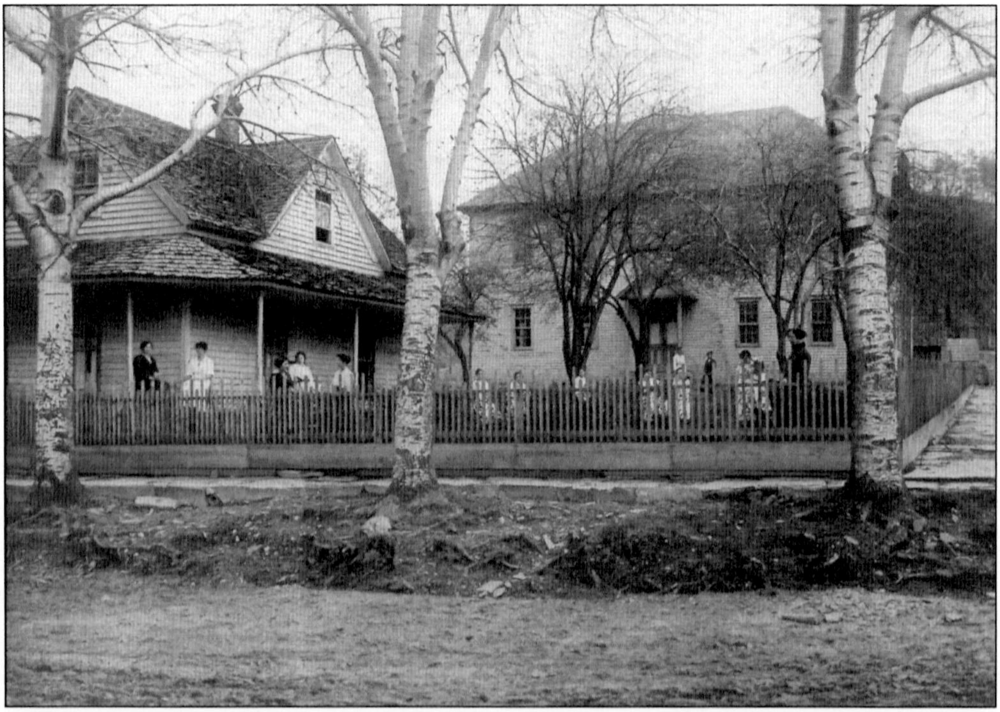

These buildings housed the Mineral Bluff Industrial School for Ladies in the early 1900s. (Courtesy Wilson and LaVerne Cobb.)

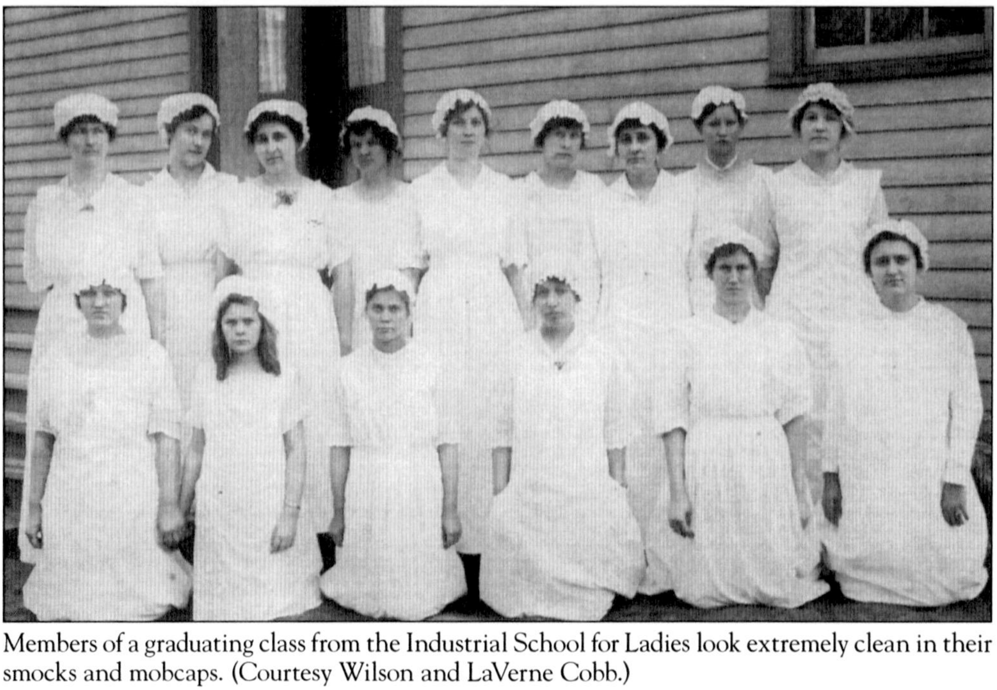

Members of a graduating class from the Industrial School for Ladies look extremely clean in their smocks and mobcaps. (Courtesy Wilson and LaVerne Cobb.)

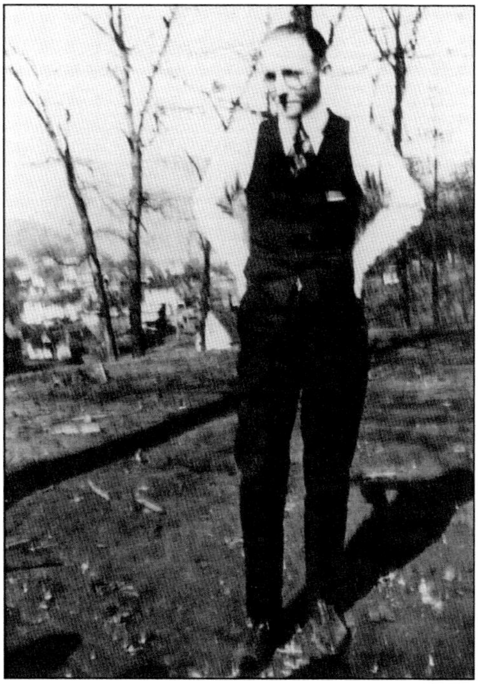

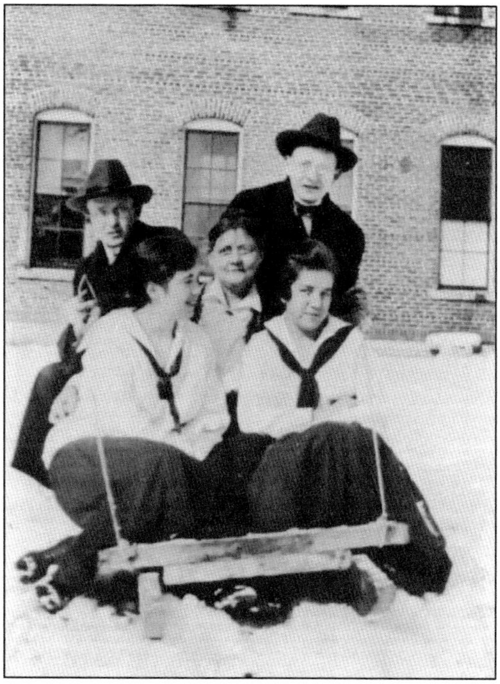

Above left is Loomis Clinton "L.C." Cutts in 1920. He served the Mary P. Willingham School as basketball coach, business manager, and French teacher. Eventually, he became Reverend Dr. Cutts, succeeding his father upon the latter's death as pastor at the First Baptist Church of McCaysville, Georgia, and Copperhill, Tennessee. He remained pastor there until 1946 when he was selected as the first president of Truett-McConnell College, which opened in September 1947. Above right, sledding near the main school building in the early 1920s are, from left to right, (front) Bonnie Jones, an unidentified student, Susan Saphronia Clark Cutts, and (back) two of their six sons, Clinton and Harvey. (Both, courtesy Ethelene Dyer Jones.)

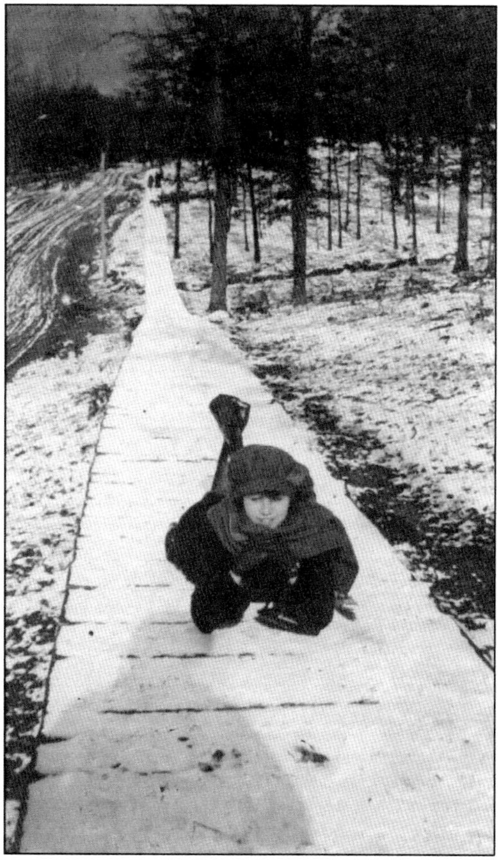

Mary P. Willingham student Mattie Tully lies on the snowy boardwalk leading from downtown to the school campus. The boardwalk was built to keep the students' boots out of the mud. Day students walked this route twice a day, and boarding students used it a couple of times a week when they had permission to visit town and buy a few supplies. All students were required to attend church on Sundays. (Courtesy Ethelene Dyer Jones.)

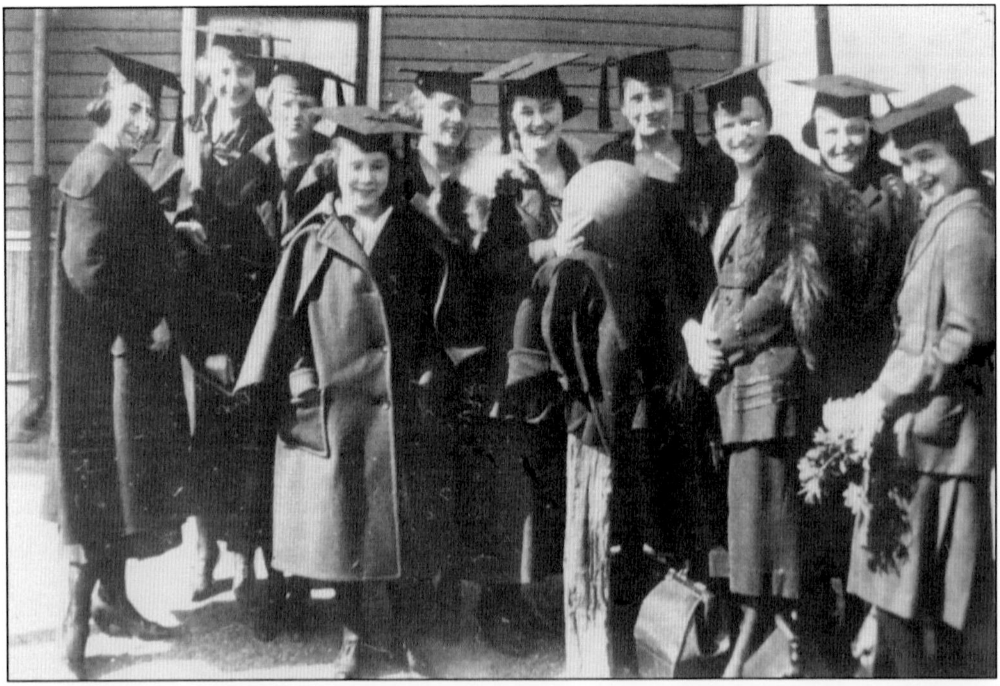

Seniors of the Mary P. Willingham school class of 1918 pose near the school. Note the basketball that appears in the photograph, indicating that the students may have wanted to commemorate a win over rival academies in Ellijay or Hiawassee. They are, from left to right, unidentified, Margaret Black, Mae Couch, Bonnie Higdon, Vertie Lee Dodd, Ella Sellers, Laura Walls, Dorothy Loretta Califf, Mattie Fuller, and Rae Herring. (Courtesy Ethelene Dyer Jones.)

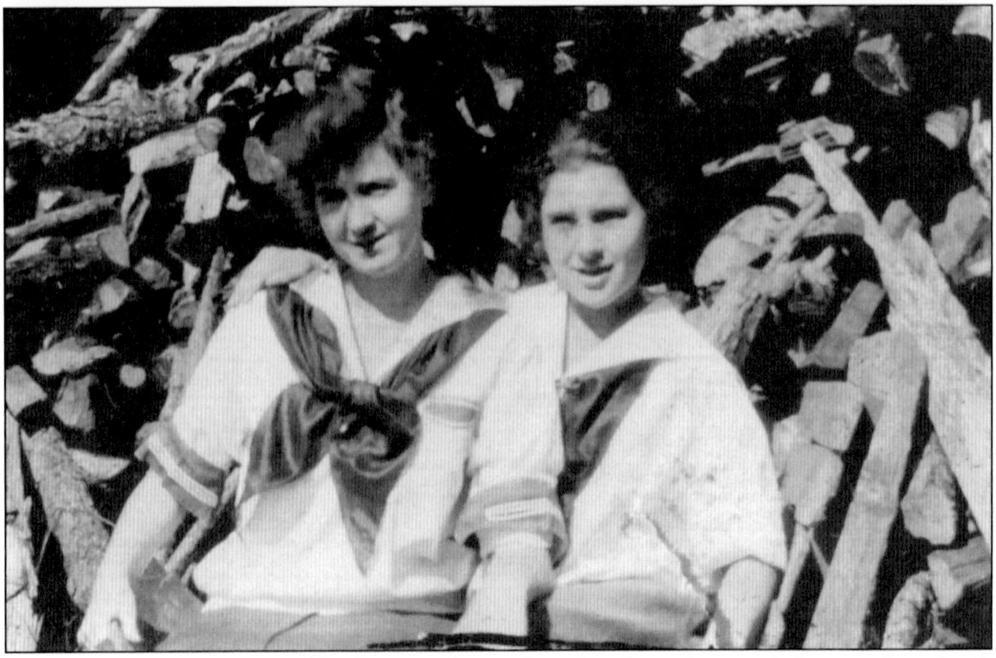

Two unidentified Mary P. Willingham students take a break on the woodpile near the school. (Courtesy Ethelene Dyer Jones.)

Mattie Fuller and Mary Esther McLean, students at Mary P. Willingham School, pose while on holiday at Epworth Park on July 4, 1917. (Courtesy Ethelene Dyer Jones.)

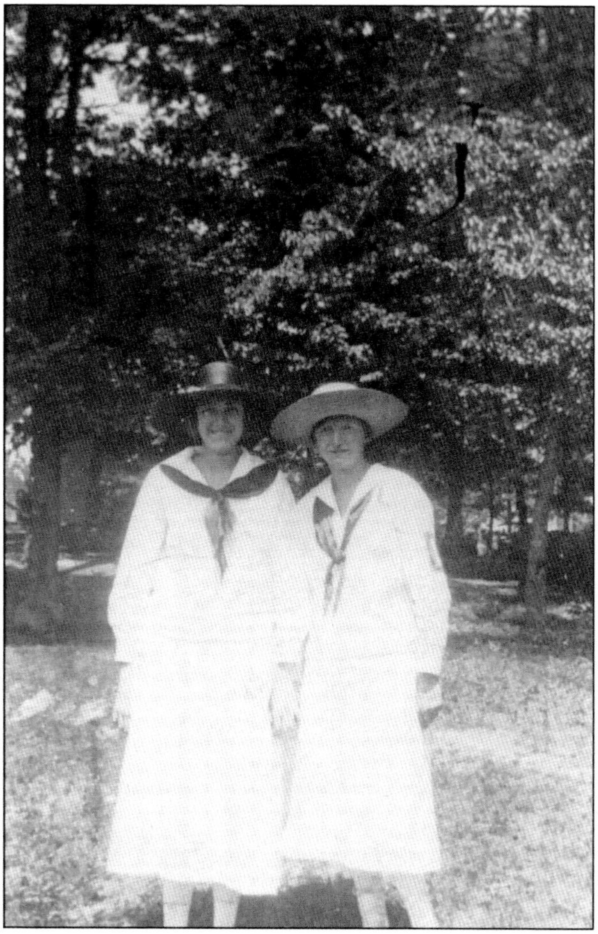

This house was provided as the parsonage for the minister at Epworth Methodist Church, who usually also served as president of Epworth Seminary, a school founded in 1898. This campus later served as a public high school and elementary school, then became the Bonnie Hidgon Reaves campus, and has also hosted satellite locations for several institutions of higher learning. The house, much modified, still serves as Epworth Methodist's parsonage. (Courtesy William Turner and Epworth Methodist.)

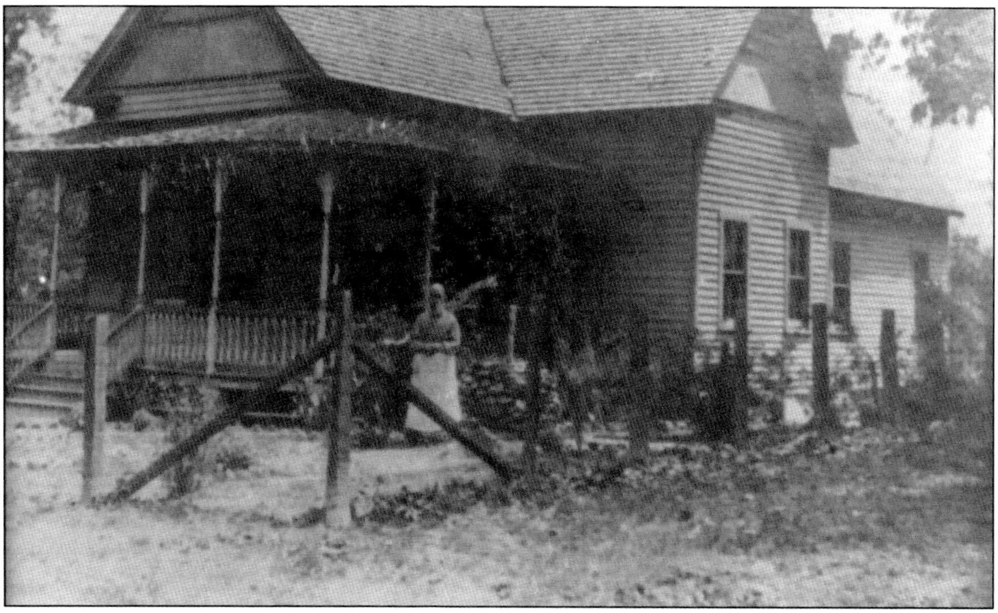

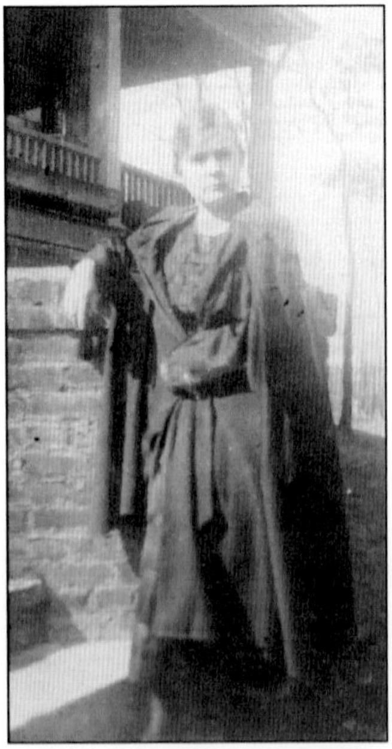

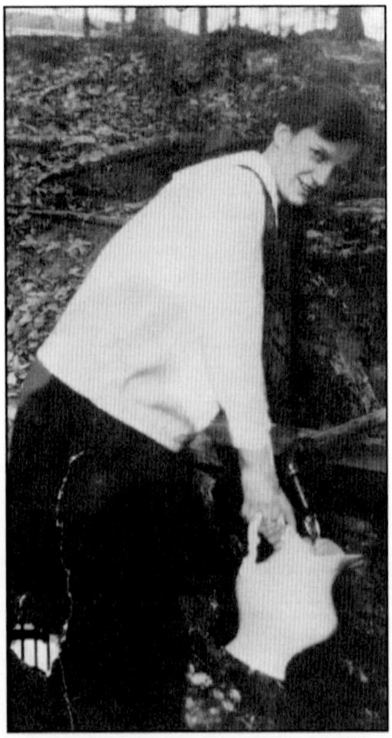

At far left, Vera Harrison Cutts stands by the front steps of Mary P. Willingham School sometime after returning from her home in Scott, Georgia, to serve as music teacher. Perhaps her stern expression is to impress on her former fellow students that she is now in charge. At left, Marie Roberts fills her pitcher at the Mary P. Willingham School spring. She later became executive secretary–treasurer of the Loeb-Goldstein Company of Atlanta, a large broker/ distributor of food products. (Both, courtesy Ethelene Dyer Jones.)

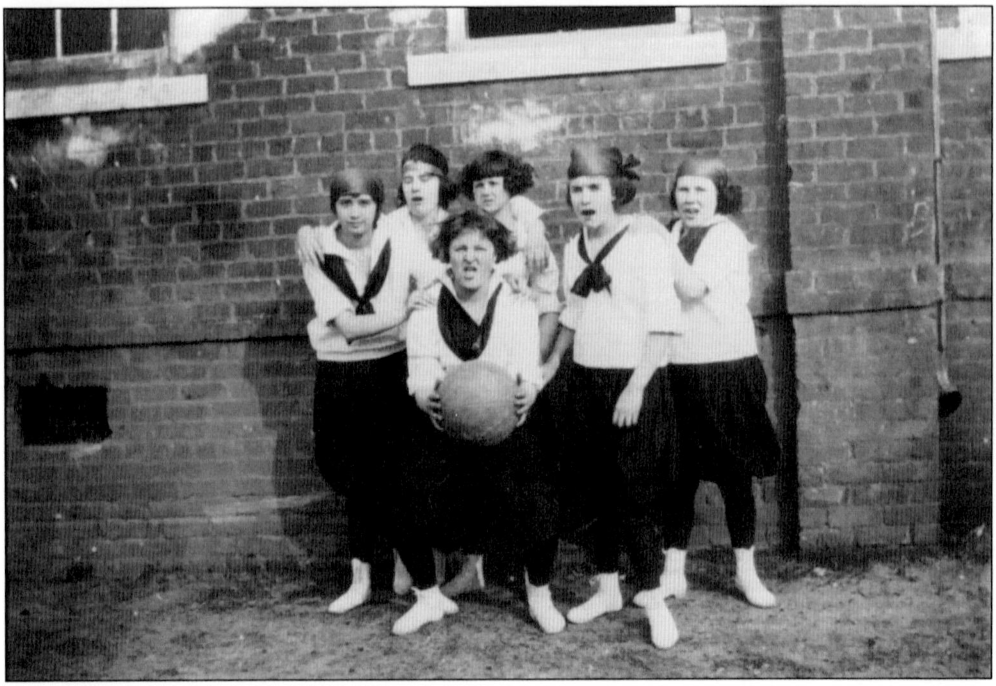

The 1920 girls' basketball varsity team from Mary P. Willingham School strikes a fierce pose for the camera. (Courtesy Ethelene Dyer Jones.)

Lorene Crawford was the daughter of Col. Tom H. Crawford, a noted Blue Ridge attorney, and Isabelle Butt, a native of Morganton. This may be Lorene's 1920 senior picture from Mary P. Willingham School. (Courtesy Ethelene Dyer Jones.)

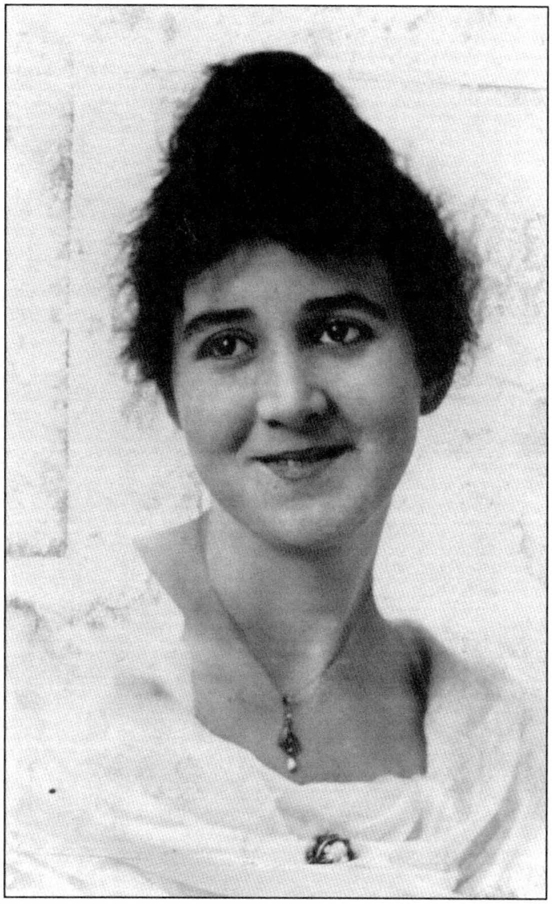

This building served as the domestic science building at Mary P. Willingham School. Seniors ran it as if it were a home, in order to learn various aspects of home economics. After the demise of the school, this became the residence of the Dobbs family, Wesley and Ruby Carney, Phil Hallum, and Hugh and Ann Gibson. It is modified but still standing in 2011. (Courtesy Ethelene Dyer Jones.)

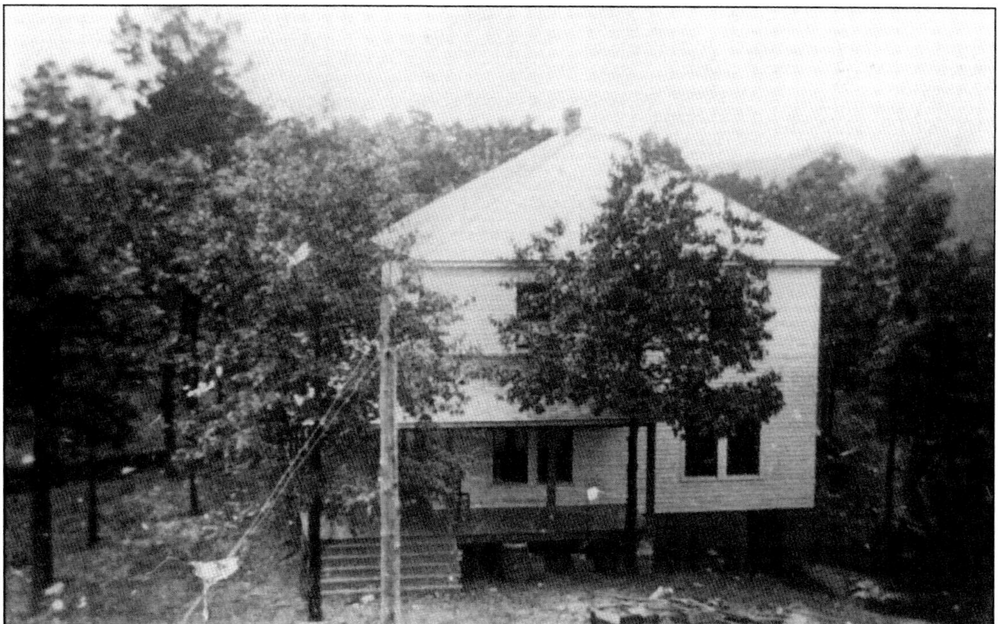

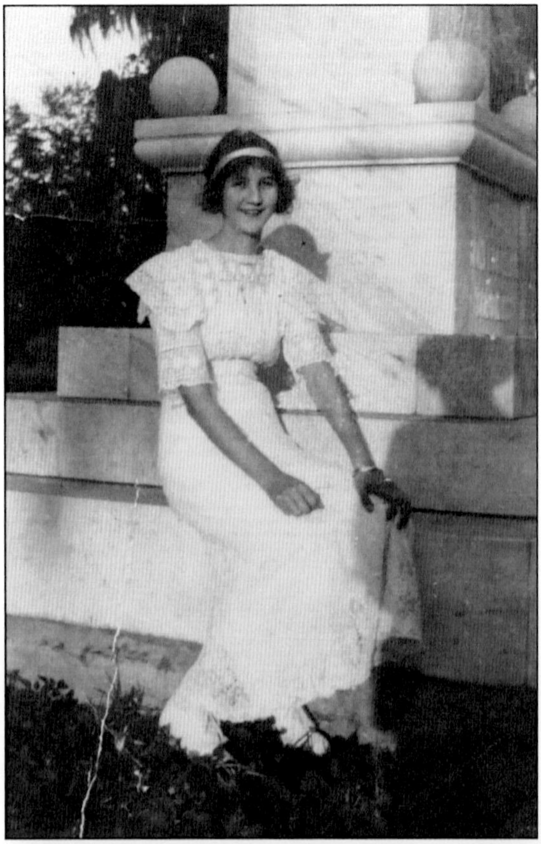

Lorene Crawford, shown here at the monument in Blue Ridge downtown park, married John Wall in 1920. In 1923, he became the local agent for Standard Oil, delivering kerosene through the mountain region, at first using a horse-drawn wagon. He retired from Standard Oil in 1948. He later was a partner in Kiker Oil and founded what became A.J. Trotter Oil Company. Their son Thomas was a US Navy fighter pilot who was lost at sea in 1945 during the Battle of Lingayen Gulf off the Philippines. Their daughter Barbara Anne married E.L. Barron and reared three children in Blue Ridge. (Courtesy Ethelene Dyer Jones.)

Members of the 1922 graduating class of Mary P. Willingham pose on the front steps of the administration building. The child in front is class mascot Sarah Frances Allen. (Courtesy Ethelene Dyer Jones.)

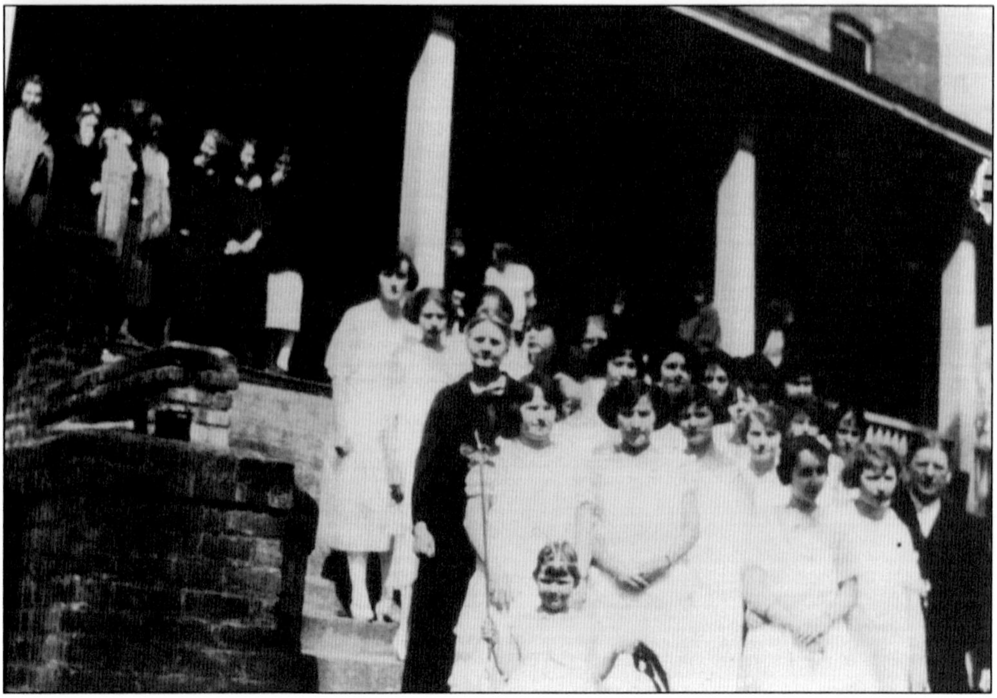

Dr. W.L. Cutts performs a baptism service in Weaver Creek around 1920. (Courtesy Ethelene Dyer Jones.)

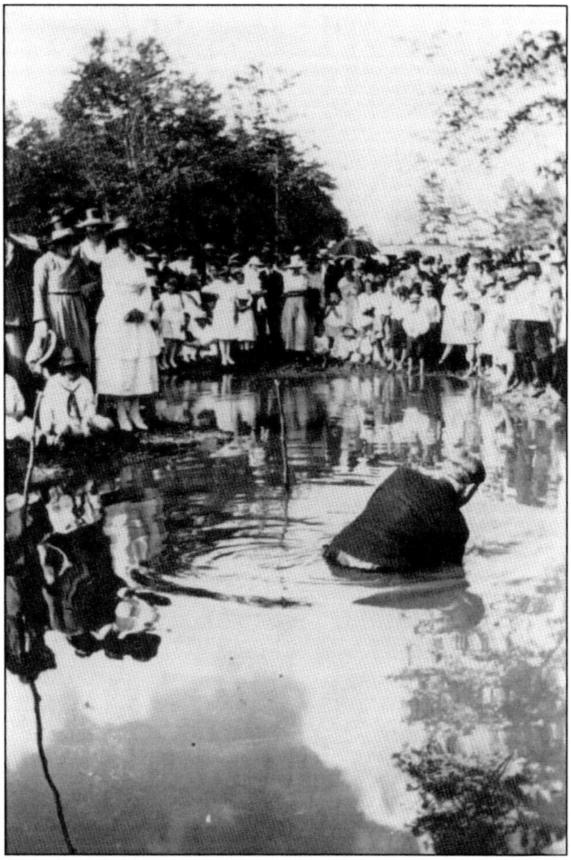

Vera Harrison stands beside a carload of Mary P. Willingham students. E.G. Willingham of Atlanta (patron of the school) brought the first automobile to Blue Ridge to transport guests to Georgia Baptist Assembly. (Courtesy Ethelene Dyer Jones.)

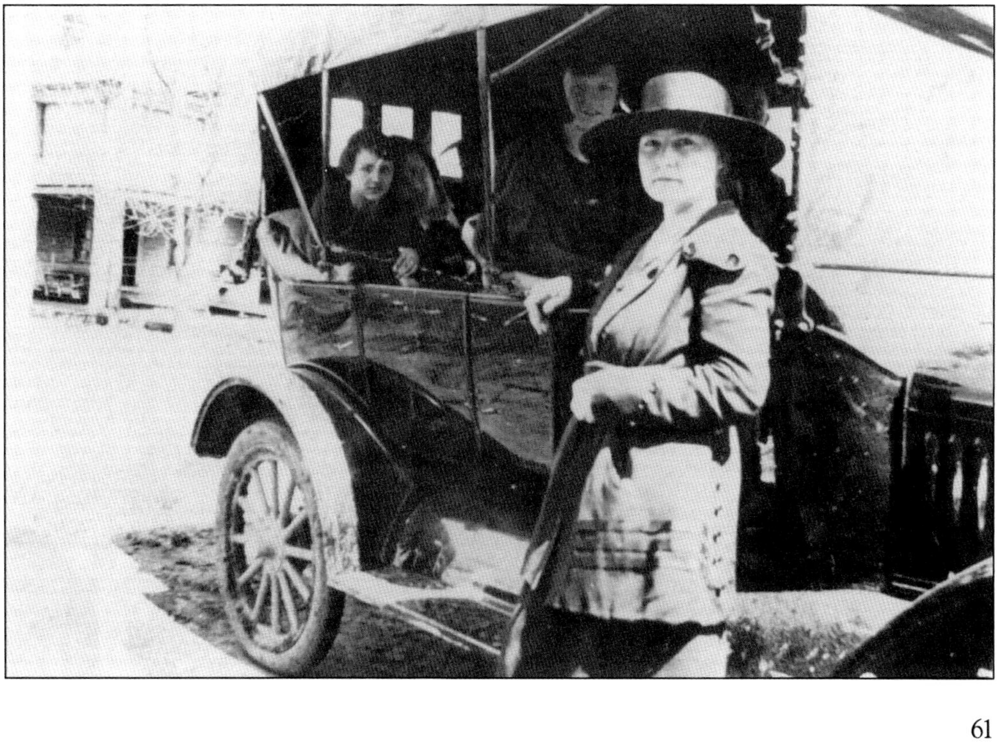

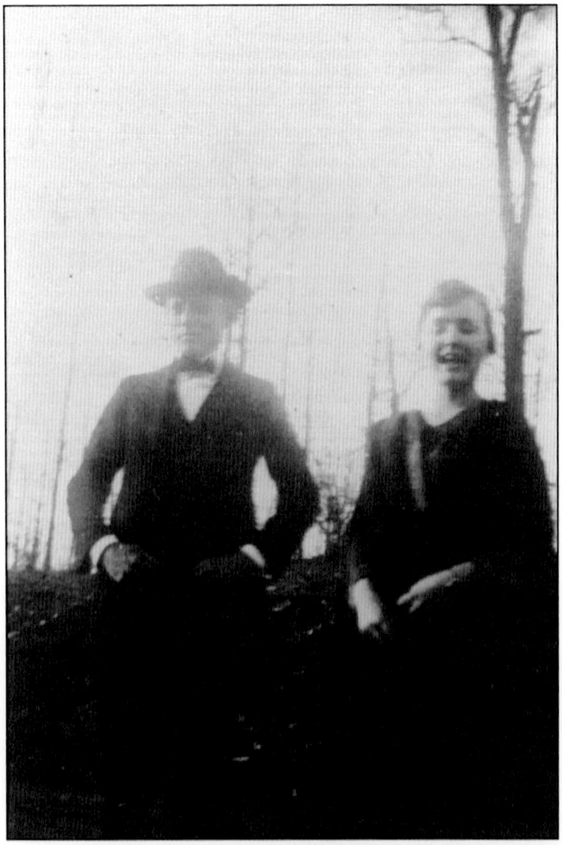

Dr. L.C. Cutts and Vera Harrison Cutts are shown here shortly before or after their wedding on May 30, 1922. (Courtesy Ethelene Dyer Jones.)

Dr. W.C. Cutts lines up with his six sons for a portrait. From left to right are Harvey Clark Cutts (b. 1900), Allen Sherwood Cutts (b. 1898), Paul Cutts (b. 1897), Loomis Clinton "L.C." Cutts (b. 1895), Warren Gibson Cutts (b. 1892), Dr. William Clinton Cutts, and Jesse Mercer Cutts (b. 1889). Dr. W.C. Cutts and his wife, Susan Saphronia Clark Cutts, also had one daughter. Note the chains on the tires; roads were still mostly unpaved around Blue Ridge. (Courtesy Ethelene Dyer Jones.)

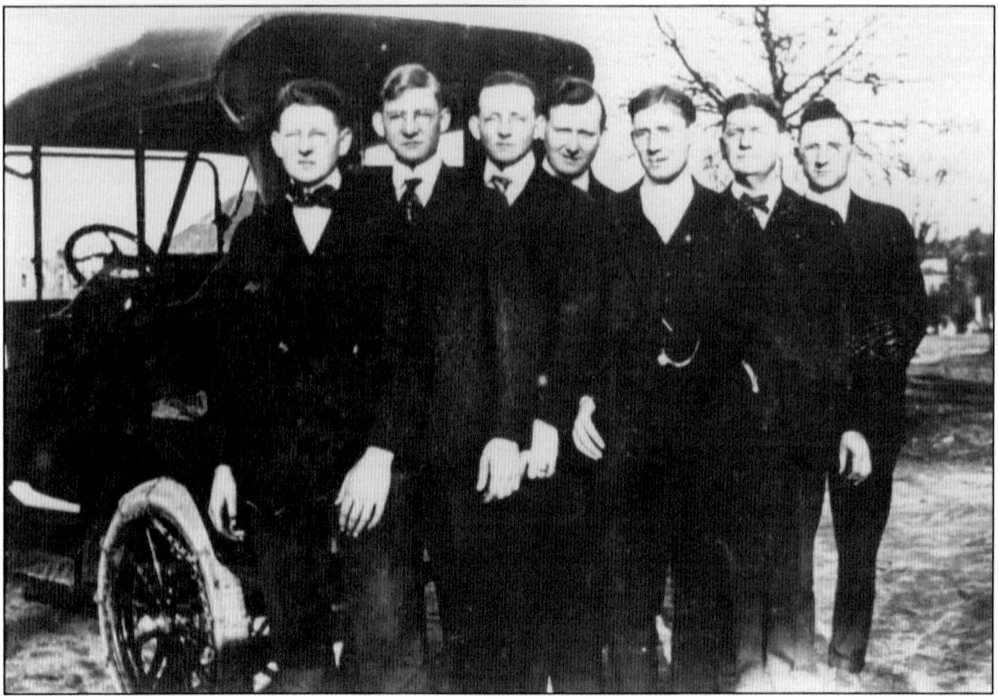

Rev. Marcus C. Lunsford (1872–1944), president of North Georgia Baptist College, was pictured in the 1919 college catalog. He and his wife, Dona, are buried in Morganton Baptist Cemetery. (Courtesy Ethelene Dyer Jones.)

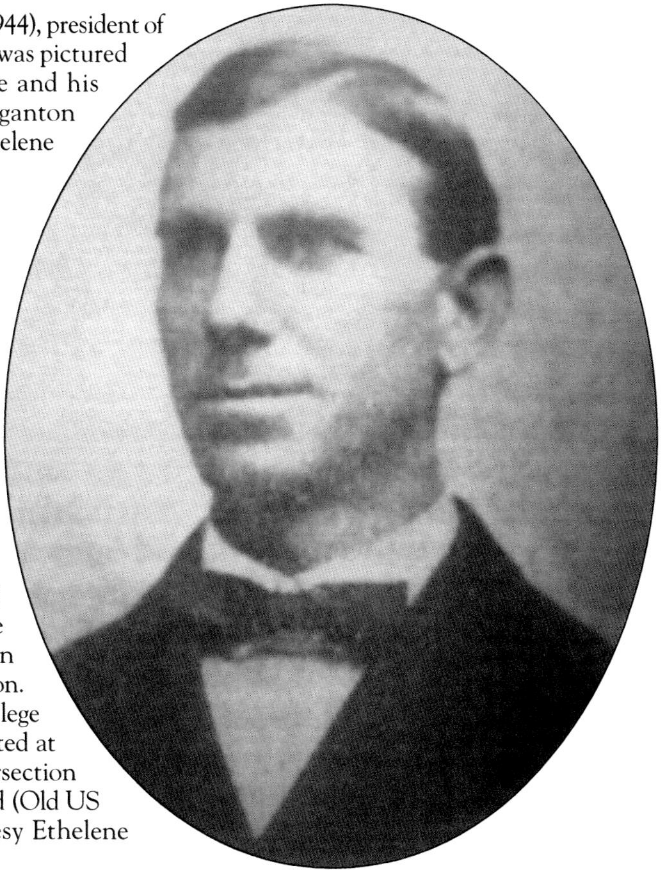

Students, faculty, and friends of North Georgia Baptist College gather at the former Fannin County Courthouse in Morganton. This building was used for the college while buildings were being erected at the campus located at the intersection of Blue Ridge to Blairsville Road (Old US 76) and Loving Road. (Courtesy Ethelene Dyer Jones.)

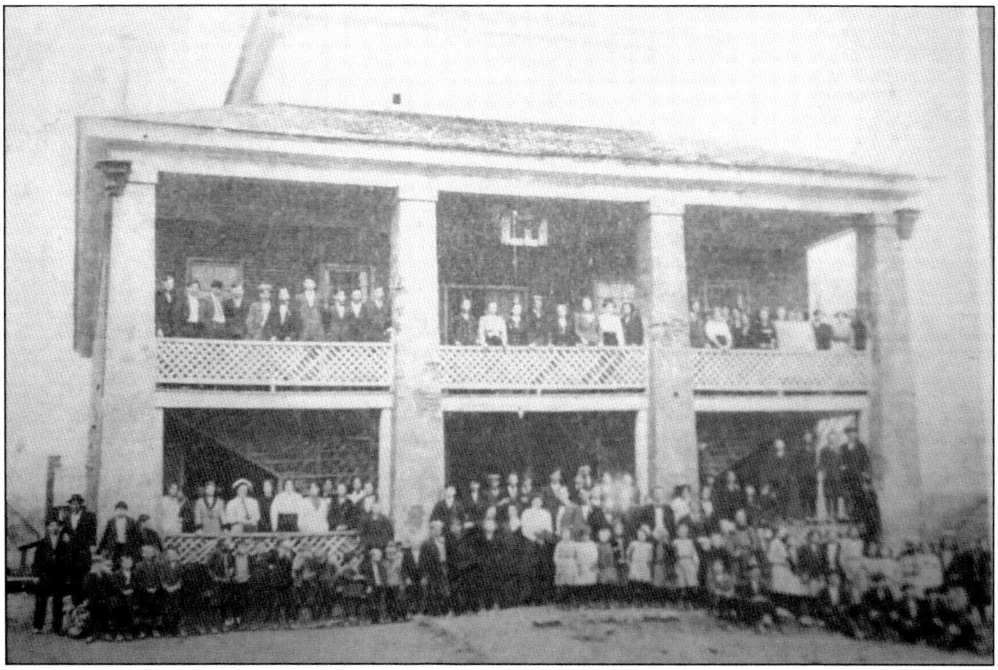

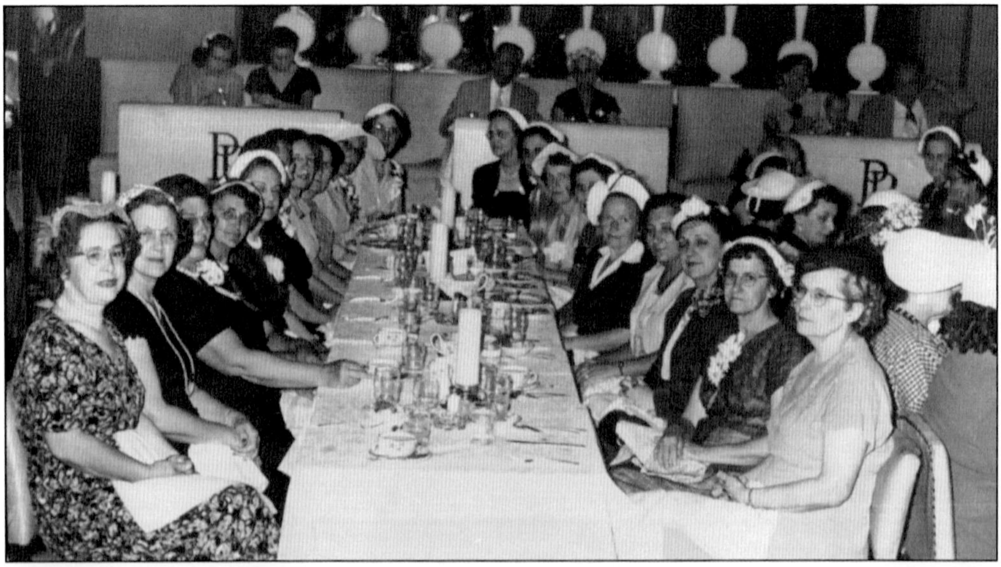

In 1967, alumnae of the Mary P. Willingham School gathered at the Henry Grady Hotel in Atlanta to celebrate the 40th anniversary of the class of 1927. Present around the table are, from left to right, Nelle Jo Bowers, Estelle Cagle, Helen Haskins, Eula Eaves, Grace Anderson, Jane Keeter, Sarah Chandler, Vera Harrison, Lorene Crawford, Vertie Lee Dodd, Bonnie Abercrombie, Mattie Jane Sexton, Ruth Crawford, Eva Mooney, Marie Hitt, Mary Bess Price, Eva Mae Lloyd, Gertrude Dunn, and Ruth Drake. (Courtesy Ethelene Dyer Jones.)

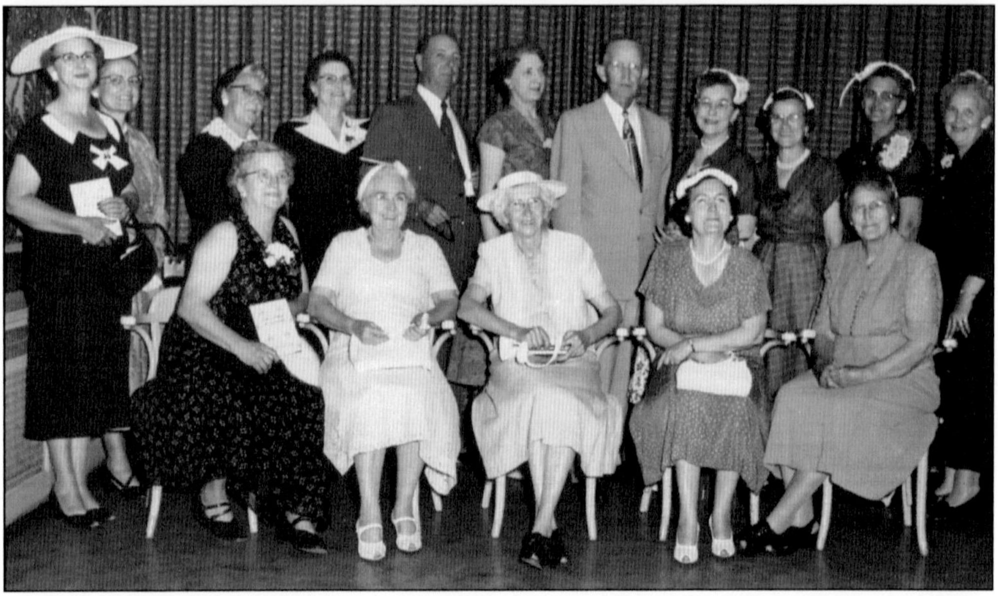

On June 9, 1976, Jackie Vertie Lee Dodd Alverson of Atlanta and Conyers, Georgia, organized a reunion of the Mary P. Willingham School that was attended by 44 alumnae from 22 towns in Georgia, plus the states of Florida, North Carolina, Tennessee, and Virginia. This picture was taken at the American Motor Hotel in Atlanta. All those in the first row are unidentified except Vera H. Cutts, seated at the far right. Standing in the second row, from left to right, are two unidentified, Lorene Crawford Wall, Helen Haskins Hall, Col. T.H. Crawford, unidentified, and Dr. L.C. Cutts. Following Dr. L.C. Cutts are four unidentified women. (Courtesy Ethelene Dyer Jones.)

Five

War, Boom, Bust, and War

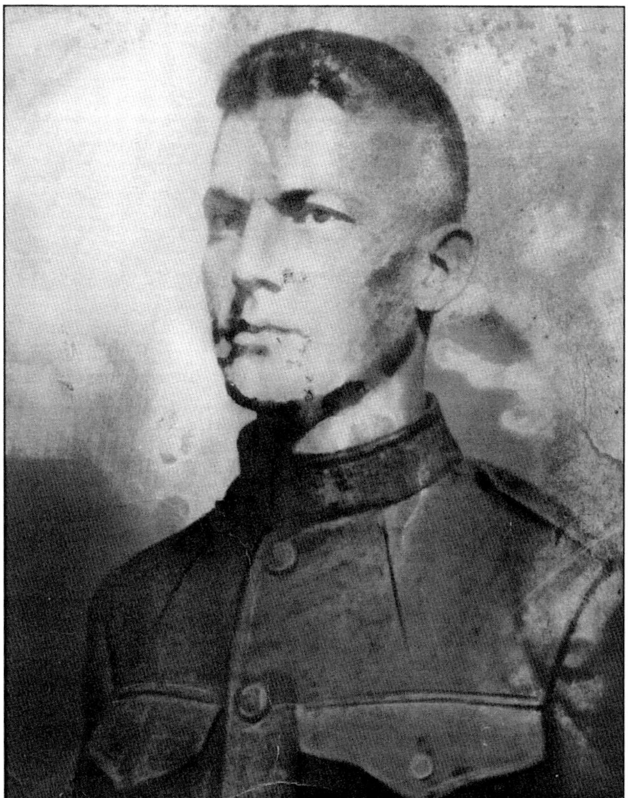

William Bascom Carter was born March 22, 1893, and was killed October 6, 1918, in the Argonne Forest of France, just over a month before the Armistice. Symbolic of many Fannin Countians who served in time of war, and especially of those who gave the supreme sacrifice, he was the son of Rev. Joseph Marion Carter and his wife, Stacy L. DeWeese Carter. Rev. Carter was pastor at several churches in the county, including Toccoa, Wilscot, and Morganton Baptist. (Courtesy Glenda Wattenbarger.)

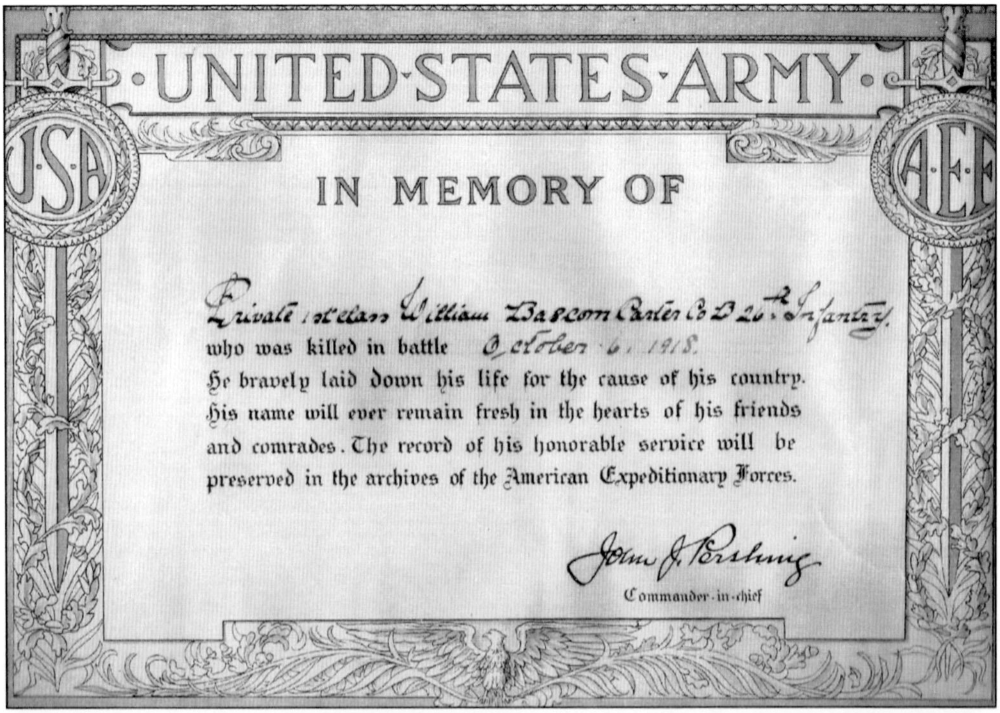
·UNITED·STATES·ARMY·

U·S·A

A·E·F

IN MEMORY OF

Private 1st class William Bascom Carter Co D 20th Infantry
who was killed in battle October 6, 1918.
He bravely laid down his life for the cause of his country.
His name will ever remain fresh in the hearts of his friends
and comrades. The record of his honorable service will be
preserved in the archives of the American Expeditionary Forces.

John J. Pershing
Commander-in-chief

This certificate from Gen. John J. "Black Jack" Pershing, commander of the American Expeditionary Forces in World War I, was lovingly preserved by the family of Bascom Carter. (Courtesy Glenda Wattenbarger via Baugh House collection.)

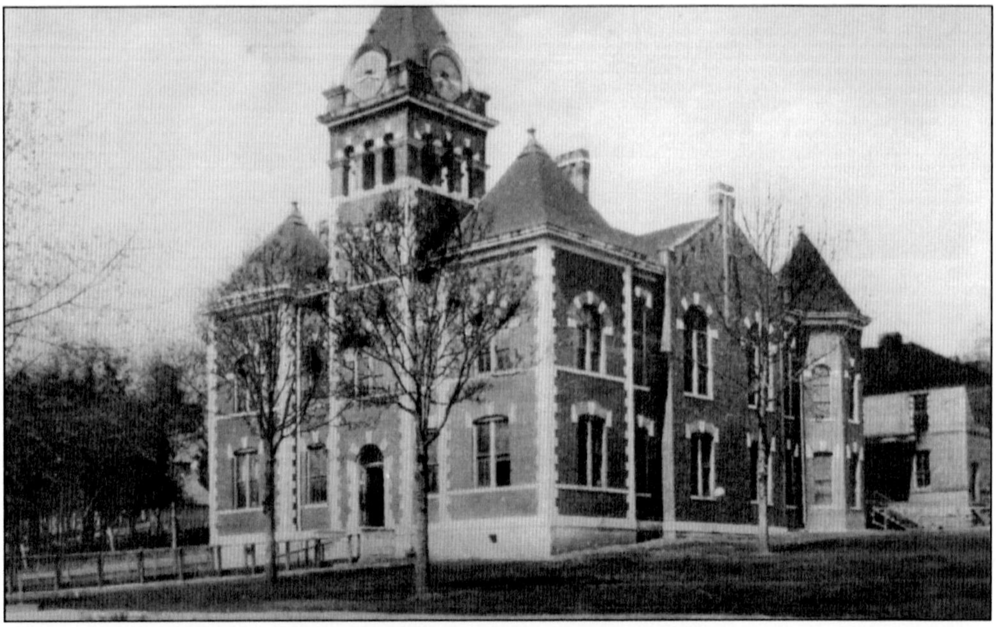

The county seat was removed from Morganton to Blue Ridge in 1895. Court must have been held in temporary quarters until completion of this structure in 1901. Many people consider this to be the most beautiful of all the courthouses Fannin County has possessed. Unfortunately, it burned to the ground in 1936. (Courtesy Don and Carolyn Hall.)

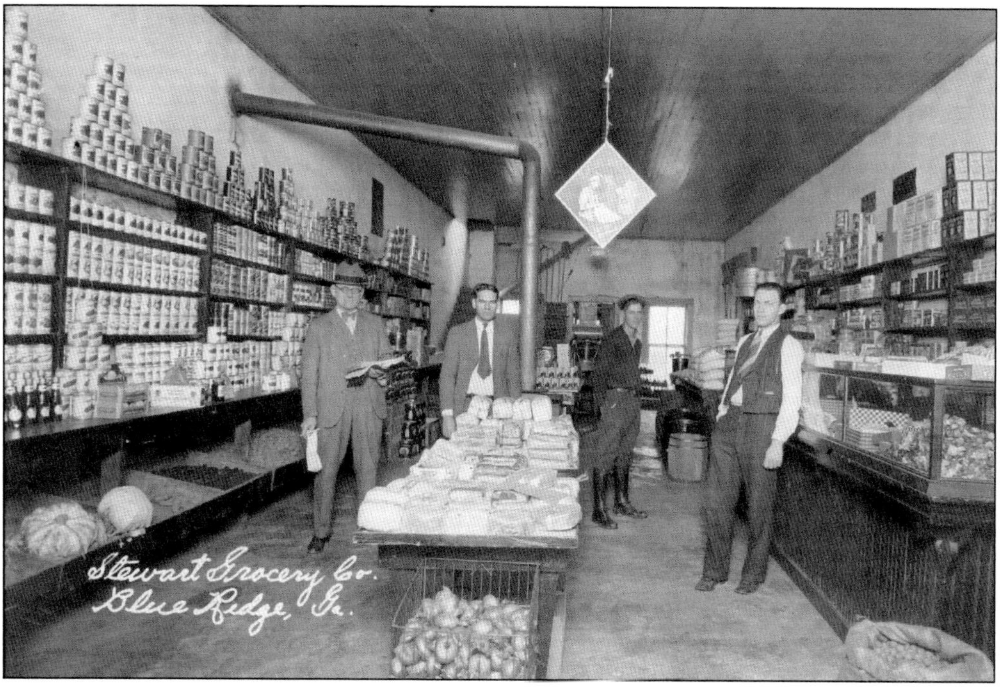

Shown here, owner Oliver Stewart (left) and salesmen Joe Hopper and Otis Hall are hard at work at the Stewart grocery in Blue Ridge, probably in the 1920s. The person second from the right at the back of the store is unidentified. (Courtesy Don and Carolyn Hall.)

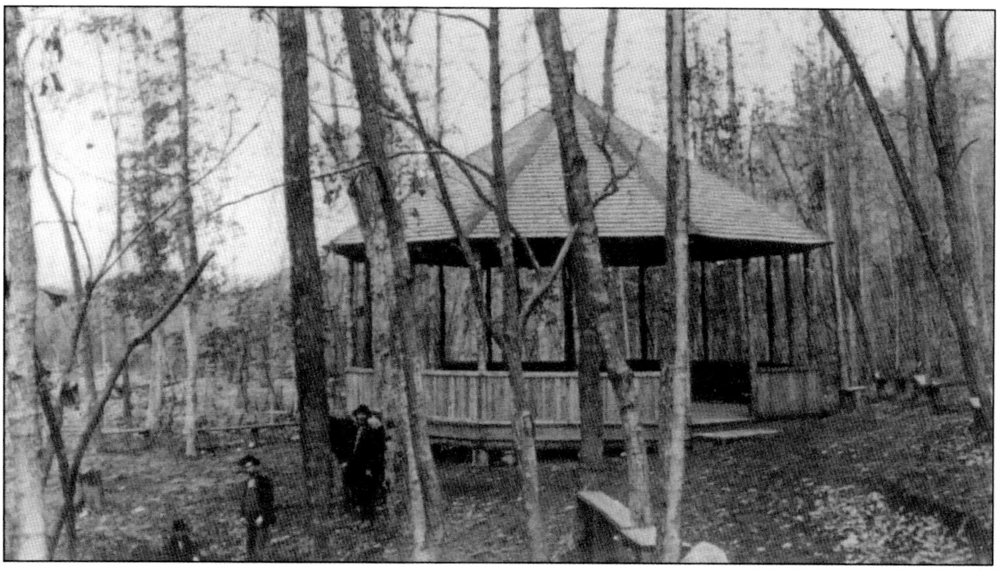

This pavilion near the Mineral Springs served the Georgia Baptist Assembly and Mary P. Willingham School through the 1920s. In 2011, plans were underway to make a park in the Mineral Springs area and to perhaps reproduce this structure. Note the rough-hewn bench in front of the structure is just a plank wedged between two trees. (Courtesy Don and Carolyn Hall.)

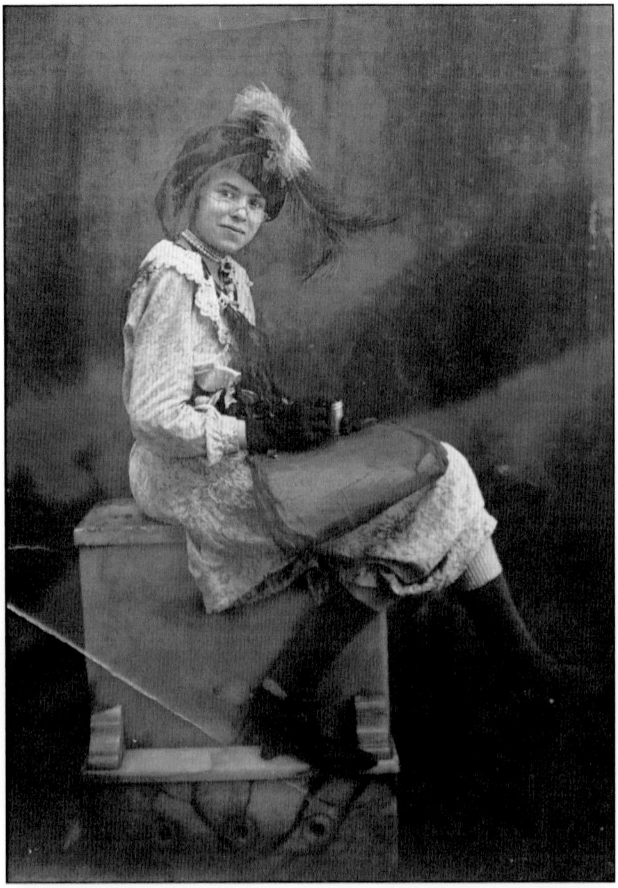

Emma Louise Beam surely must have won top honors at the 1929 "Tacky Party." (Courtesy Michael Eaton.)

A train makes a snowy run from Copperhill, Tennessee, south toward Blue Ridge in the early 19th century. According to folklore, as relayed by Rev. Grover D. Jones, conductors gave this cry (all in one breath!) as the train moved southward from the "loop" (where the line circled a mountain, looping over itself to gain and lose altitude): "The next turtle is Turtletown, the next duck is Ducktown, the next hill is Copperhill, the next 'ville' is McCaysville, the next son is Patterson, the next ridge is Blue Ridge, the next log is Cherry Log, the next jay is Ellijay!" (Courtesy Ethelene Dyer Jones.)

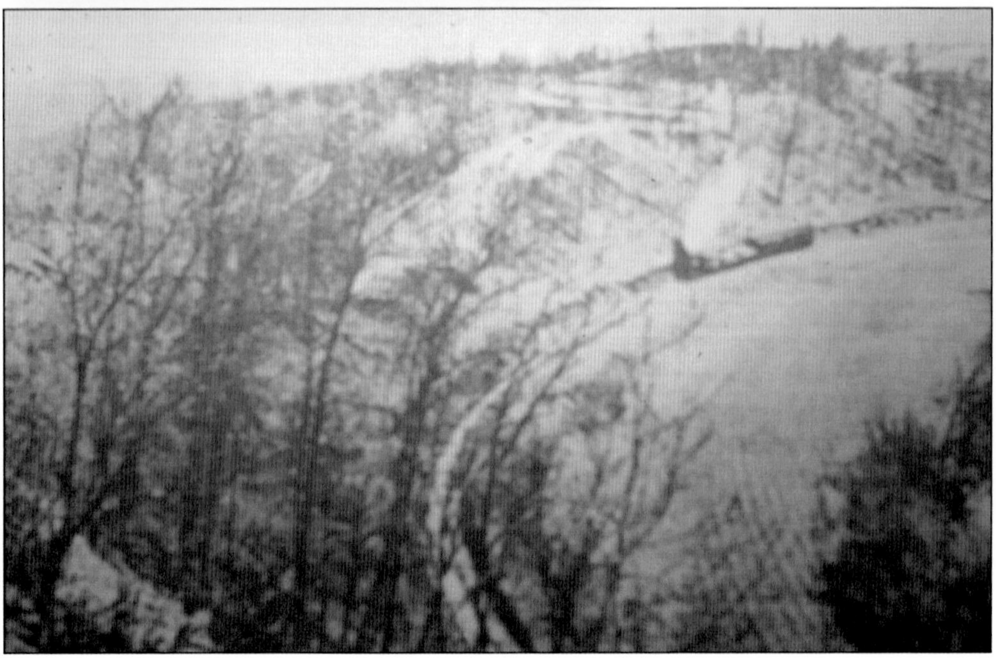

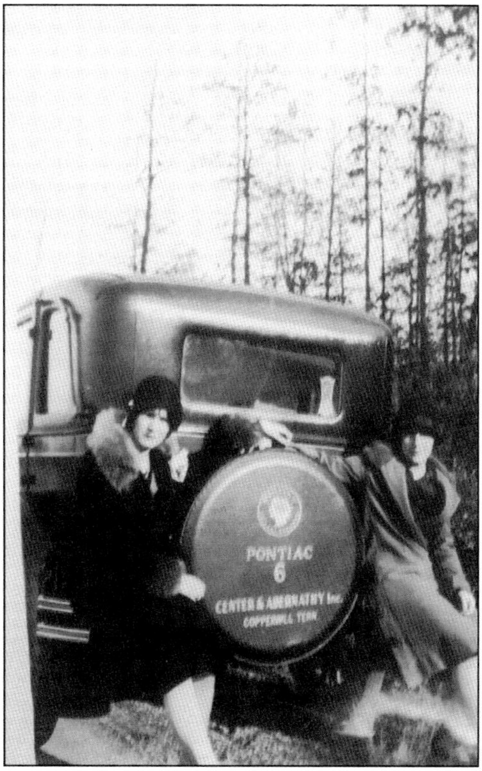

Two ladies seem pleased with their Pontiac purchased from Center and Abernathy in Copperhill, Tennessee, in the Roaring Twenties. Luther H. Abernathy was a partner in this business. He also sold furniture and ran a funeral home. Later, the business was moved to Epworth, Georgia, where it continues operation as of 2011. Their motto is "You marry the girl, we'll furnish the home." (Courtesy Michael Eaton.)

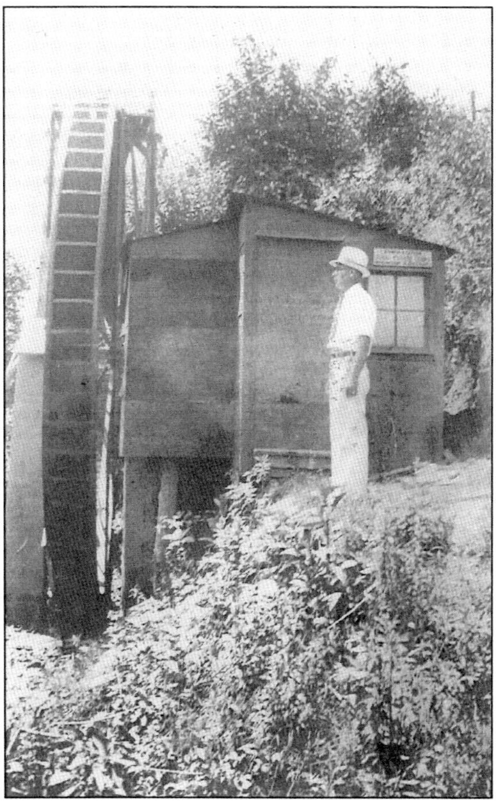

Lewin Cobb stands by an 18-foot water wheel that generated electrical power in the Hemptown community. It provided electricity to the Sword Printing Company, which published the *Fannin County Times* newspaper in the early 1930s. (Courtesy Wilson and LaVerne Cobb.)

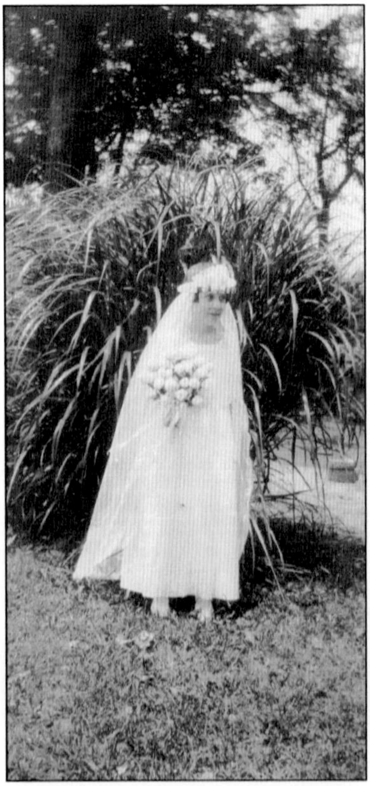

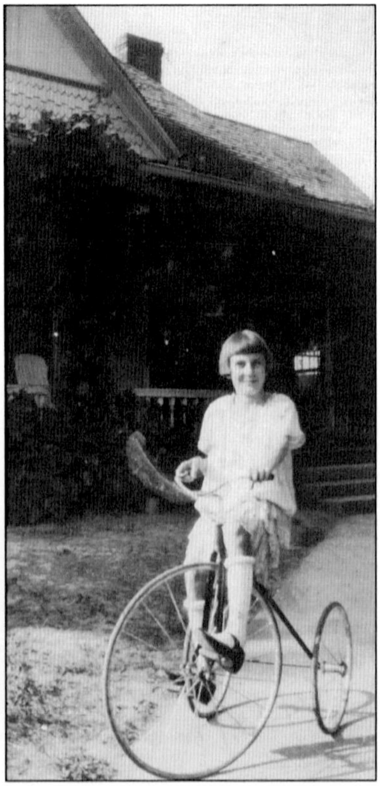

In the 1921 image at far left, Dorothy Lloyd is dressed to star as the bride in a "Tom Thumb wedding" in Blue Ridge. In the c. 1923 photograph at left, Lloyd rides her tricycle atop one of Blue Ridge's hills. Sadly, Lloyd only lived from 1915 until 1926, passing away from a heart condition. (Both, courtesy Michael Eaton.)

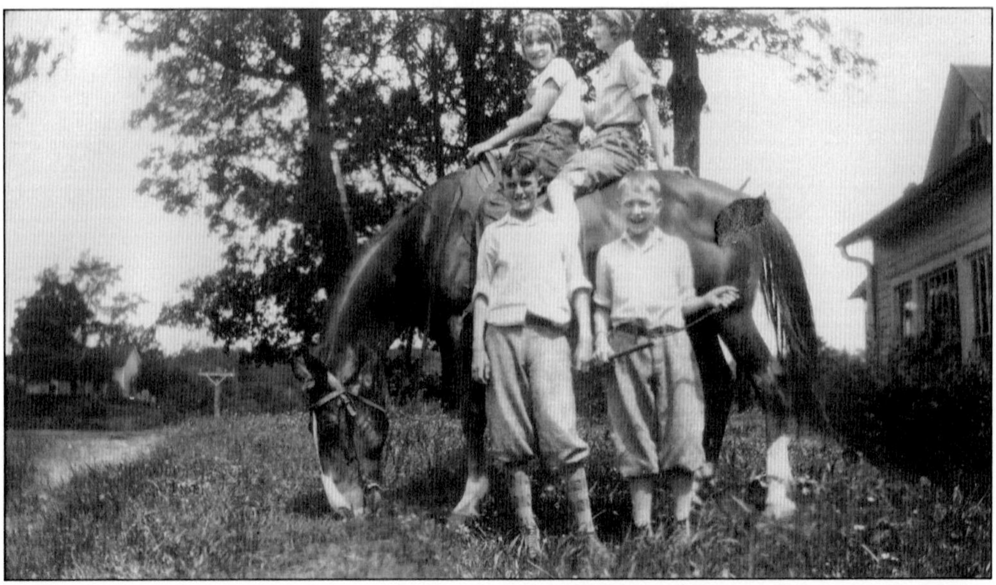

Suella Lloyd (at the reins) and three unidentified friends enjoy riding and playing in the yard of the Lloyd home in Blue Ridge around 1923. (Courtesy Michael Eaton.)

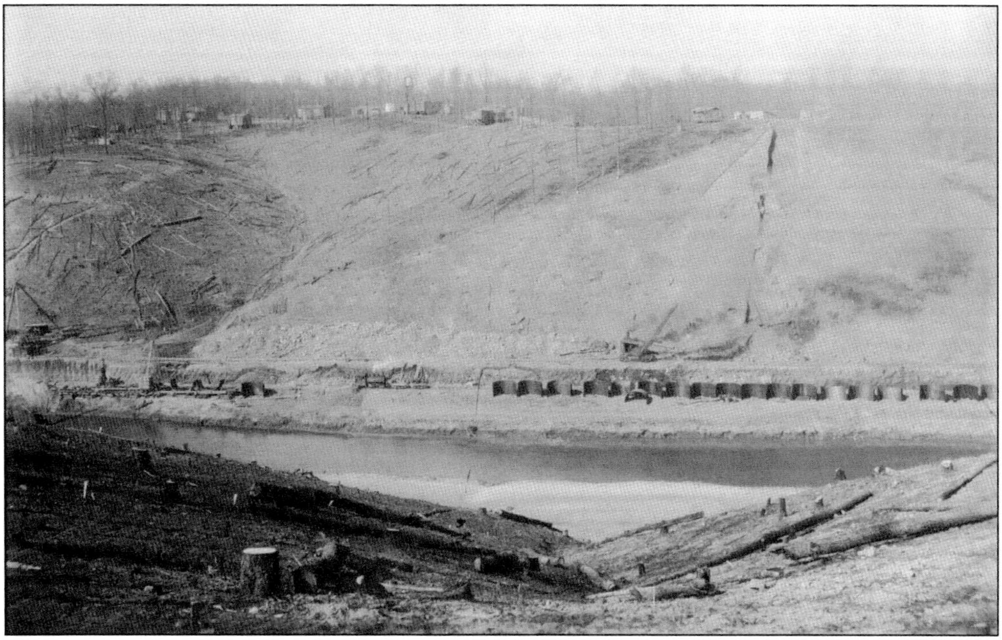

Massive amounts of soil and rocks had to be moved to construct the Toccoa Dam in the 1920s. Here, the Toccoa still flows unchecked, but much work is taking place along the adjacent narrow bluffs. (Courtesy Tennessee Valley Authority.)

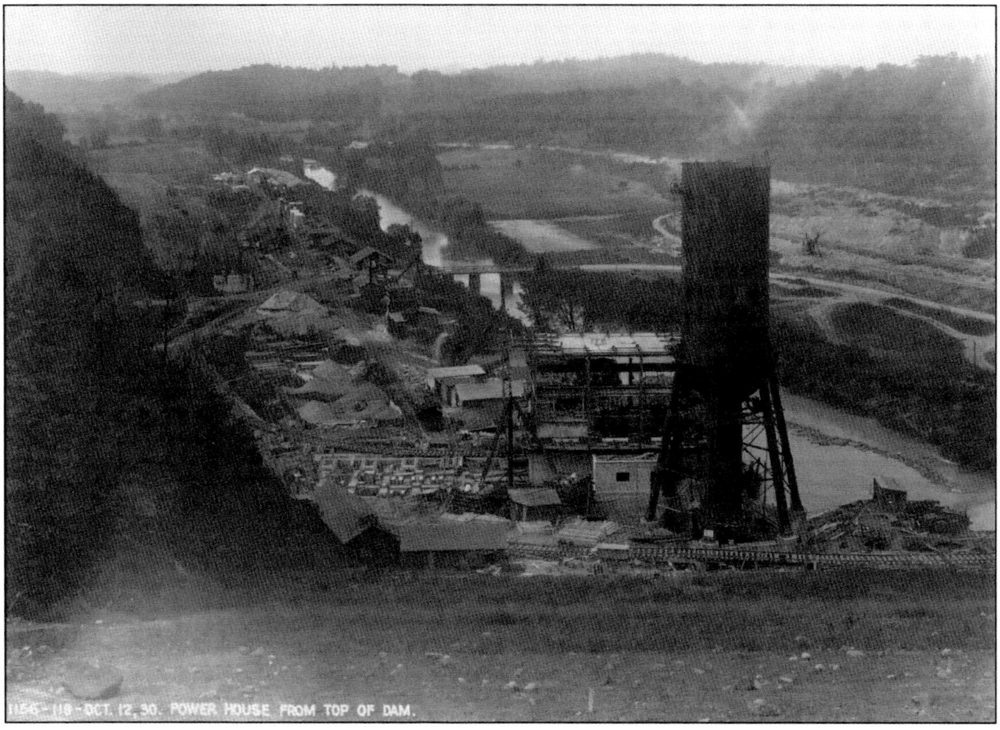

Steam or smoke billows from the almost-completed surge tank during the construction of the Toccoa Dam in the late 1920s. The surge tank helps regulate the pressure of water passing through the penstock to the turbines. (Courtesy Tennessee Valley Authority.)

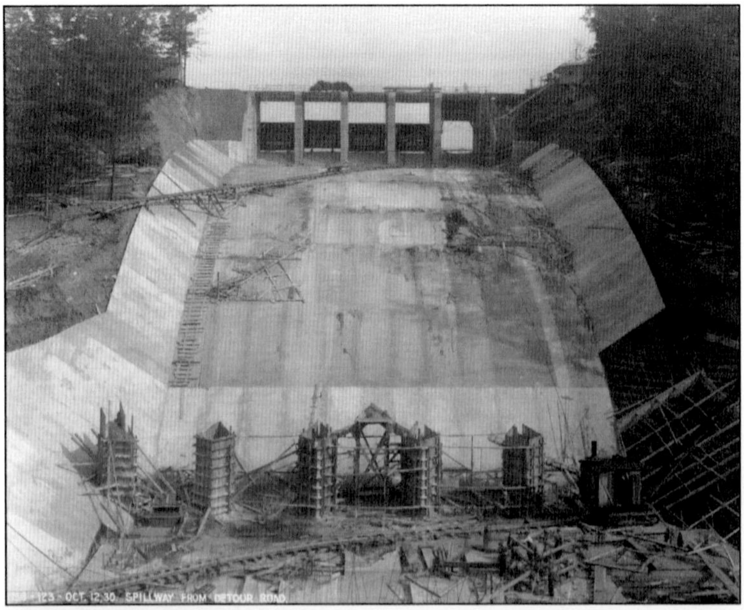

The massive spillway of the Toccoa Dam is nearing completion. Note the concrete forms are still in place near the bottom of the photograph, and the almost-finished bridge is visible at the top. Massive retractable curved steel doors will be placed below the bridge to hold back floodwaters. (Courtesy Tennessee Valley Authority.)

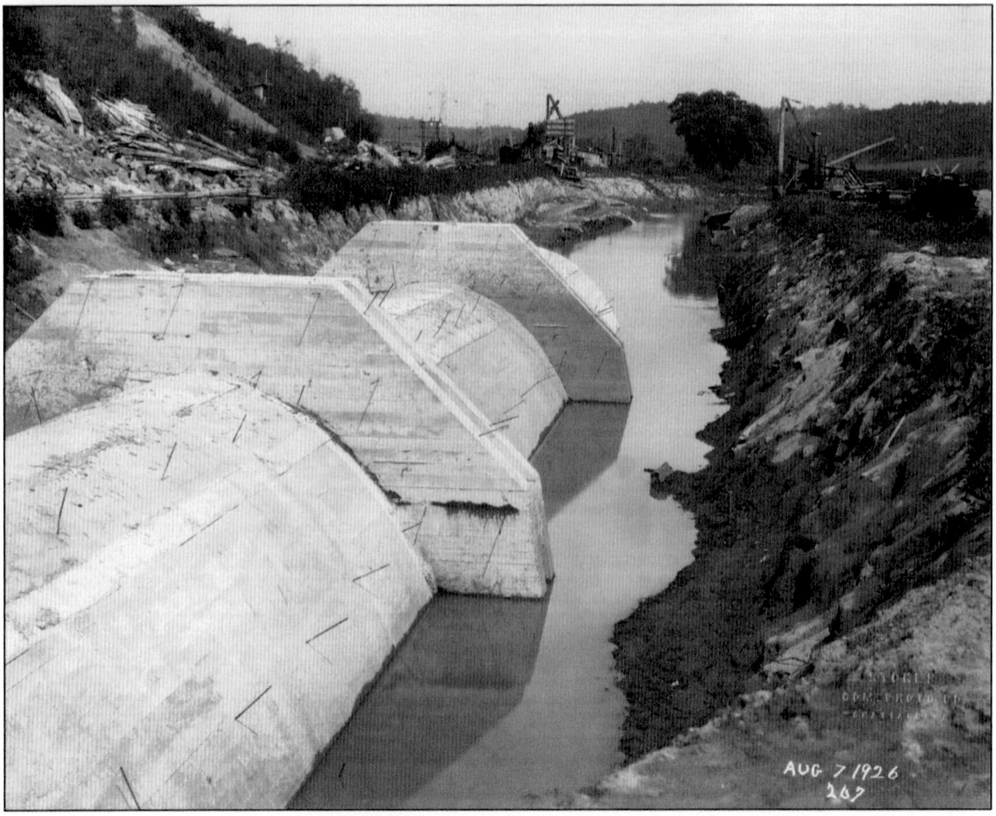

By August 7, 1926, much work had been completed on the Toccoa Dam project. What appears to be a large culvert is the horizontal part of the penstock assembly, which conducts the water from the "tower" in the center of the lake down to the water turbines. What must the old-time gristmill operators have thought of such an operation? (Courtesy Tennessee Valley Authority.)

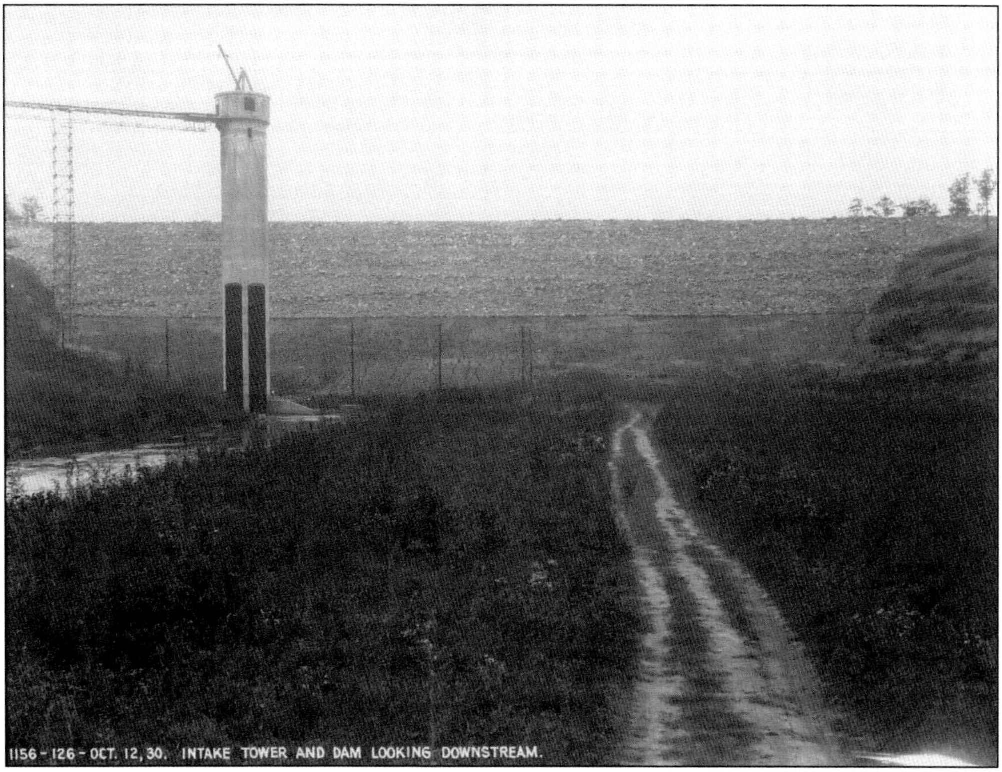

The penstock stands here in solitary glory, revealing its true height since the lake has not yet begun to fill. Water enters the penstock, falling through a massive pipe to drive the turbines that spin the generators when the powerhouse is in operation. (Courtesy Tennessee Valley Authority.)

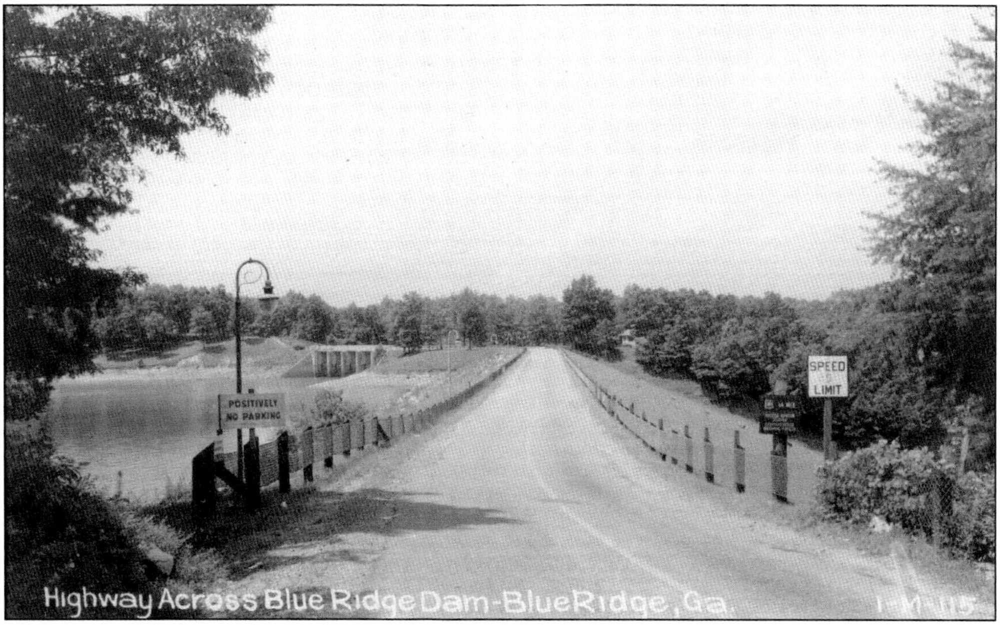

This postcard shows the highway crossing the dam, ready for travel. (Courtesy Don and Carolyn Hall.)

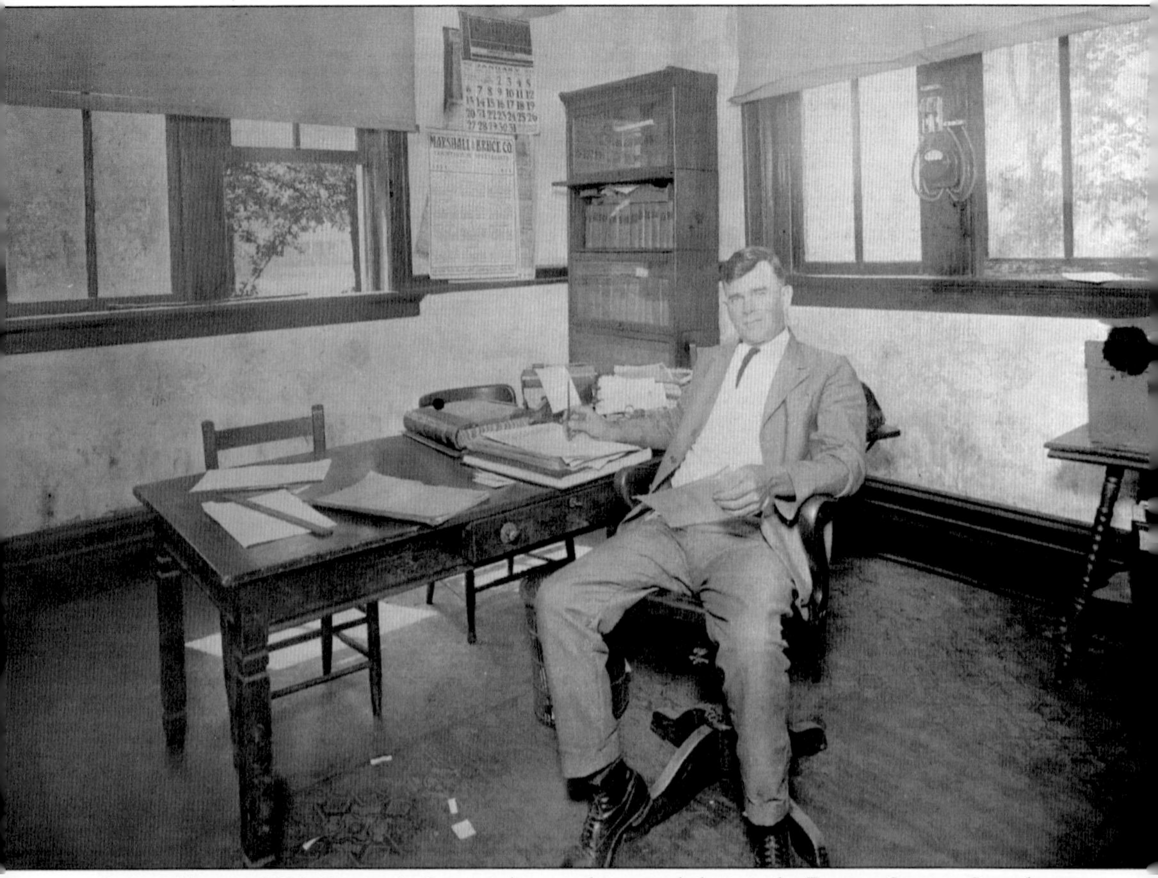

Pictured here in 1924, George A. Curtis relaxes in his swivel chair at the Fannin County Courthouse. Age 46 at this time, Curtis served as clerk of superior court from 1910 to 1916, ordinary from 1916 to 1924, and as commissioner of roads and revenue from 1924 to 1932 and again from 1936 to 1946. The ordinary essentially had duties similar to modern county commission chairs. (Courtesy Georgia Archives, Vanishing Georgia Collection, image fan018-83.)

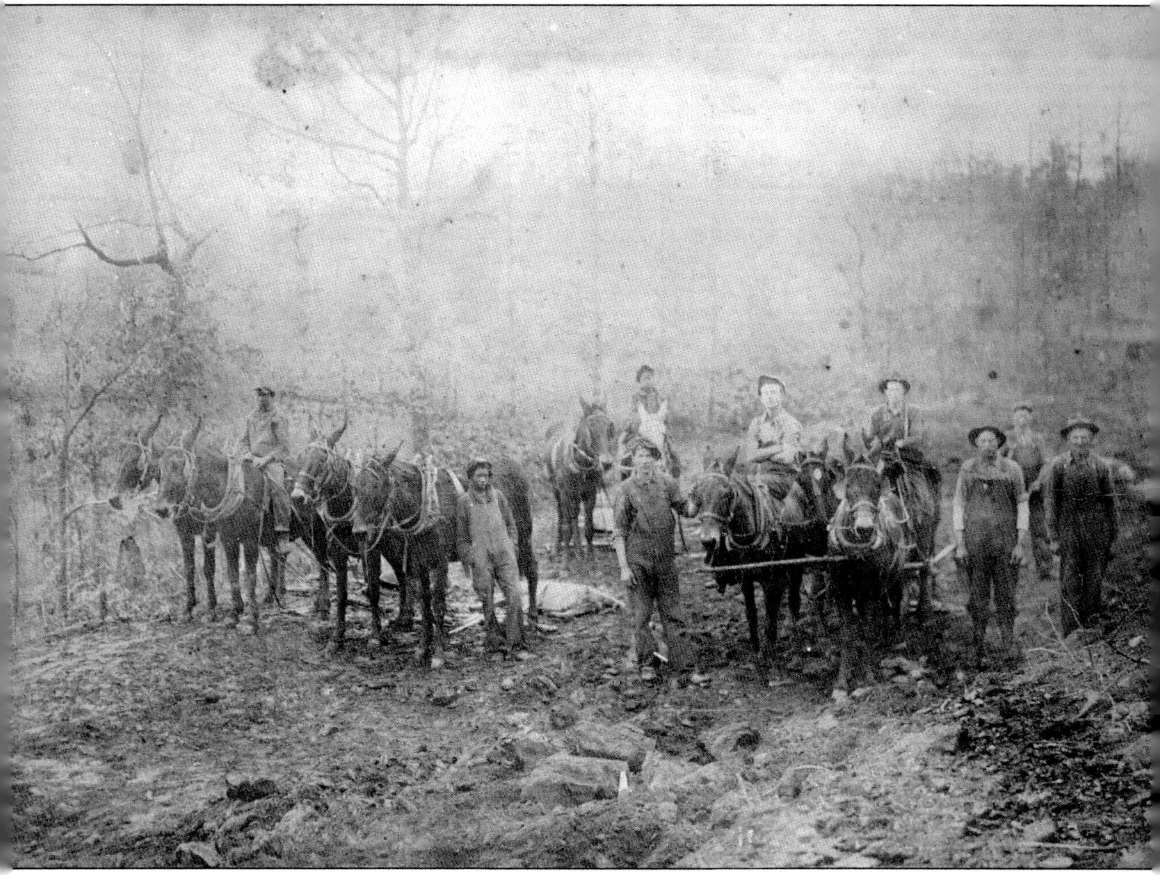

In this 1930s image, men use mule teams to construct a road through the rugged mountains of Fannin County. Note the two African Americans on the left. At the time, the black population of the county was very small. Some or all of these men may be providing labor on the roads in lieu of cash payment for their property taxes. Some may also be county or state prisoners serving hard labor. (Courtesy Georgia Archives, Vanishing Georgia Collection, image fan007-83.)

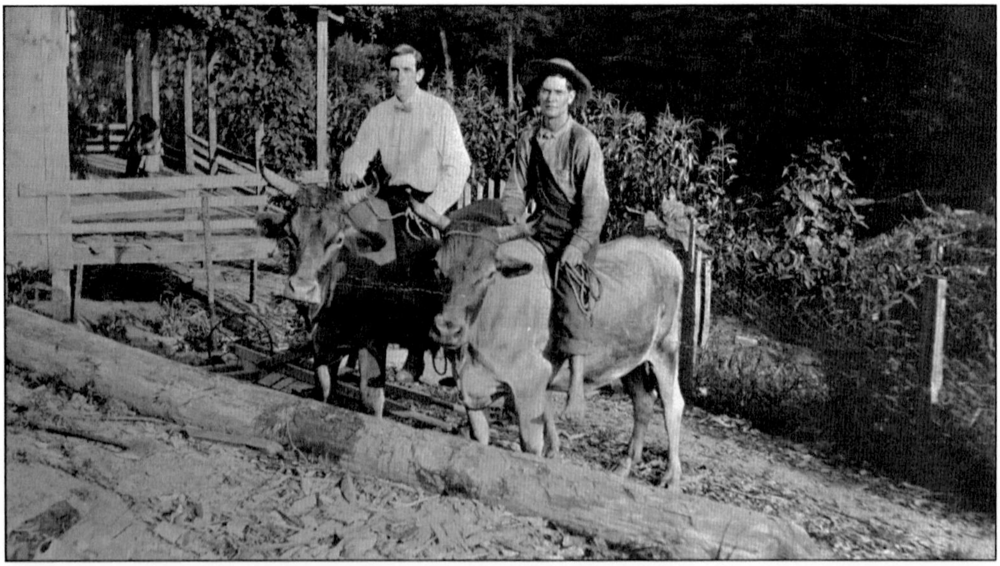

Two unidentified Fannin County men are riding oxen in this snapshot from the 1920s. Oxen were used to haul felled timber, drag sleds full of rocks from fields, and other heavy tasks. (Courtesy Georgia Archives, Vanishing Georgia Collection, fan008-83.)

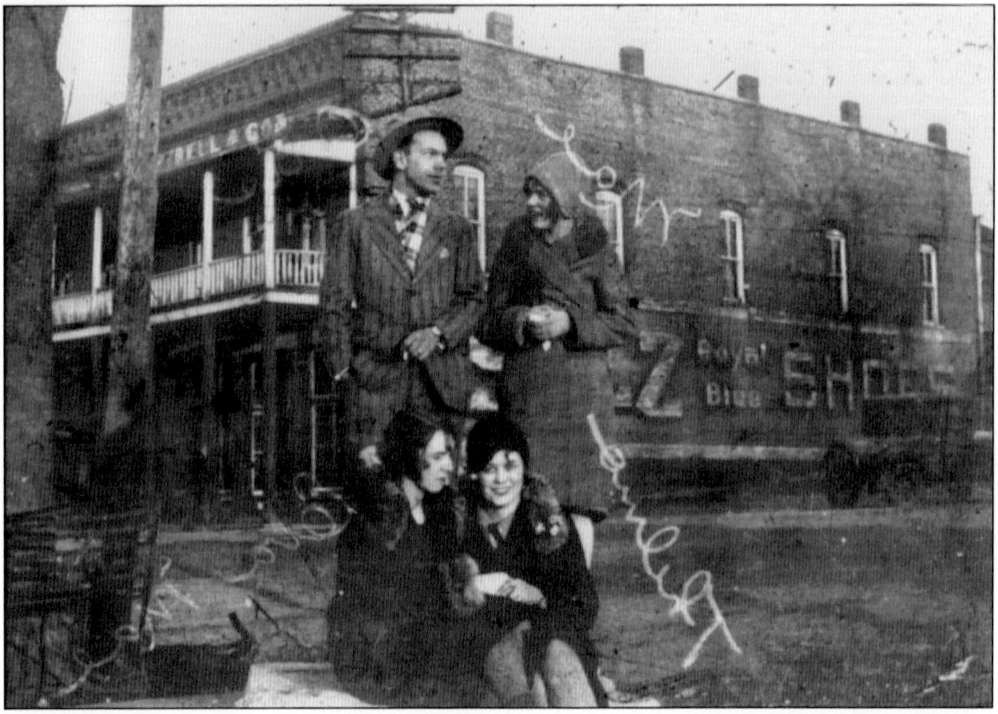

Otis Hall is very nattily dressed in this c. 1928 photograph, standing in front of Blue Ridge's Gartrell Hotel. Hall later founded a haberdashery. Mae Brackett (later Mae Hall, but it was another Hall she married, not Otis) is standing next to him. Seated is Eva Mae Lloyd (later Eva Mashburn) on the front left and Thelma Reece (later Thelma Middleton) on the right. The reversed handwriting on the image was caused when the names were written on the back of the photograph with heavy pressure, causing the ink to flake off the obverse. (Courtesy Don and Carolyn Hall.)

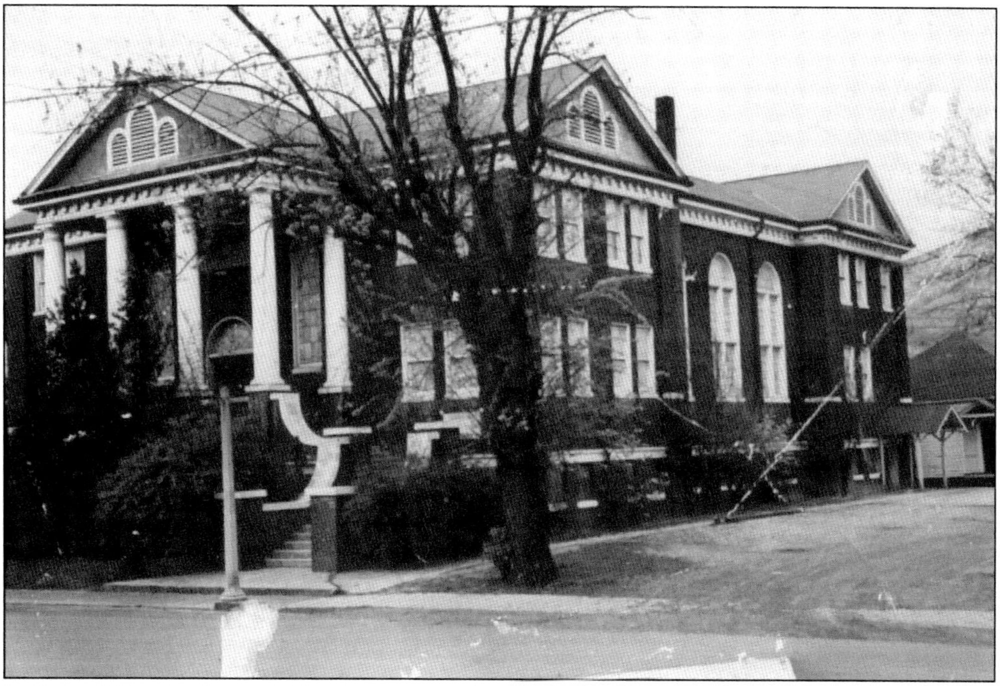

Built in 1926, this beautiful brick sanctuary building was home to the First Baptist Church of McCaysville, Georgia, and Copperhill, Tennessee, until it was destroyed by fire on Christmas 1960. That event, plus several floods of the adjacent Toccoa River, inspired the name of the church's history book, *Faith Through Flood and Fire*. (Courtesy Ethelene Dyer Jones.)

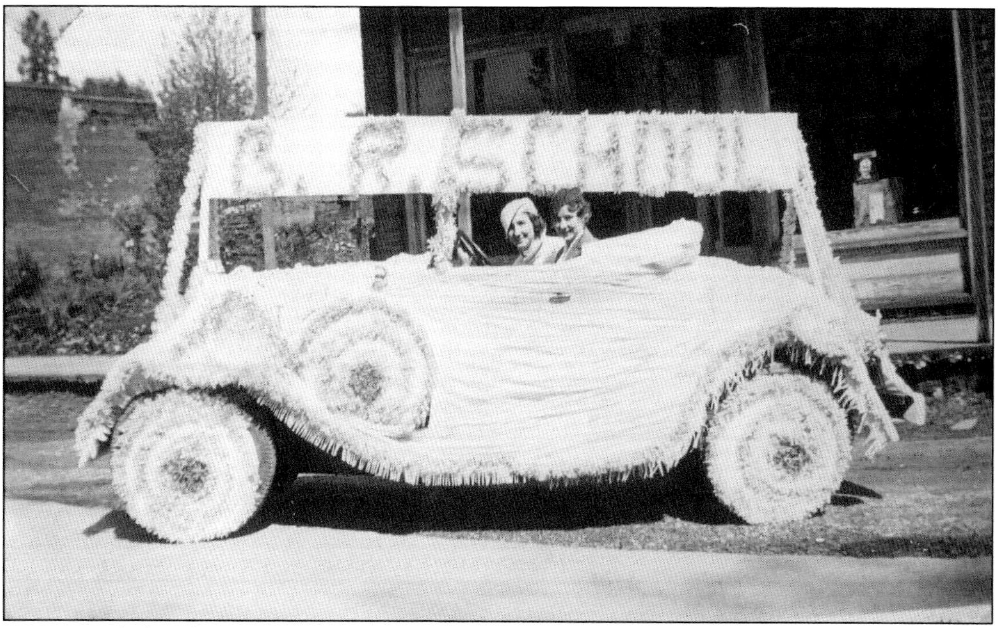

Two young ladies drive some kind of roadster in a school spirit parade in the mid-1920s. (Courtesy Michael Eaton.)

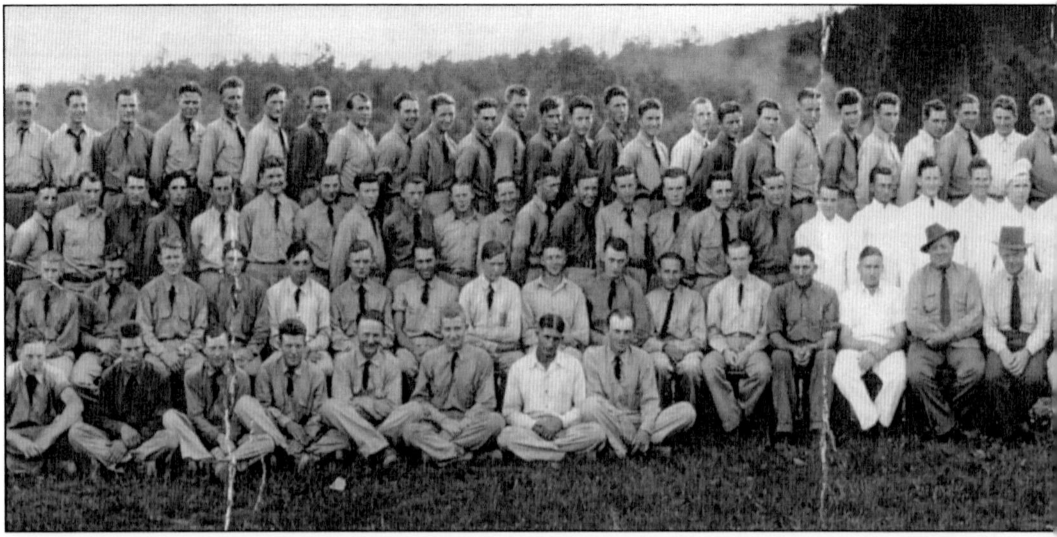

Civilian Conservation Corps "boys," their military commanders, and camp staff members gather on the grounds of Camp Lawrence W. Young near Higdon's Store on July 8, 1937. Those pictured are as follows, in alphabetical order: (officers) Lawrence L Boyd, Captain, 324th Military Police Battalion, Commanding Officer; Dondell C. Cotter, Second Lieutenant, 323rd Infantry, Junior Officer; C.D. Stovall, C.E.A.; H.M. Chester, C.E.A.; J.A. Abercrombie, Project Supervisor; O.B. Hooper, Truck and Trail Foreman; E.J. Avery, Truck and Trail Foreman; Tobie Green, 'Locator' ; Paul C. Barnes, Machine Operator; Bert Gooch, Machine Operator; (leaders) Starnes, Homer L, Senior Leader; Byrd, Will H, Mess Steward; Huskey, Cecil, Storekeeper; Crocker, D.H, 1st Cook; Pollinzi, Dominico; Sargent, Bennett; Davidson, Frank; Kirkland, Johnnie; Cadle, Clarence; Norrell, Thomas; Mosely, John; (assistant leaders) Allen, Lawrence; Black, Rex; Burke, Jimmie; Grizzel, Vernon; Harris, A.G.; Hightower, Marion; Jessup, Cadwell, Company Clerk; Jolley, Emmett; McCay, T.J.; McEver, Frank; Nichols, Horace; Pope, Lenior; Porter, Luther; Price, William B.; Queen, Garnett; Self, Jay B.; Wilson, H.S.; Holt, Theodore; Stover, J.C.; (members) Allison, James; Allred, Clinton; Anderson, David; Andrews, Grant; Andrews, Major; Barkley, Paul; Barnes, Ralph; Barrett, Vaughn; Beasley, Bennie L.; Beavers, Elisha; Blackwell, Paul; Blaylock, Arnold; Bloodworth, Thomas; Brackett, Morris; Brawley, Mark; Brown, Clarence; Brown, Harless; Brown, H.J.; Bruce, James C.; Cabe, George; Callihan, Mark; Campbell, Clarence; Cantrell, Hugh; Cantrell, Boyd; Cantrell, William; Canup, Clyde; Carroll, Arthur; Carroll, Floyd; Carroll, Roy; Carter, Ira; Childers, Otis; Cleek, Robert; Clements, Cecil; Clements, Hubert; Coker, Paul D.; Corn, John H.; Couch, Howard; Crawford, Clem; Davenport, Loyd; Edalgo, Talmadge; Evans, Truman; Fain, Hoyt; Fain, John; Fair, Winfred; Foster, Royce; Fox, Ralph; Galloway,

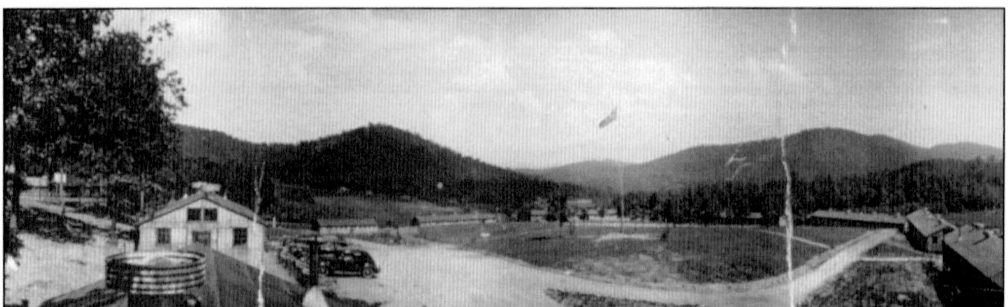

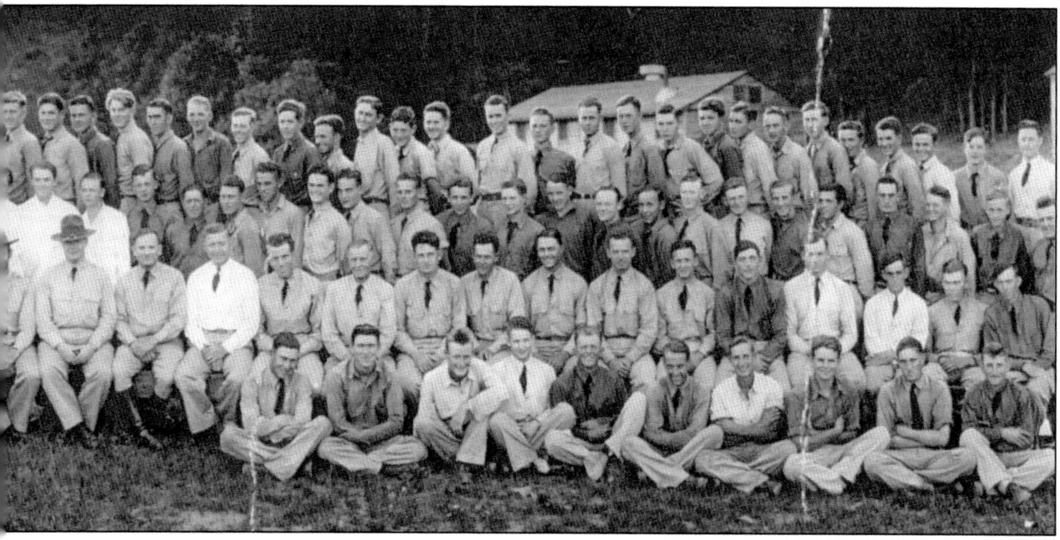

Earl; Galloway, Edward; Garland, James; Garrett, Lillard; Gayton, William; Gee, Elmer; Gilliam, Hobert; Goss, Luther T.; Green, Samuel; Gregory, George; Groves, Ernest; Hamrick, C.C.; Hancock, Robert; Hardy, Brunnell; Harkins, Lonnie; Harper, Albert; Harrison, Earl; Hembree, Quinton; Hendrix, Lee; Higgins, Rollie J.; Hill, Fain; Holloway, Homer; Horton, Claude R.; Howell, Troy; Hughes, Buster; Hunicutt, Void; Hutson, Jay E.; Human, Noah; Ingram, Howard; Johnson, Buster; Johnson, Charlie; Johnson, Gearlie; Jones, Harold; Jones, Herbert B.; Kaylor, Samuel D.; Kelley, Paul C.; Key, Winston; Kilgore, Andrew; King, Ondus C.; King, Vaughn; Ledford, Martin; Lock, Henry; Long, C.J.; Long, Trammell; Mappin, George; McCallister, Wayne; McClure, Walter; Miller, Willie L.; Mize, Joe Jr.; Mulkey, Loyd; Mullinax, Paul; Nelson, Cecil; Nichols, Glen; Nicholson, Dewey; Nix, Garlin; Norton, Thomas; Odom, Hue Floyd; Olvey, Jim; O'Neal Chas. W.; Orton, Gober H.; Oxford, William A.; Pack, John F.; Palmer, Hugh L.; Parks, Hue; Patterson, Clyde; Patterson, Jesse; Payne, Harley; Payne, Jep; Payne, Loyd; Payne, Lush; Peacock, E.B.; Peck, Ray; Pendley, Wayne; Pendland, Robert; Petty, Bascom; Pope, Roy; Postell, Reno; Powell, T.J.; Qualls, Robert; Queen, Deward; Queen, Ray; Queen, Ross; Quinton, Lawrence; Rainey, John H.; Rector, Elon; Richards, Howard; Roland, Gordon; Rolin, Curtis J.; Satterfield, Henry; Sealey, Claude L.; Self, George; Sikes, John D.; Sims, Frank; Sluder, Lester; Smith, Felder; Sosebee, Grady; Standridge, Gilliam; Stewart, Leemar; Stewart, Otis; Strickland, Grady; Talley, Howard; Thomas, Jack; Thomas, John H.; Thomas, Willie Frank; Tinsley, Harrison; Trippe, William H.; Walden, Claude A.; Walker, Arnold; Williams, Ernest; Wilson, Clifford; and Wimberley, Windell. (Courtesy Baugh House collection.)

Opposite: Perhaps a visiting photographer from Spencer & Wyckoff of Detroit climbed to the roof of a Camp Lawrence W. Young building to take this wide-ranging image of the camp's surroundings. The Cohutta Mountains are in the distance. After its use as a CCC camp, this facility was pressed into service in World War II as an internment camp. Most of the detainees were Italian, and some made strong friendships with the people of the nearby Higdon community. (Courtesy Baugh House collection.)

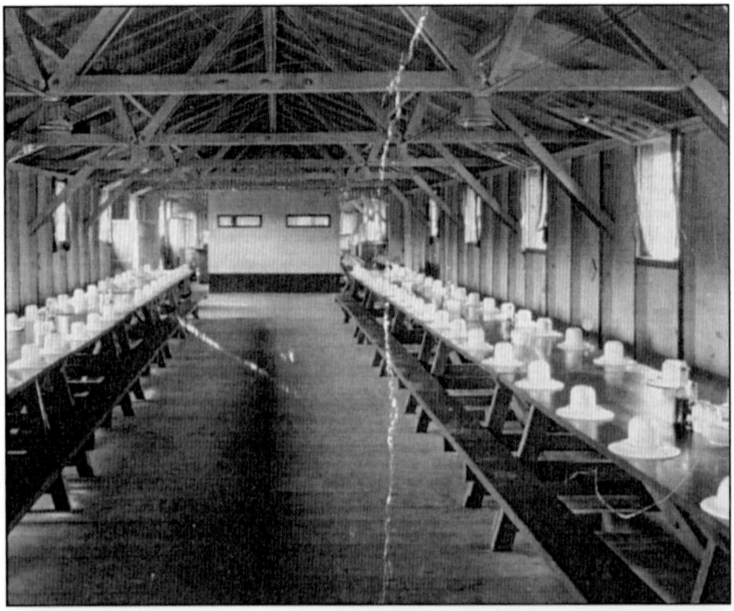

Plates and mugs stand with soldierly neatness in the mess hall at Lawrence W. Young CCC Camp, emphasizing the quasi-military nature of the Civilian Conservation Corps. Note that there is no insulation between the widely spaced wall studs, and the building shows evidence of its hasty construction. (Courtesy Baugh House collection.)

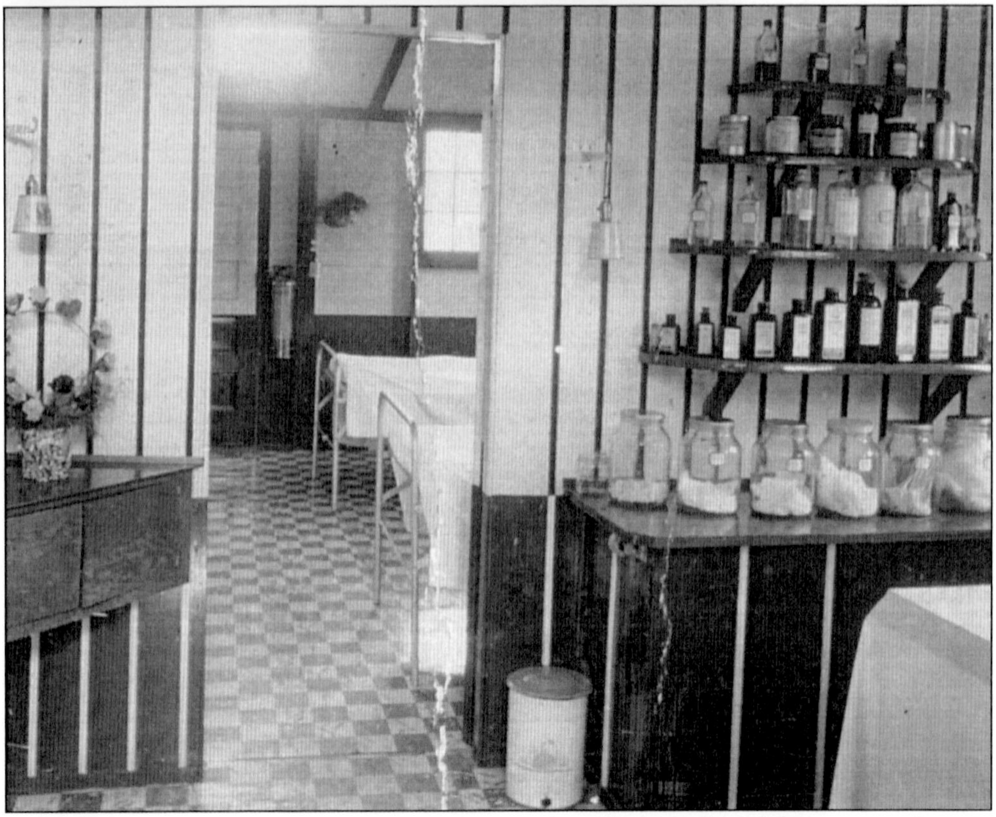

The infirmary at the CCC Camp near Higdon stands ready to render aid for axe wounds, cuts, contusions, and even snakebites. A fire extinguisher stands ready in case a young patient happens to start a fire by smoking in bed. One wonders if the infirmary treated many cases of homesickness. (Courtesy Baugh House collection.)

World War II draftees with CCC experience must have felt right at home in the barracks of training bases, since they had been living in buildings like this one at Camp Lawrence W. Young near Hidgon. (Courtesy Baugh House collection.)

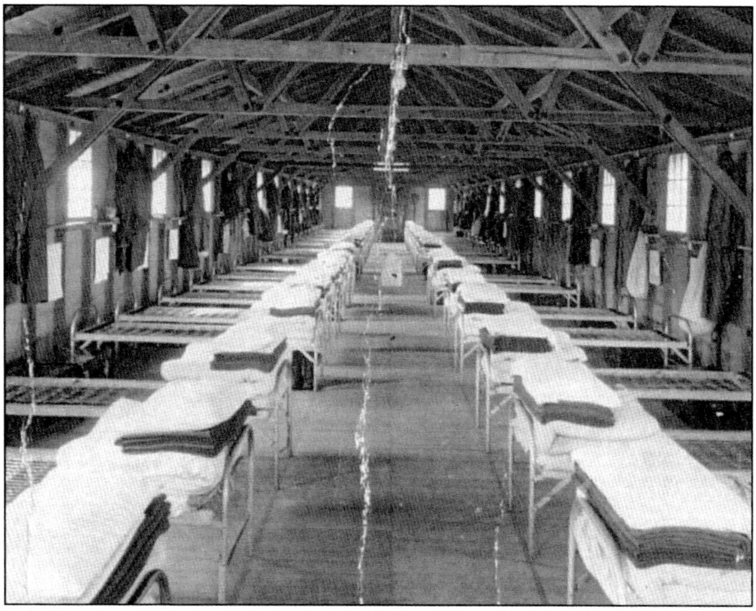

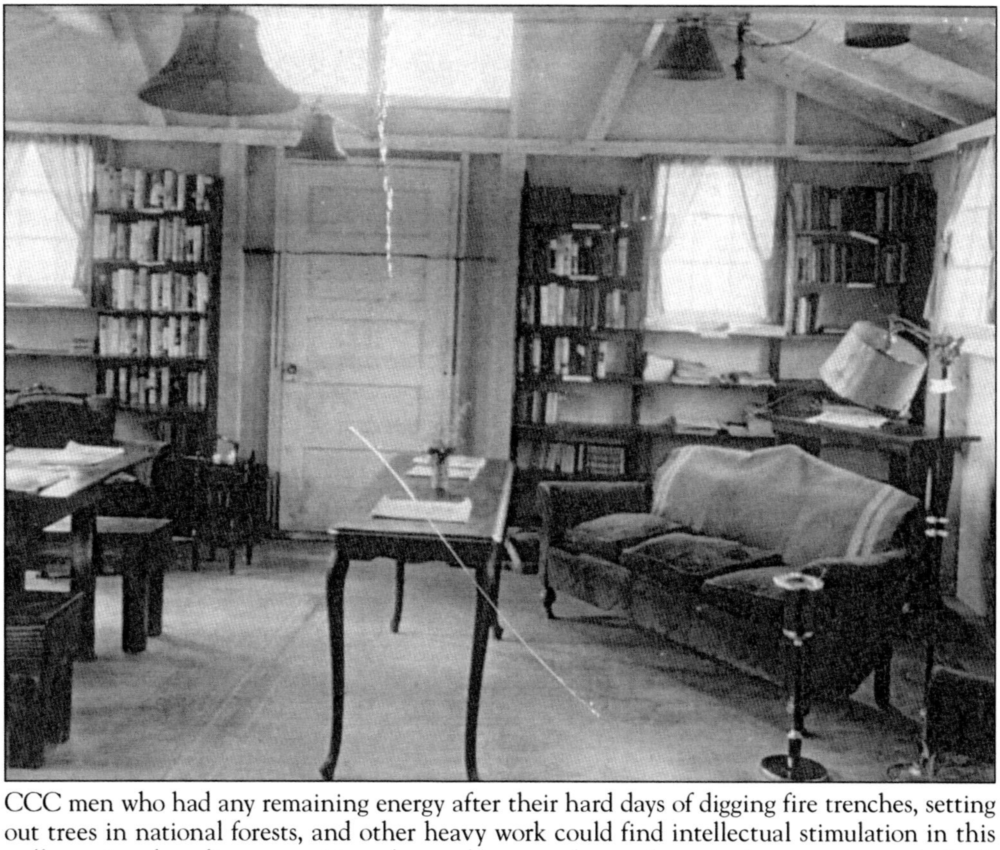

CCC men who had any remaining energy after their hard days of digging fire trenches, setting out trees in national forests, and other heavy work could find intellectual stimulation in this well-appointed reading room. Note the smoking stand near the sofa, the magazine racks built between the wall studs, and the curtains that give a touch of home to the rough-and-ready camp. (Courtesy Baugh House collection.)

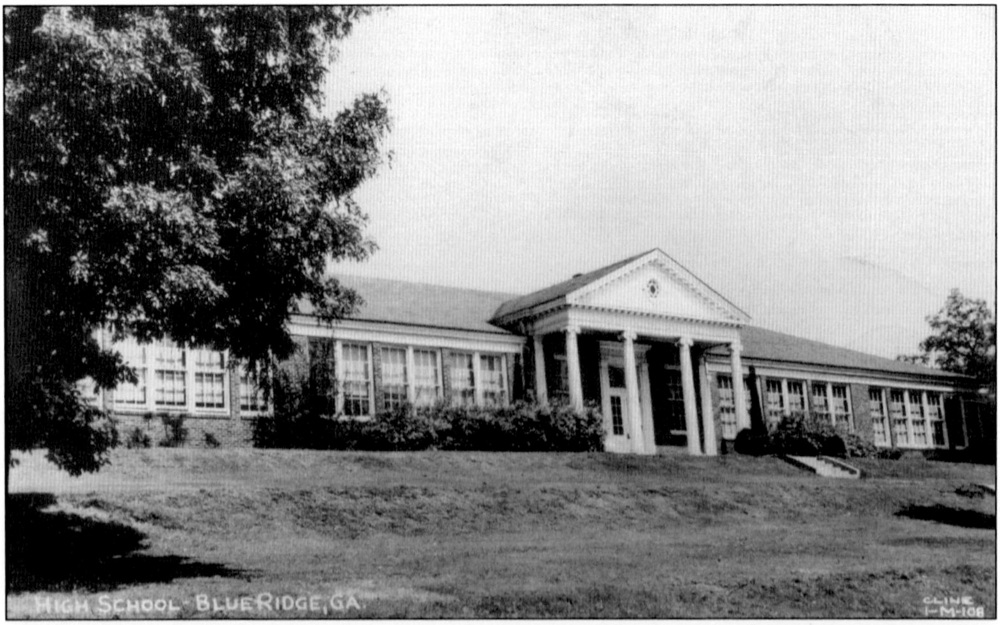

The city of Blue Ridge must have been very proud of its new brick high school. Except for the lack of a steeple or cupola, it might almost have been a twin of the grammar school. Unfortunately, this building burned down in the 1990s. (Courtesy Don and Carolyn Hall.)

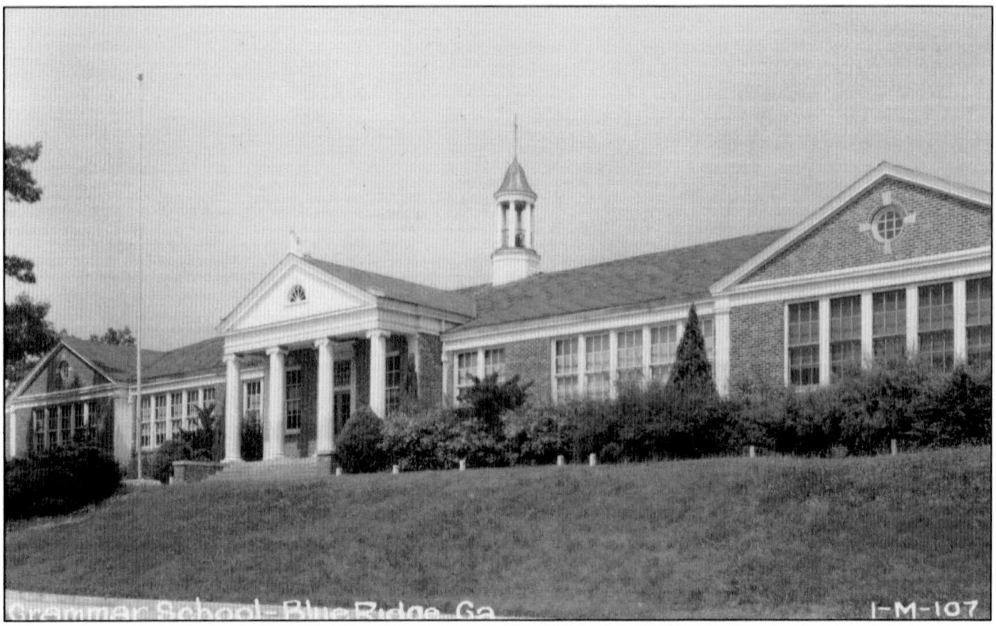

The grammar school at Blue Ridge has seen service for eight decades and is still going strong in 2011 as Blue Ridge Elementary. (Courtesy Don and Carolyn Hall.)

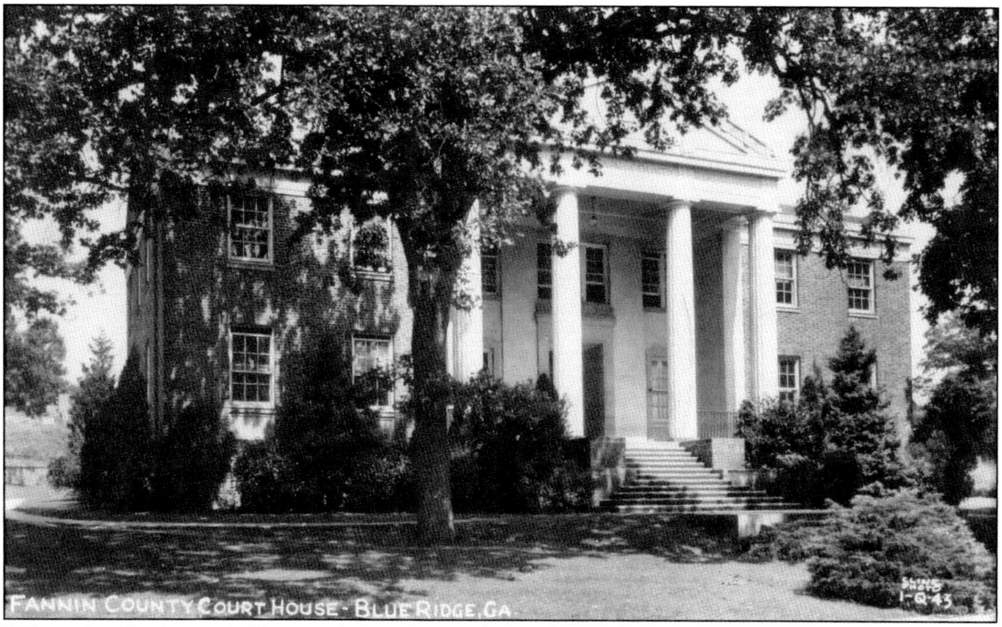

When the Gothic-style Fannin County Courthouse burned in 1937, it was very quickly replaced by this new structure, built with money from Pres. Franklin D. Roosevelt's New Deal. Many in what was rumored to be the most Republican county in the Deep South found it highly ironic that most of the money for the building came courtesy of the century's most famous Democratic president. This historic building now serves as the home of the Blue Ridge Mountains Arts Association. Many locally and even nationally known artists have work on display in its galleries. (Courtesy Don and Carolyn Hall.)

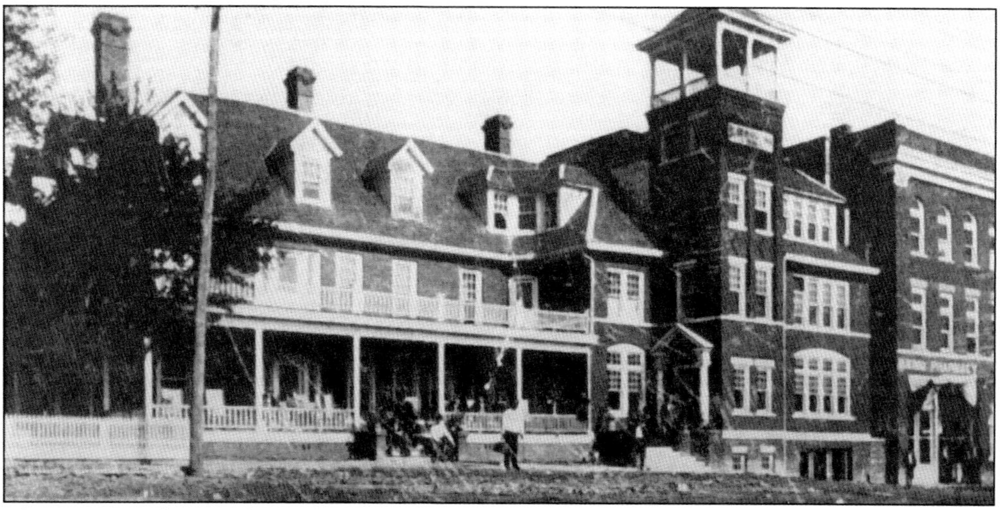

The spacious, elegant Blue Ridge Hotel occupied the center of the block between the Blue Ridge depot and the Fannin County Courthouse. This towered building was the first of two Blue Ridge Hotels, both of which burned. Perhaps the owners felt the spot was prone to conflagrations—the space is now occupied by a concrete parking lot for Blue Ridge Methodist. The building to the immediate right of the tower is the L&N building, constructed by the railroad of the same name. At some point in its long history, the structure lost its top floor. Now beautifully restored, in 2011 the building houses a real estate office. (Courtesy Don and Carolyn Hall.)

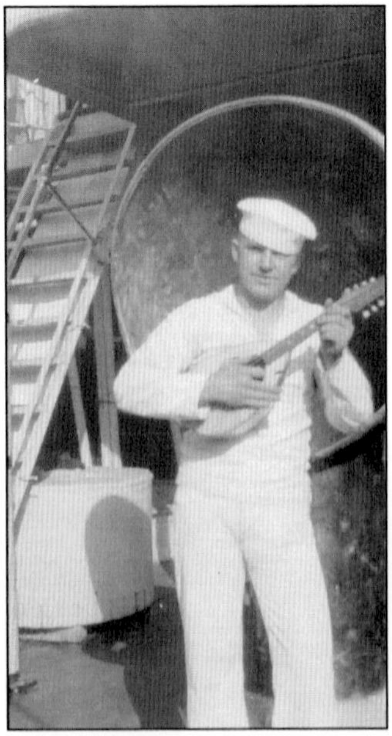

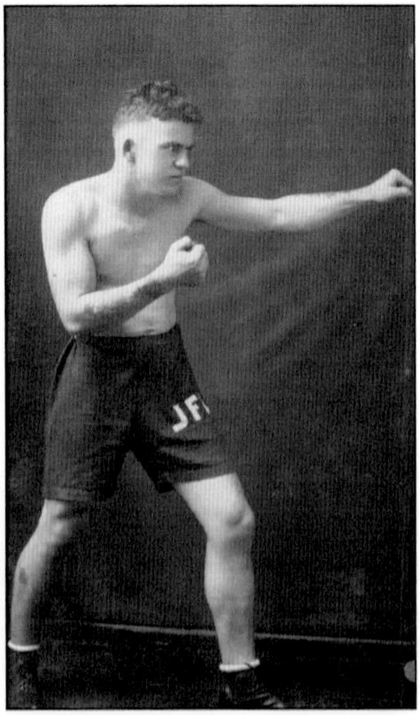

At far left, jaunty sailor Jack Lloyd plays a mandolin aboard a US Navy ship sometime in the 1920s. The ship may be the USS *Pittsburgh*, since a photograph of that ship appeared a few pages later in the same photo album. In the image at left, Lloyd, striking a much more pugnacious pose, advertises his skills in the squared circle. It is unclear if Jack is representing the Navy as a pugilist or is a professional, semiprofessional, or amateur fighter. (Both courtesy Michael Eaton.)

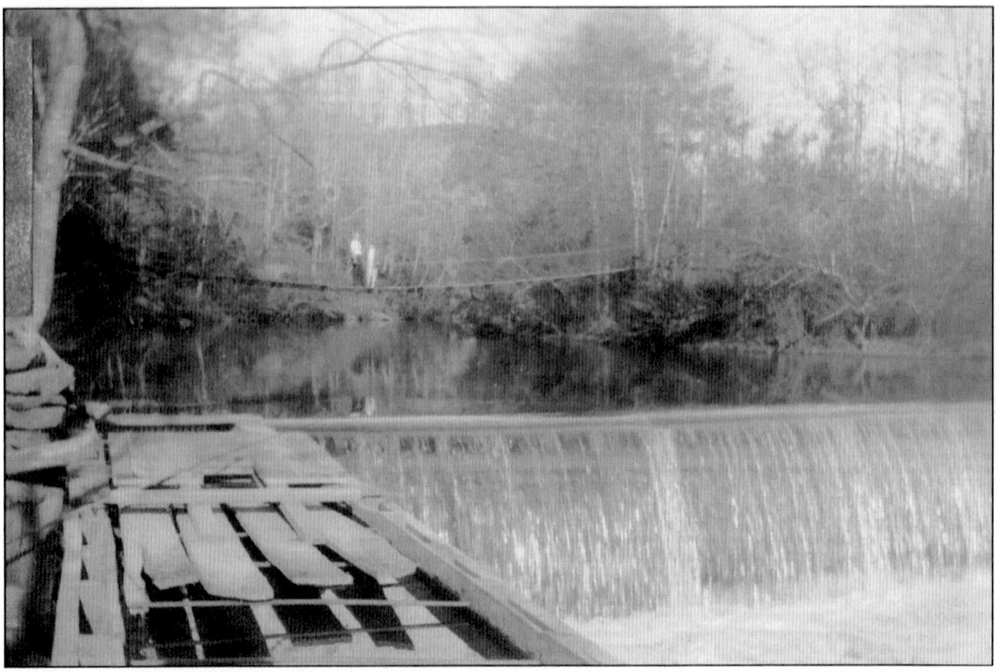

Despite the construction of Blue Ridge Dam, many small mills continued to operate in Fannin County. A couple in this photograph enjoys the view over the millpond as they stroll across the swinging bridge. The boards in the foreground cover the sluice leading to the mill wheel. This is believed to be the Forge Mill operation. (Courtesy Michael Eaton.)

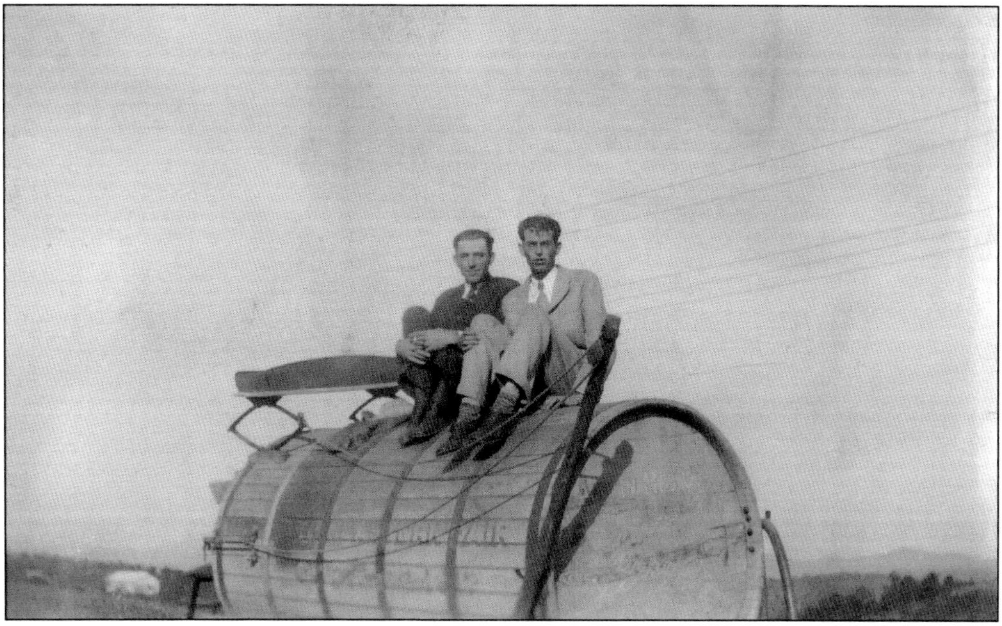

Harry ? and Eddie ? pose atop a huge, wooden water tank (or tar barrel) wagon in 1928 near Blue Ridge depot. (Courtesy Michael Eaton.)

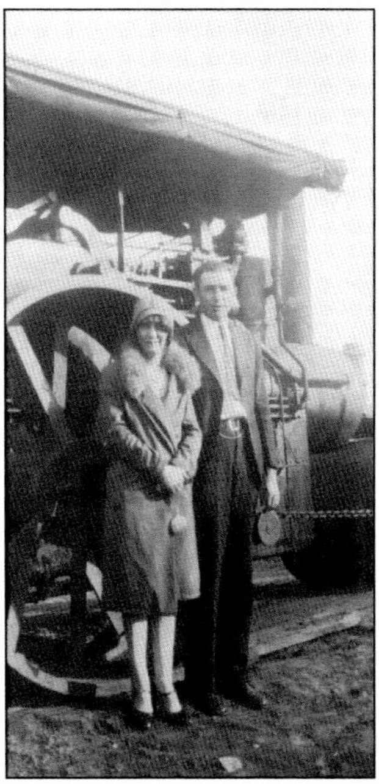

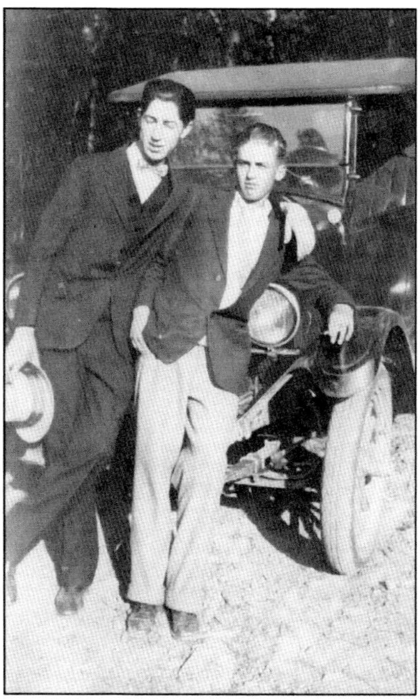

In the 1920s image at far left, Eva Mae Lloyd Mashburn and her husband, Henry Frank Mashburn (known as Frank), stand next to a steam-powered, steel-wheeled tractor. Similar tractors were the first machines to replace animals for plowing fields; they were also used to haul freight. This machine may have been brought to the area to work on Blue Ridge Dam. In the 1926 image at left, two men identified as Joe and Tasker lounge against their automobile. (Both courtesy Michael Eaton.)

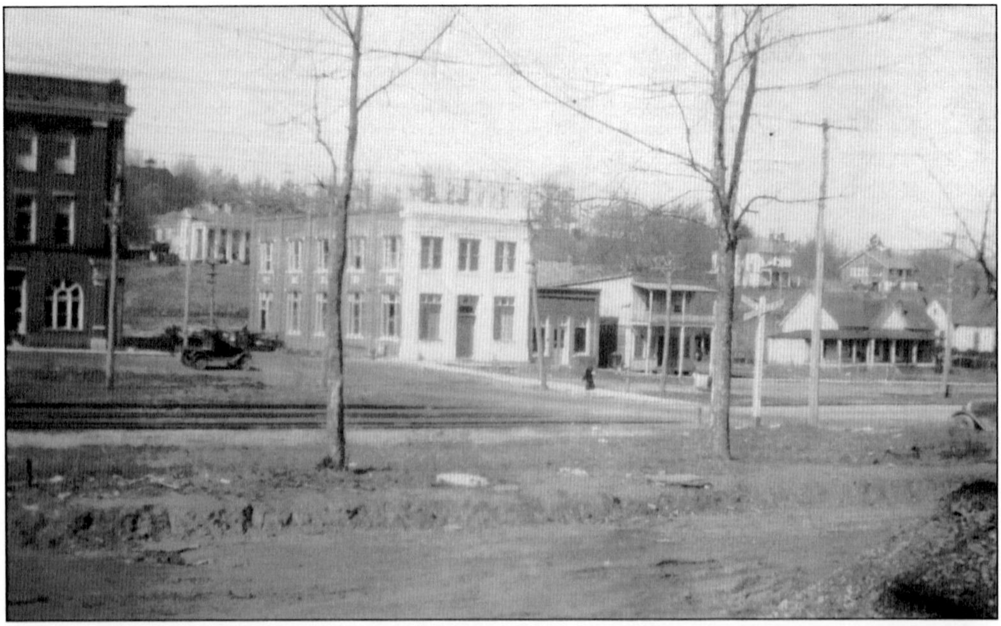

Putting its best face forward, the marble-faced Fannin County Bank took its place on East Main Street in 1926. This image from the following year shows the L&N building to the left. On the knoll behind the bank stands the Butt home. In later years, the bank would move to a new building on the Butt property, which now houses Blue Ridge City Hall. The original bank building is now a coffeehouse/restaurant. (Courtesy Michael Eaton.)

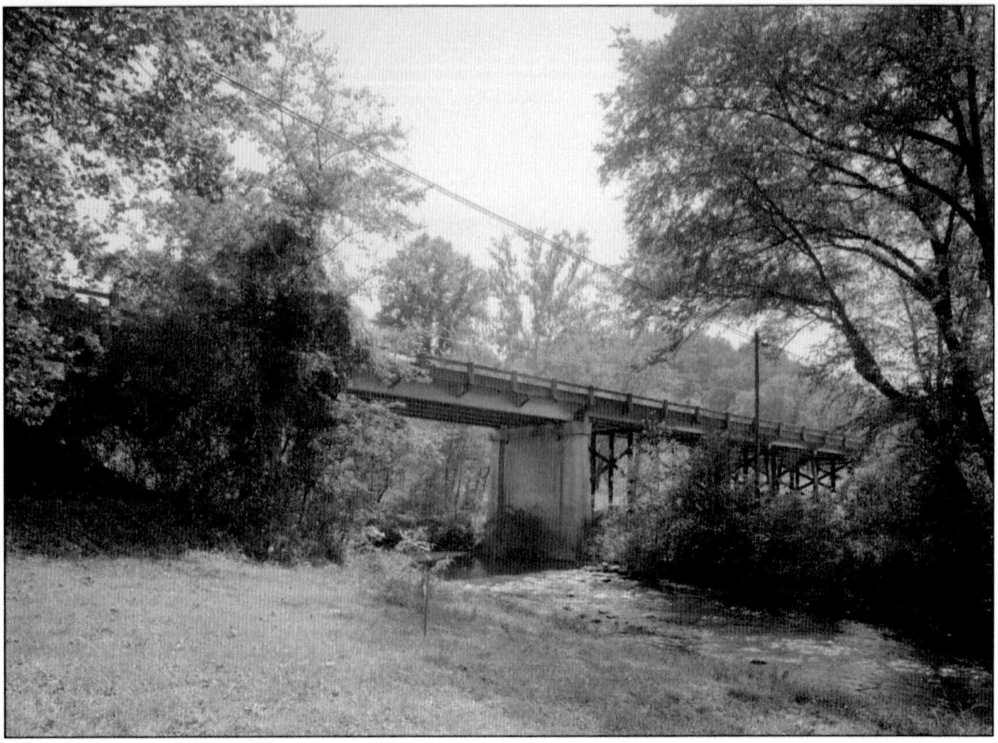

This bridge near Mineral Bluff spans Hemptown Creek. (Courtesy Library of Congress.)

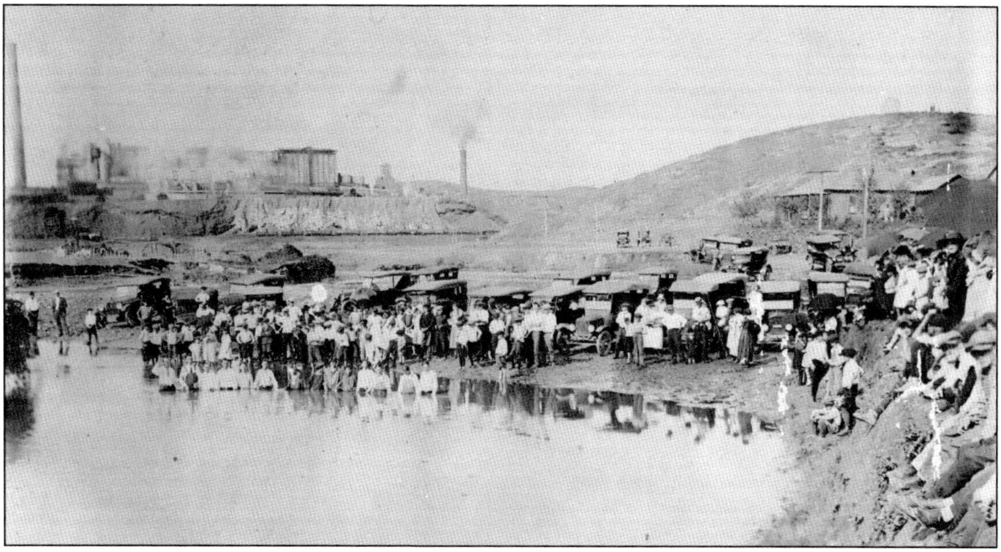

A crowd gathers for a baptizing that took place in the Toccoa River near Copperhill, Tennessee, around 1920. The photograph was taken by someone either in the river or standing on the Georgia side of the river. Note the industrial complex in the background. Operating under various names over the decades, the Tennessee Copper Company was simply called "the Company" by the many Fannin County residents who worked in its mines, smelters, flotation mills, and chemical works. (Courtesy Georgia Archives, Vanishing Georgia Collection, image fan006-083.)

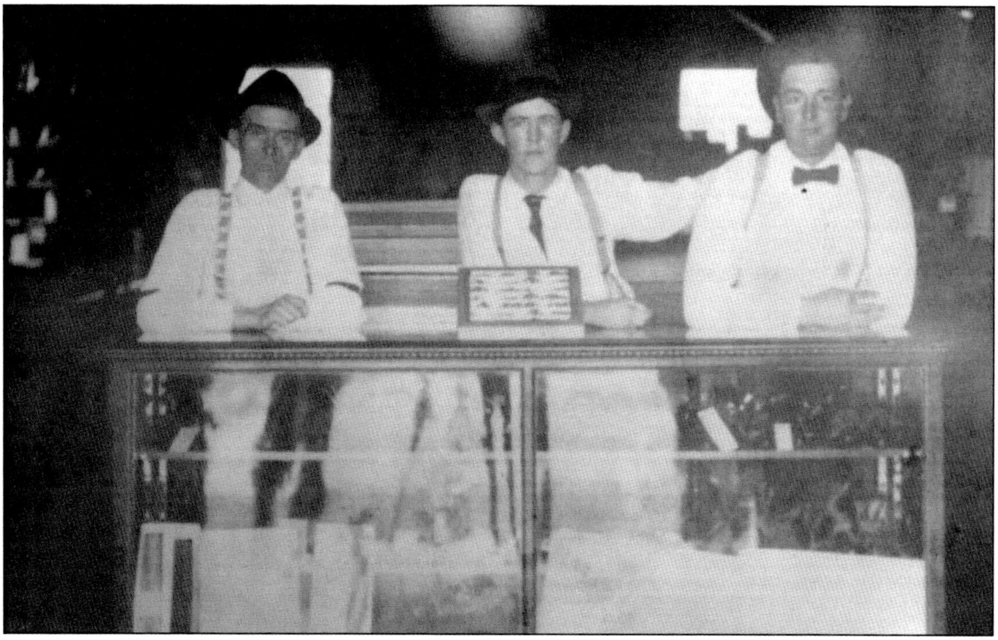

From left to right, J.W. Napoleon "Poley" Dickey, Claude Baugh, and William Arthur Black stand behind the counter of the Smelter Store in Copperhill, Tennessee, around 1920. This was a typical "company store," like the one Tennessee Ernie Ford sang about in "Sixteen Tons," the Merle Travis song popularized by Ford in the 1950s. Baugh is a member of the family that owned the brick works in Mineral Bluff and built the Baugh House in Blue Ridge. (Courtesy Georgia Archives, Vanishing Georgia Collection, fan014-83.)

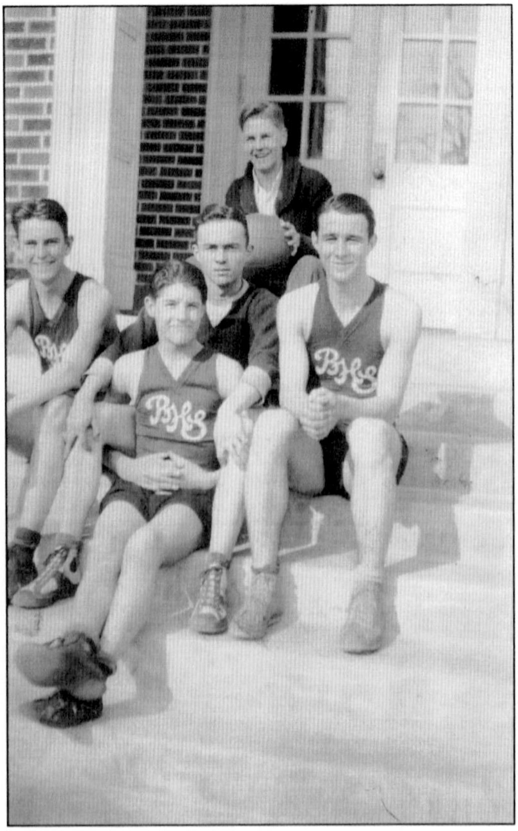

The starting (and maybe the only) five members of the Blue Ridge High basketball team seem happy—all but the frowning fellow in the center. (Courtesy Michael Eaton.)

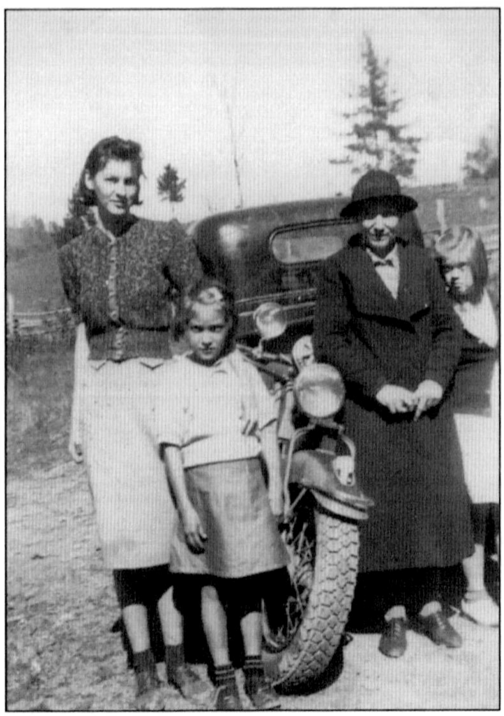

This photograph, taken on November 3, 1944, near the Margret community, shows Hazel Edmondson Fortenberry (left), her mother-in-law, and two younger sisters-in-law gathered around a snazzy motorcycle. The siren indicates the motorcycle may be a police or military surplus model. (Courtesy Betty Parker.)

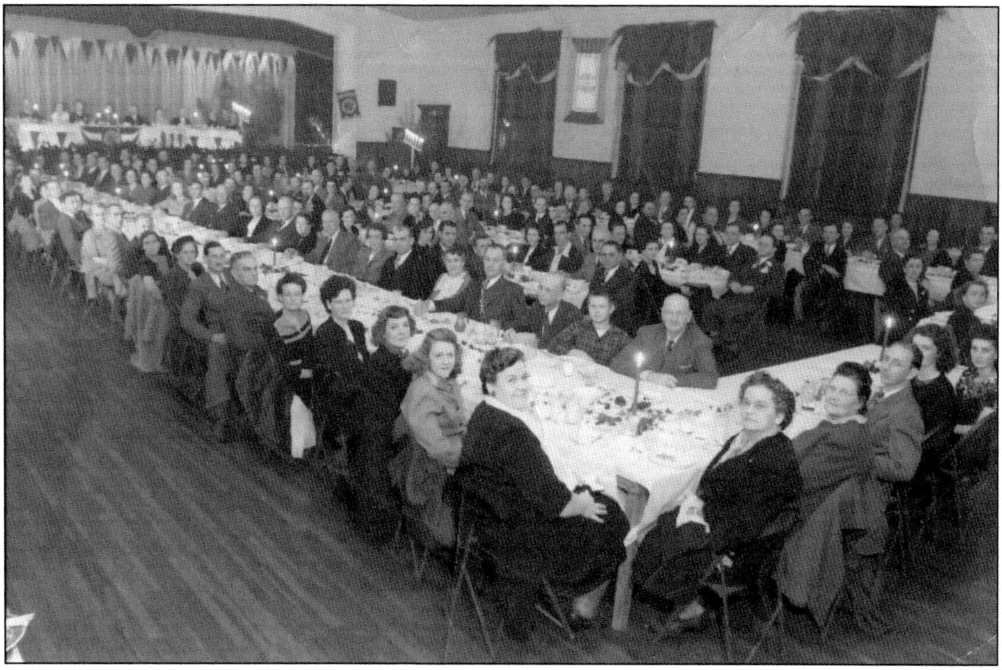

A large crowd gathered in the Blue Ridge Grammar School auditorium on July 22, 1931, as the Copperhill Kiwanis Club chartered the new Kiwanis organization for Blue Ridge. Kiwanians have been involved in activities as diverse as sponsoring the county fair and the rodeo and helping with the publication of the history book *Facets of Fannin*. (Courtesy Don and Carolyn Hall.)

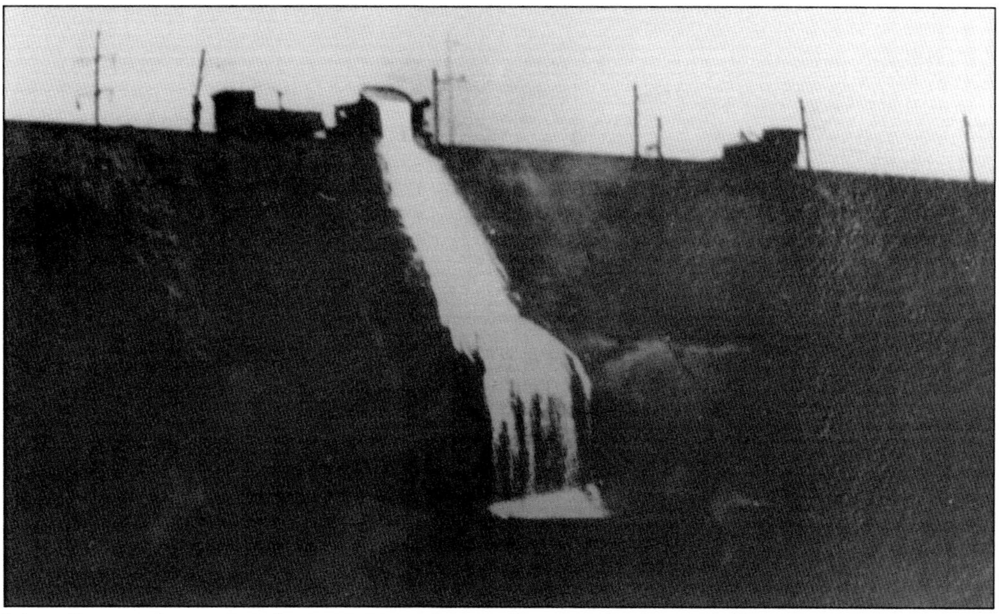

Many Fannin County residents commuted to work in nearby Copperhill, Tennessee, at what was universally called "the Company." The work was hard, hot, and sometimes spectacular, as attested by this picture of slag being poured out of a huge crucible. Such pours were common in the days before environmental awareness. Many of these slag heaps are now being mined for calcite and rich, partly refined iron ore. (Courtesy TriCities Business Association.)

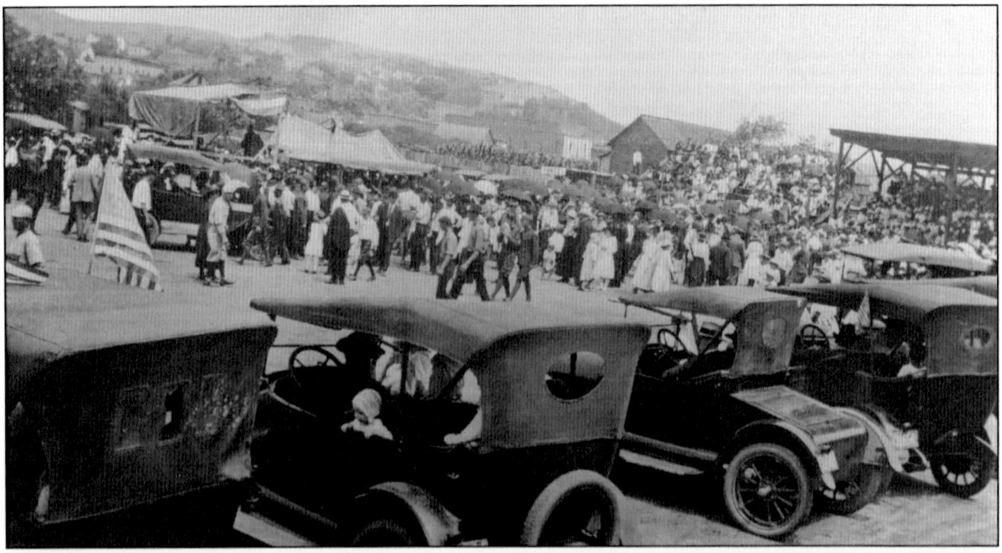

The Copperhill ball field is the gathering place for the Miners' Fourth of July celebration sometime in the 1920s. Because the state line is not congruent with the path of the river, parts of both Copperhill, Tennessee, and McCaysville, Georgia, are on each side of the river. This ball field is on the south (or "Georgia") side of the river but is actually in Tennessee. (Courtesy TriCities Business Association.)

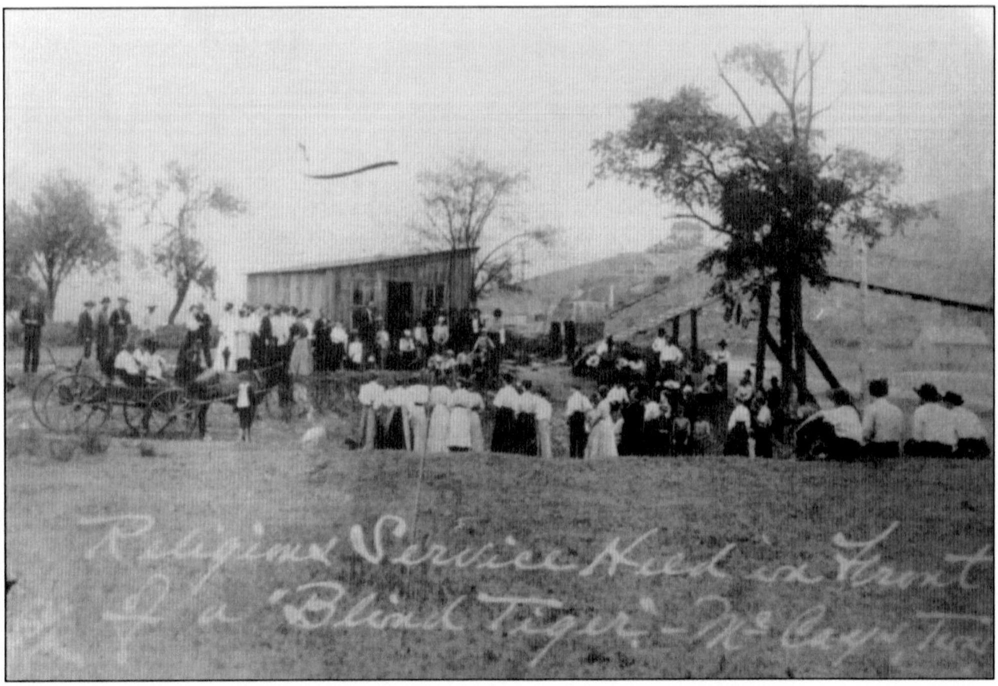

The faithful have gathered to pray and preach against demon rum! A blind tiger was a place that sold alcohol during Prohibition. Perhaps the name came from the dangers of bathtub gin, which sometimes substituted wood alcohol for grain alcohol, resulting in blindness. Or maybe drinking made the imbiber feel like a tiger? (Courtesy TriCities Business Association.)

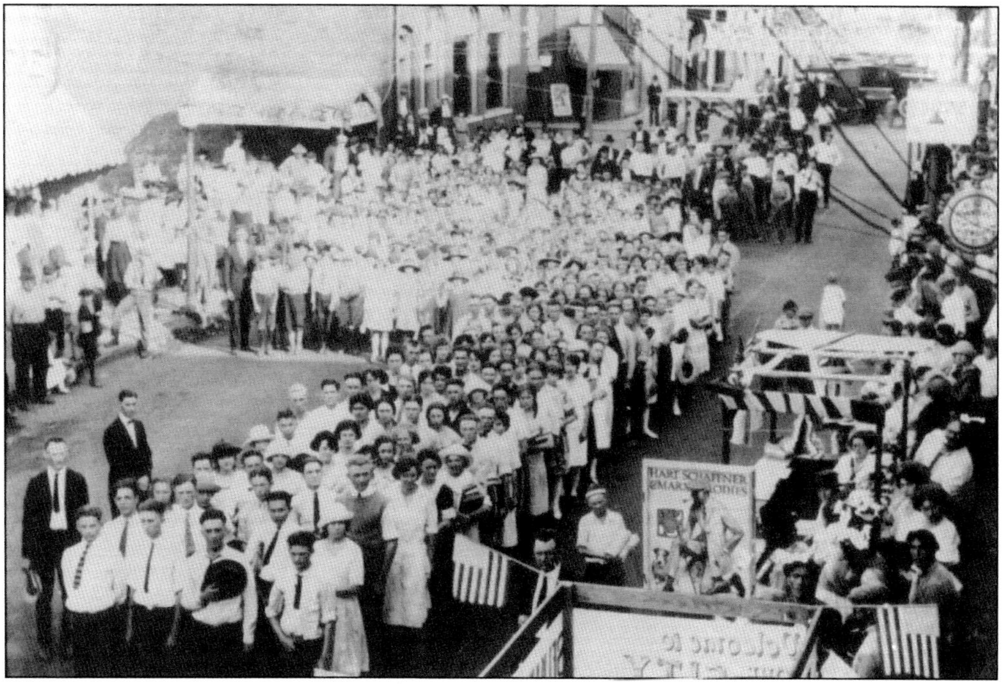

What Miner's Fourth of July is complete without a parade? It is possible that this July 4, 1922, photograph was snapped during the playing of the National Anthem. Note how many men have removed their hats and are holding them over their hearts. The parade route is on Ocoee Street, moving from Copperhill toward the state line at the corner of Blue Ridge Street. (Courtesy TriCities Business Association.)

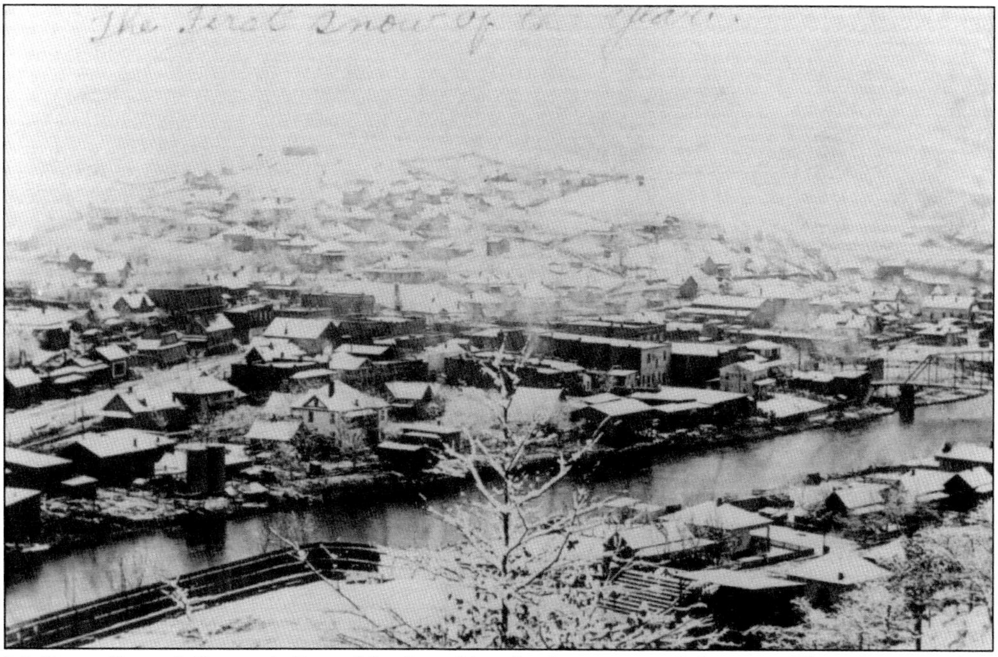

McCaysville and Copperhill are blanketed by the first snow of the year. This photograph is probably from the 1920s. (Courtesy TriCities Business Association.)

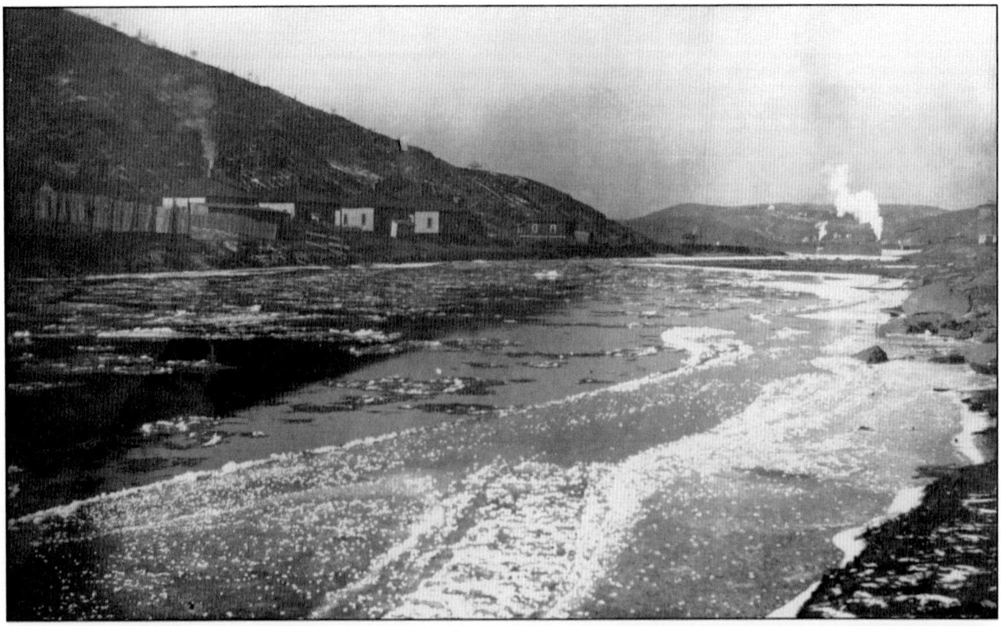

Another wintry scene reveals ice on the Toccoa River north of Copperhill and McCaysville around 1930. (Courtesy TriCities Business Association.)

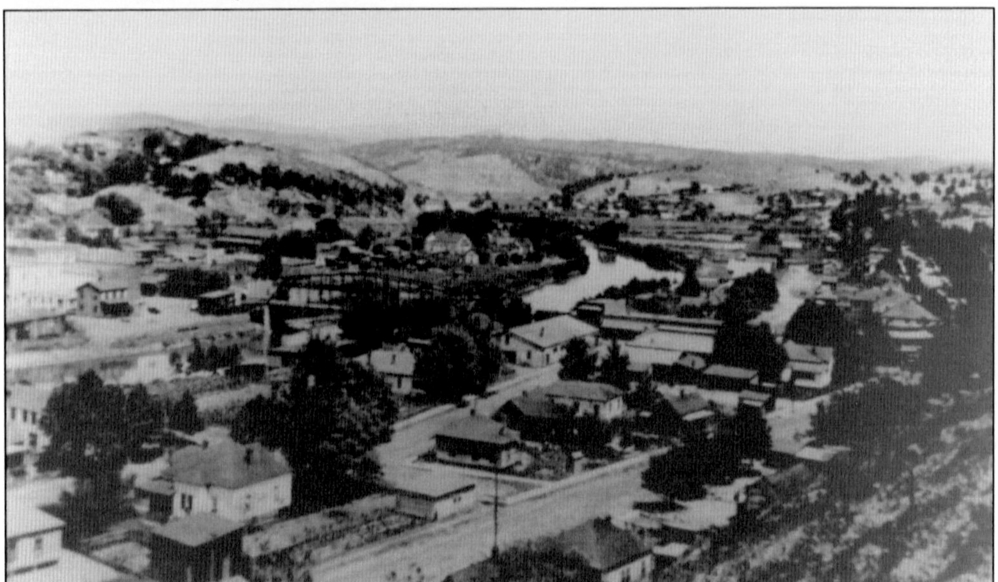

The Toccoa flows serenely through Copperhill and McCaysville sometime in the 1920s or 1930s. The steel bridge has replaced the earlier ferry and footbridge, but the later concrete bridge is not yet in place. There has been much speculation over whether the steel bridge in this image is the same bridge that once spanned the Toccoa River between Blue Ridge and Morganton. Most local lore holds that it is one and the same and that it was moved before being flooded by the rising waters of Blue Ridge Lake. Some have claimed that they floated the beams down the river, but those who have canoed or rafted the miles between the foot of the dam and McCaysville would argue that is not very likely. More likely, the dismantled beams were trucked to the new site and reassembled. (Courtesy TriCities Business Association.)

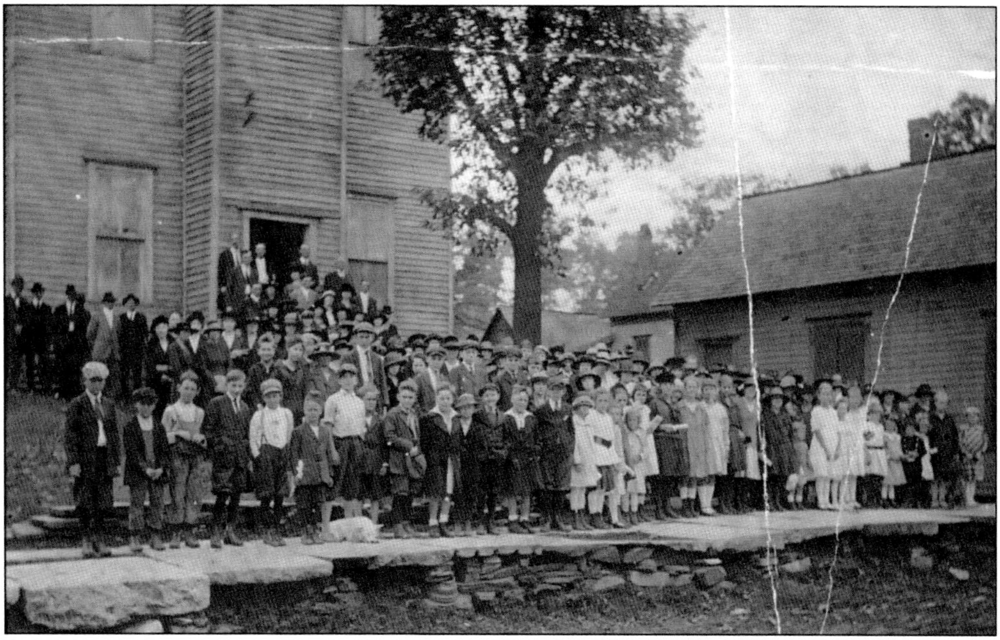

A crowd gathered in the early 1920s for a Sunday School event at First Baptist Church in Blue Ridge. (Courtesy Don and Carolyn Hall.)

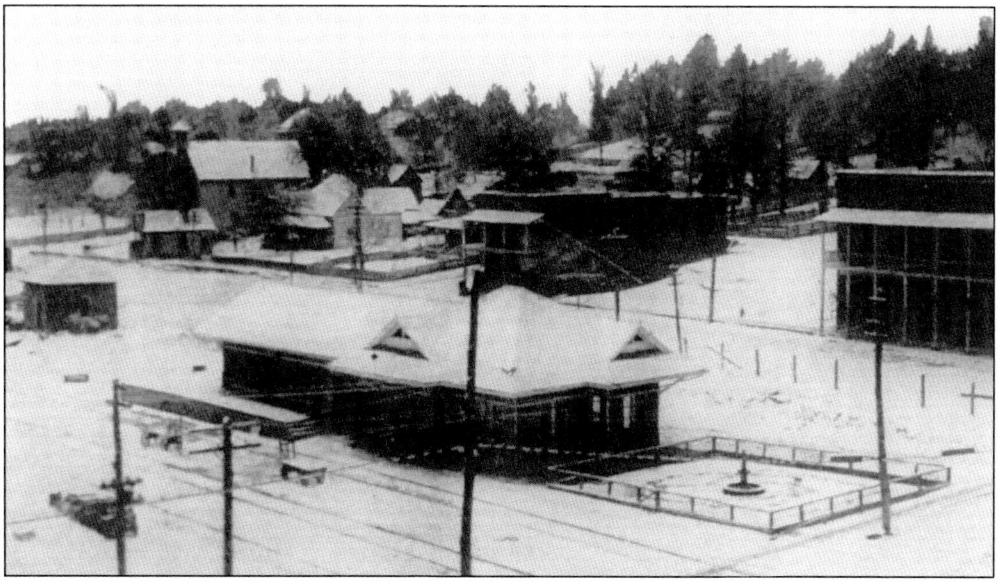

Blue Ridge is blanketed in snow in this 1920s scene. Note the fenced fountain in front of the depot. To the back left of the depot is a two-story building with a small steeple that was built and shared by the Baptists (later known as First Baptist Church of Blue Ridge) and the Masonic lodge in early 1900. The small building partly obscuring the lower view of the church is Dr. Thompson A. Terrell's dental office. The white house, next door to the right, is his family home. To the right of Dr. Terrell's house, next to the brick building, may be the home of Ed Davis. The brick building directly behind the depot, known as the Tilley Building, was originally a Ford dealership. W.H. Tilley Sr. bought this building from Mark King. On the corner is the (Thomas) Douthit building. Pinson's store was in the lower level. (Courtesy Don and Carolyn Hall.)

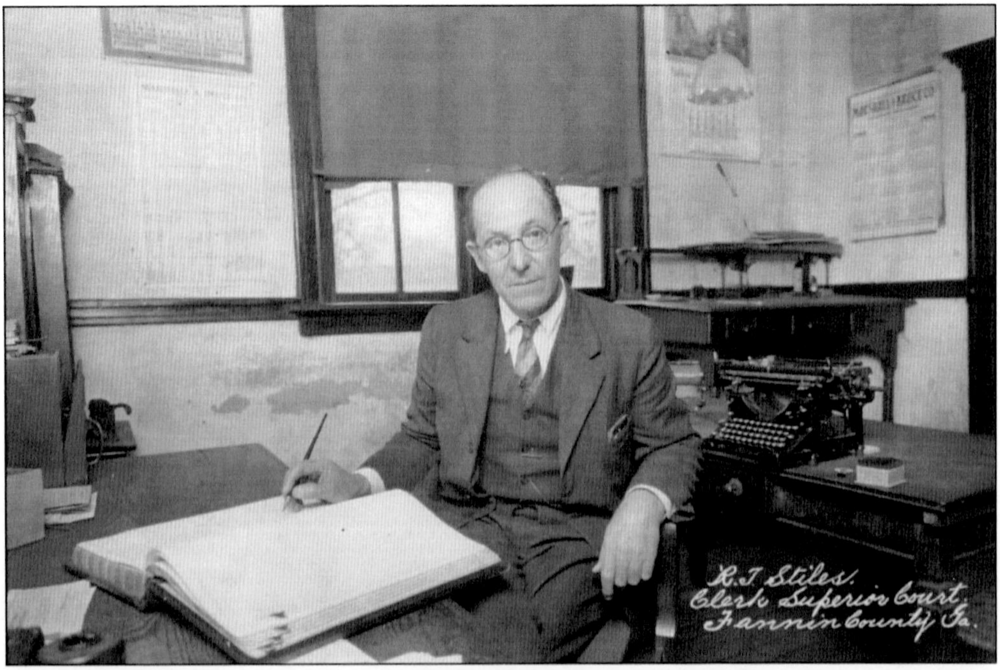

R.T. Stiles, clerk of the superior court from 1917–1933, is surrounded by the latest in office equipment in this image from December 1923, but he still chooses to enter data by hand in the ledger. The office is located in the old Fannin courthouse that burned in 1937. (Courtesy Don and Carolyn Hall.)

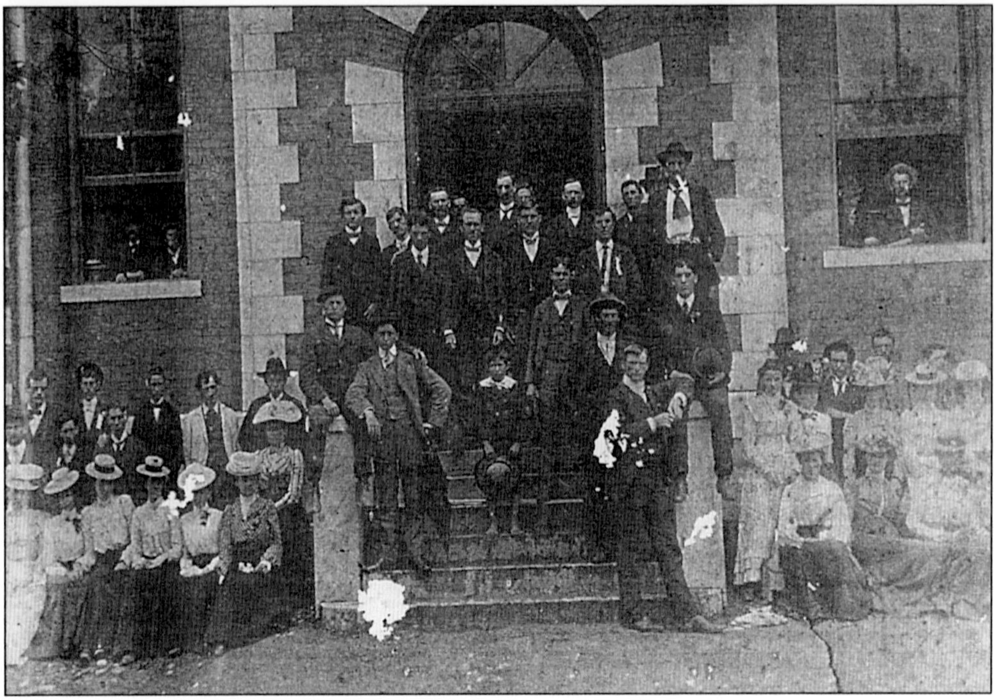

In the early 20th century, a crowd gathered in front of the old Fannin courthouse. The occasion for the gathering is not known. (Courtesy Don and Carolyn Hall.)

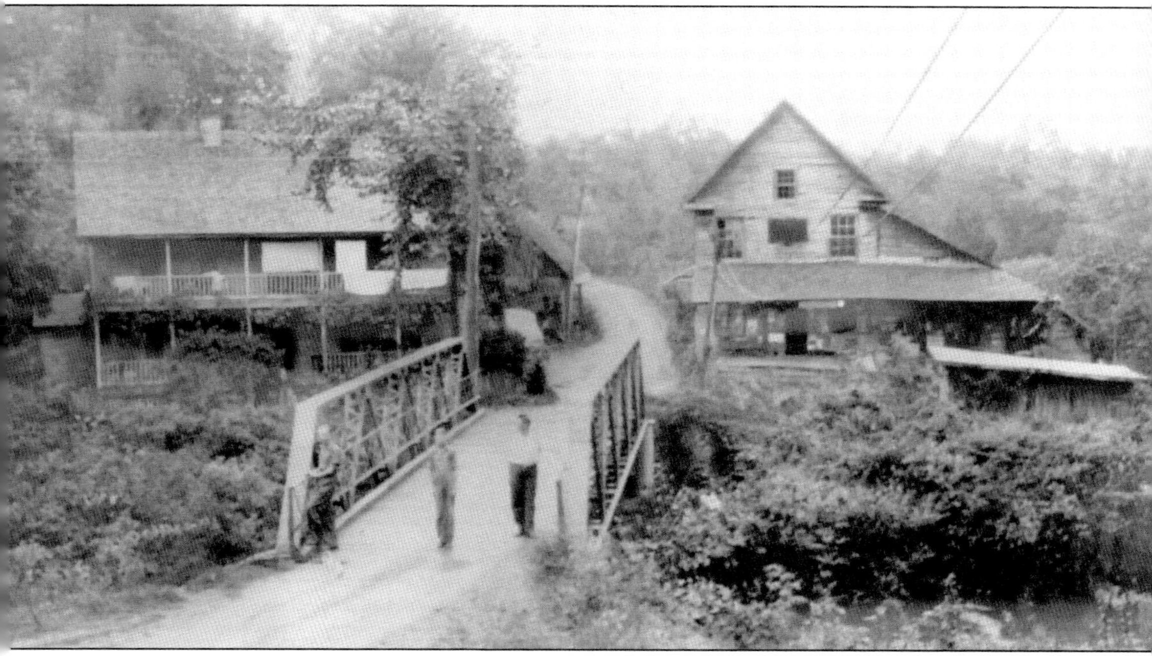

Frank Buttram, Winford McKinney, and Clyle McKinney amble across the Fightingtown Creek Bridge at McKinney Crossing in October 1937. The house at the left is the McKinney home, built after Union raiders in the Civil War destroyed the complex. To the left, beyond the bounds of this photograph, was the gristmill. Barns and various stores are to the right of the road across the bridge. (Courtesy Ron Henry family.)

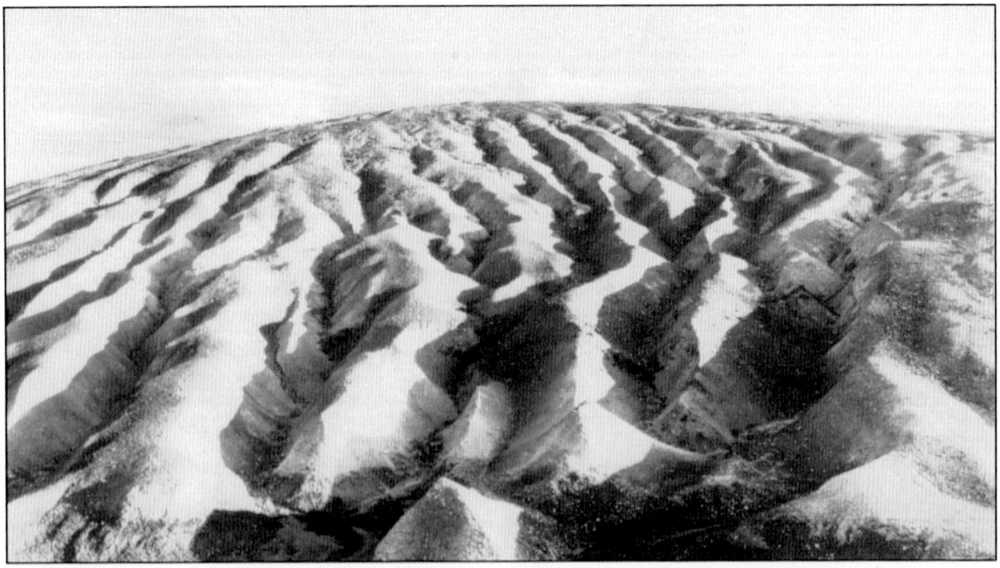

Residents of the Copper Basin area in the first three-quarters of the 20th century were familiar with sights such as this. The red clay was literally so barren and blighted by pollution that not even kudzu would grow. In the 1800s, the trees were cut to fuel the copper smelting process, which released massive quantities of sulfur into the air. This produced intense acid rain, which killed off the rest of the vegetation. With no roots to hold it, all the topsoil washed down the Ocoee River. (Courtesy Ron Henry family.)

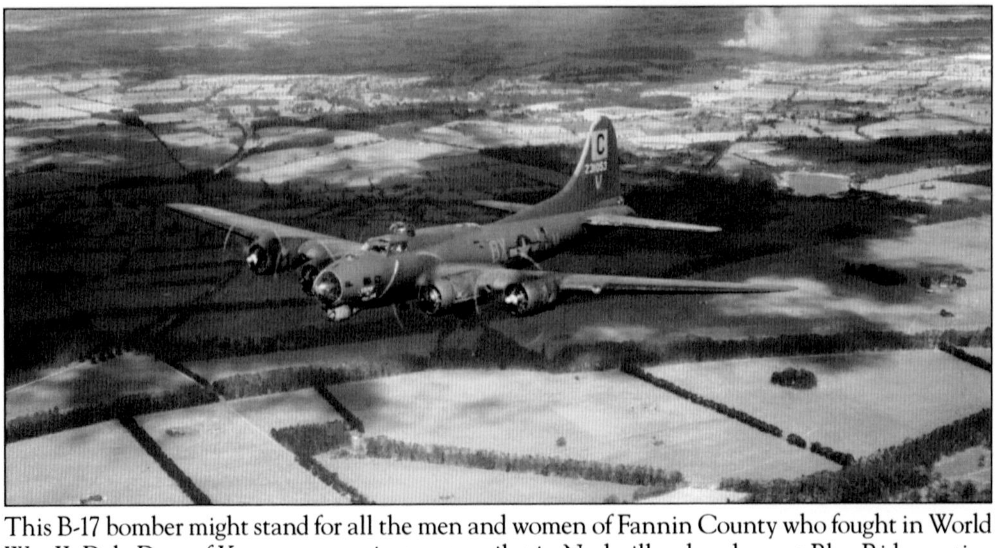

This B-17 bomber might stand for all the men and women of Fannin County who fought in World War II. Dale Dyer of Kansas was an instructor pilot in Nashville when he met Blue Ridge native Virginia Hampton at a United Service Organization (USO) dance. The day he was to travel to meet her parents, he and some student pilots "buzzed" Blue Ridge, frightening his future mother-in-law greatly. He flew many missions over Hitler's Fortress Europe, and to this day keeps a navigation map that one of his crew embellished skillfully with cartoons commemorating their experiences. After the war, he and Virginia settled down in Blue Ridge. (Courtesy Ron Henry family.)

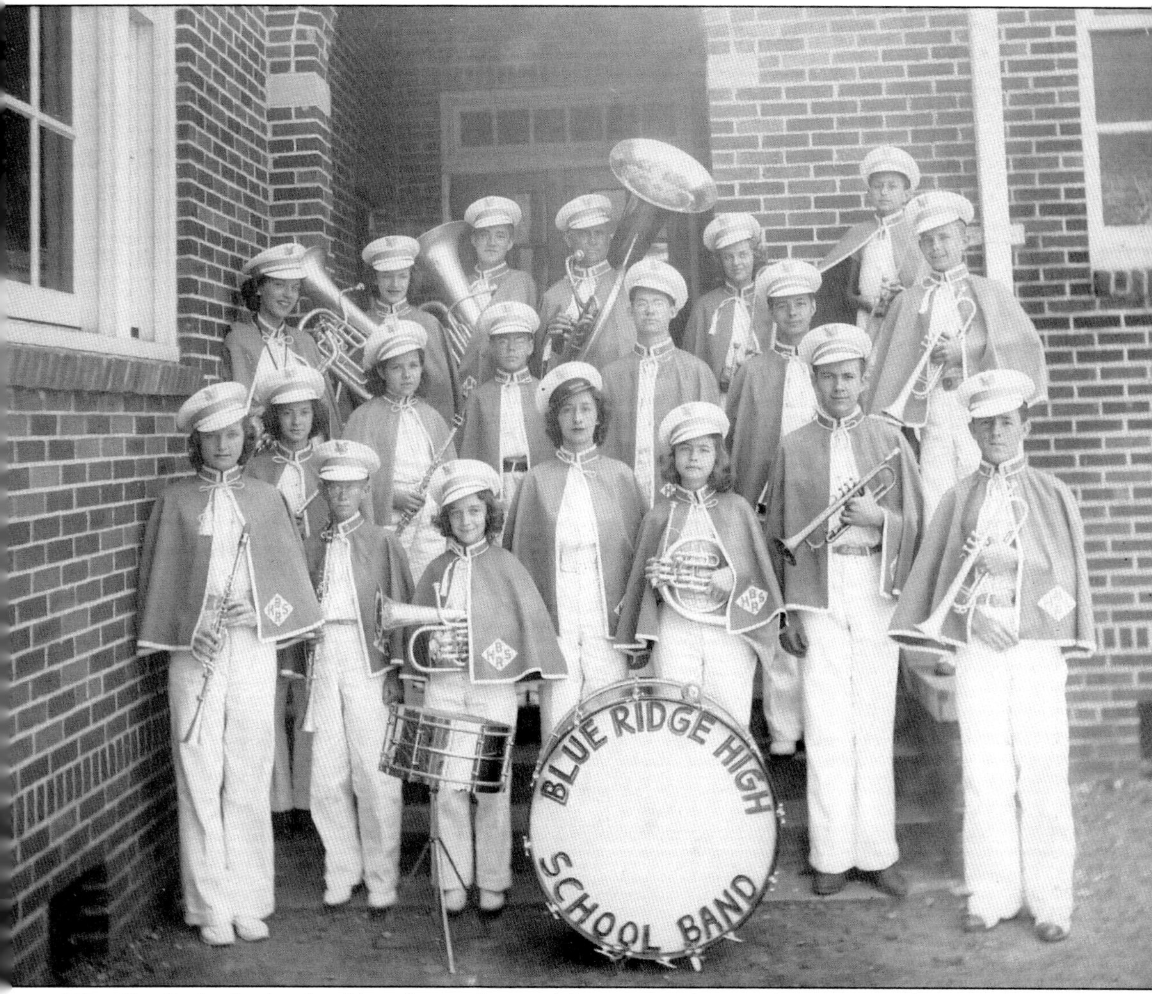

The Blue Ridge high school band is ready to celebrate something! Aline Crawford (center front) was the music teacher and director of the band. She had a long career teaching Latin and music. The following are, from left to right, (first row) Dot Corn, Harold Paige, Barbara Ann Wall, Aline White Crawford, Ruth Ann Clyburn, Jimmy Whitfield, and Blake Stiles; (second row) Violet Jo Davis, Jeanette Anderson, Bobby Stewart, Baxton Hudson, Bobby Gartrell and Roy Allen; (third row) Nita Ruth Beam, Doris Stewart, Browne Allen, John Wall, Louise Hall, and Don Ellis. (Courtesy Don and Carolyn Hall.)

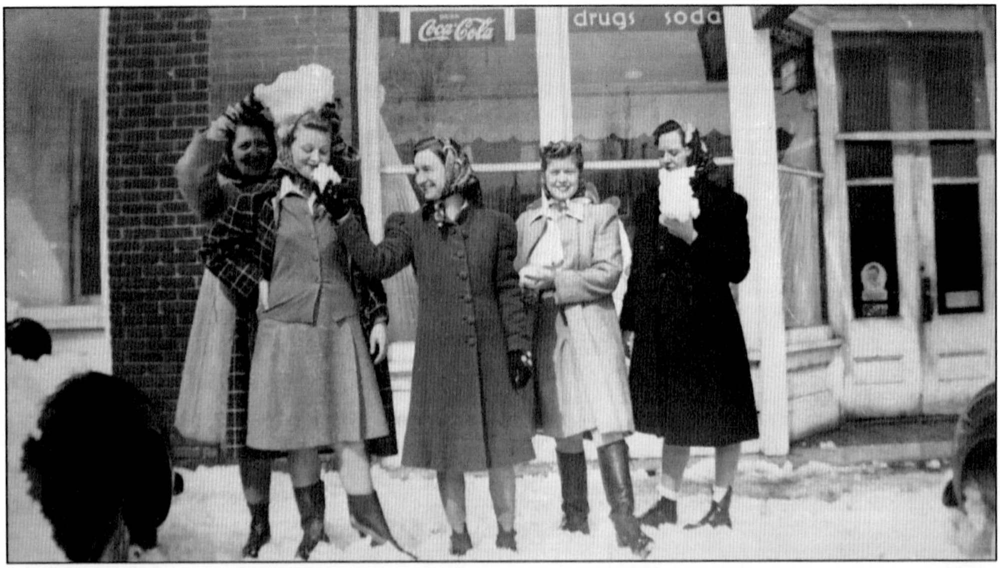

During the big snow of 1940, teachers freed from the classroom cut up a little in front of Blue Ridge Pharmacy. Doris Marshall is the second person from the right. (Courtesy Georgia Archives, Vanishing Georgia Collection, image fan003.)

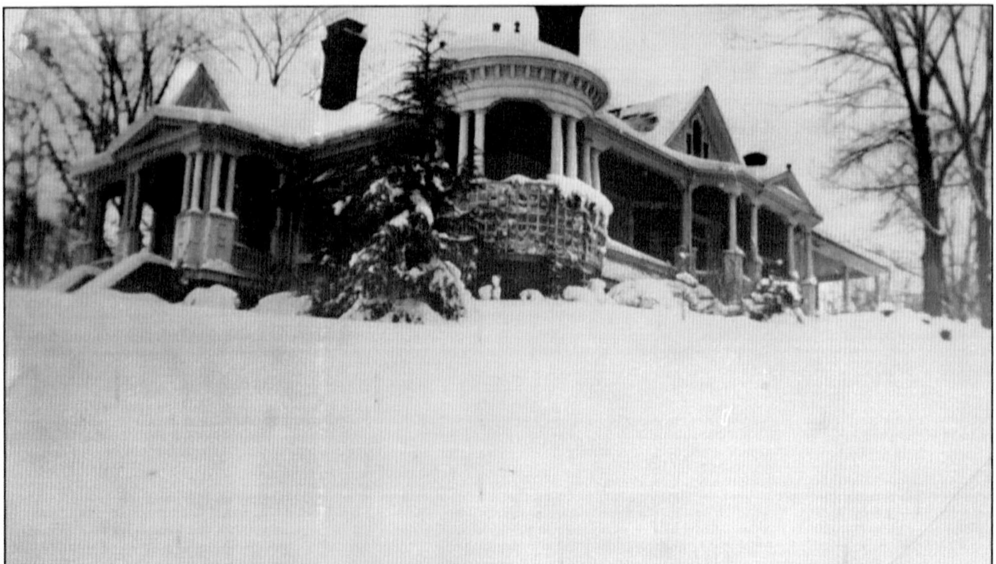
The Whitfield house looks like a snow castle in the winter of 1940. Huge snowstorms seem to hit every decade or two in the Copper Basin area. (Courtesy Georgia Archives; Vanishing Georgia Collection, fan002.)

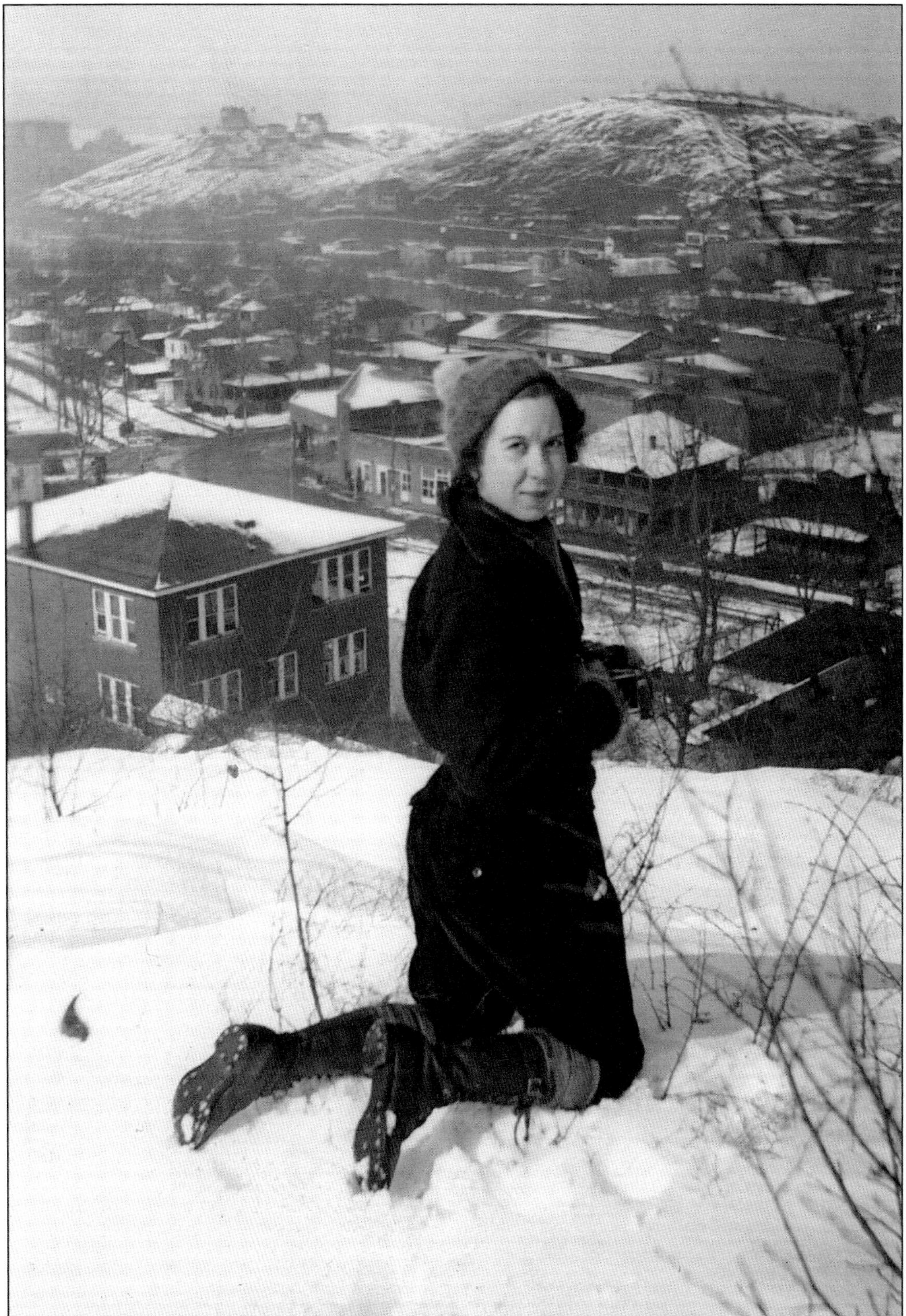

Blanche Howard found the big snow of 1940 delightful. She is pictured here atop 'Tater Hill in McCaysville, with the city spread out below her. (Courtesy Ron Henry family.)

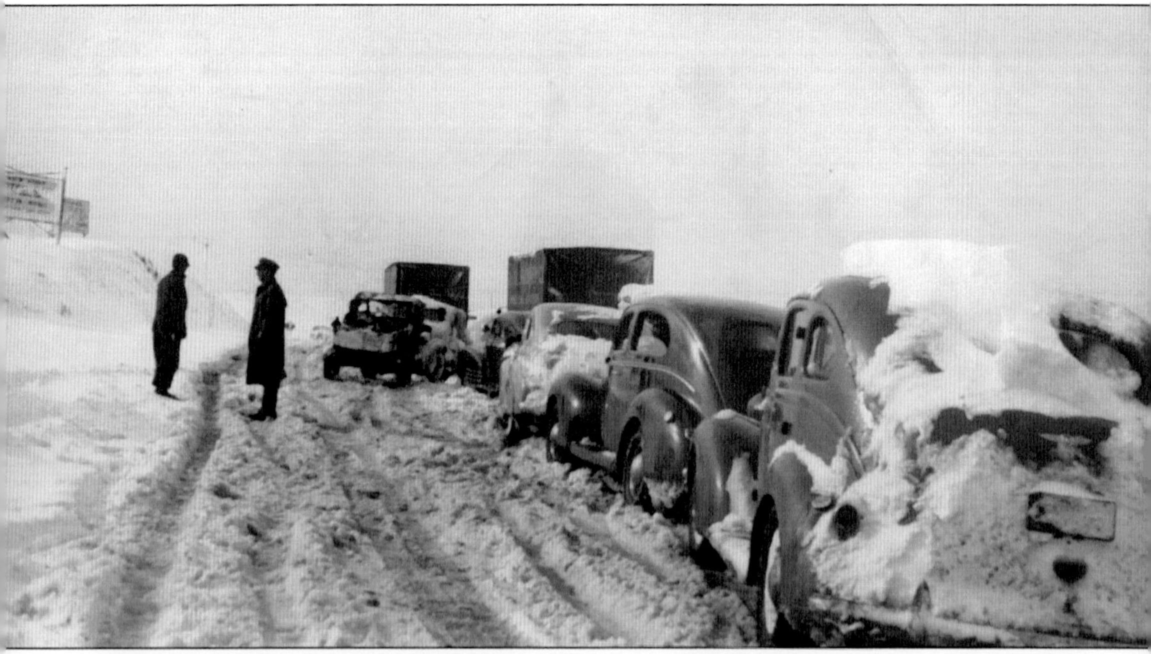

Drivers and police officers dealing with the big snow of 1940 found it much less delightful than teachers out of school or young ladies hiking to hilltops. This tangle seems to be headed up Harpertown Hill on Blue Ridge Drive, but the snow is falling too hard to tell for sure. (Courtesy Ron Henry family.)

Six

G.I. Joe Comes Home . . . and Gets Busy

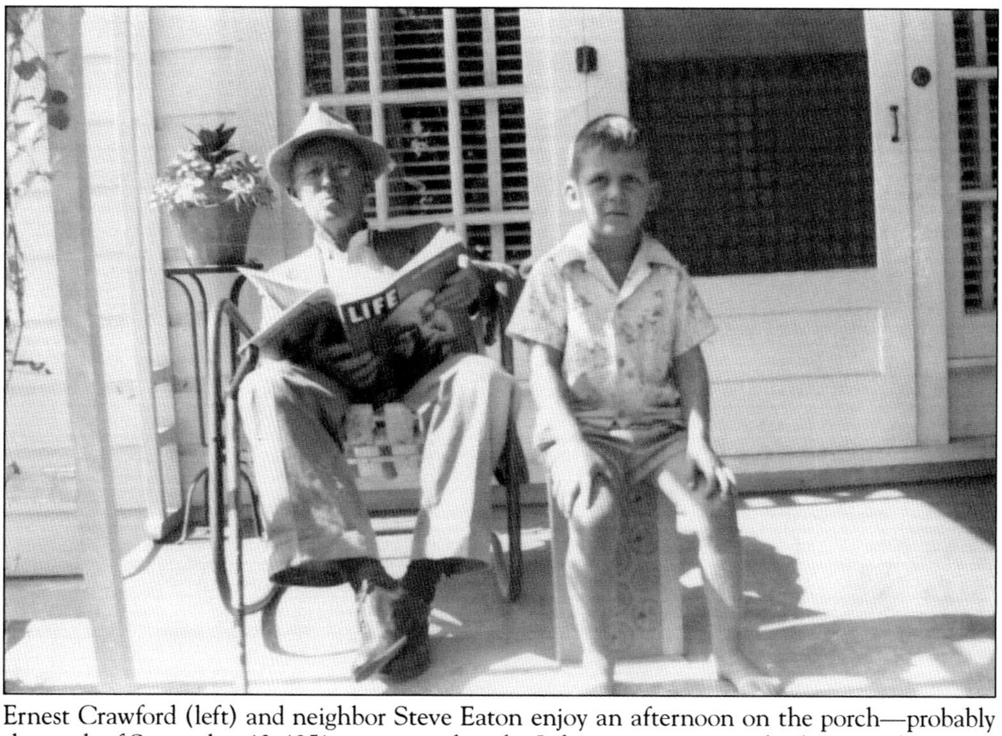

Ernest Crawford (left) and neighbor Steve Eaton enjoy an afternoon on the porch—probably the week of September 10, 1951, assuming that the *Life* magazine is not a back issue. The stogie-puffing diplomat on the cover is Japanese prime minister Yoshida Shigeru, chief of Japan's treaty delegation. The official end of World War II did not happen until several years after the end of the fighting. (Courtesy Michael Eaton.)

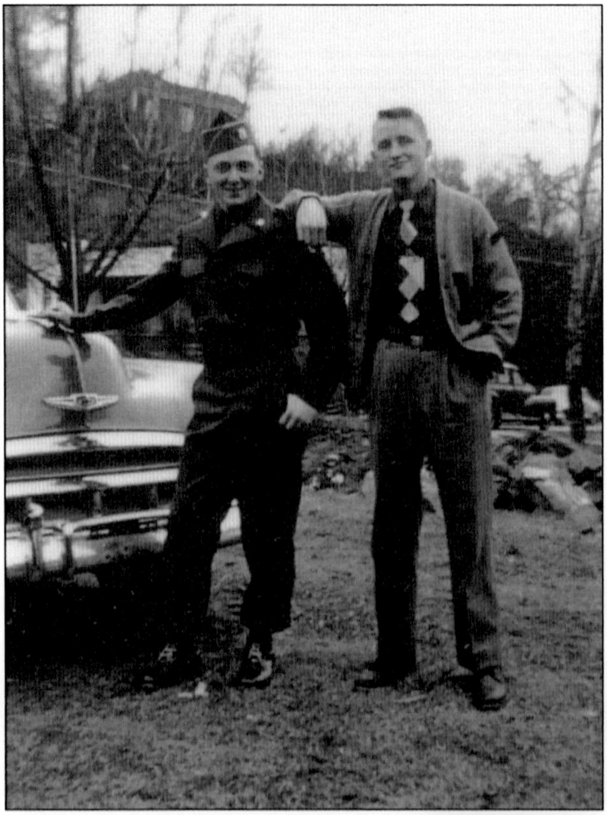

In 1950, brothers Ted DeHart (age 20, in uniform) and Harold DeHart Brown (age 18) stand in a vacant lot in McCaysville, about a quarter mile south of the foot of Harpertown Hill. This site is currently occupied by a video store. (Courtesy Ethelene Dyer Jones.)

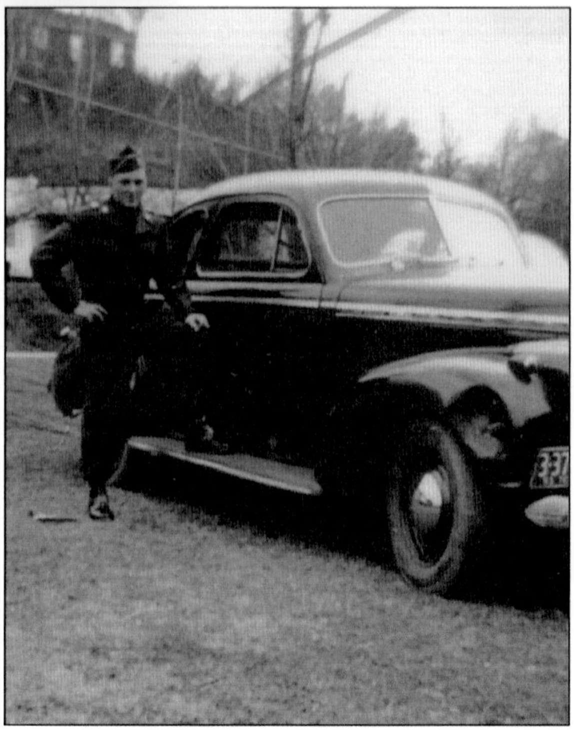

In this photograph from 1950, Ted DeHart stands on Blue Ridge Drive across from Queen's store in McCaysville. (Courtesy Ethelene Dyer Jones.)

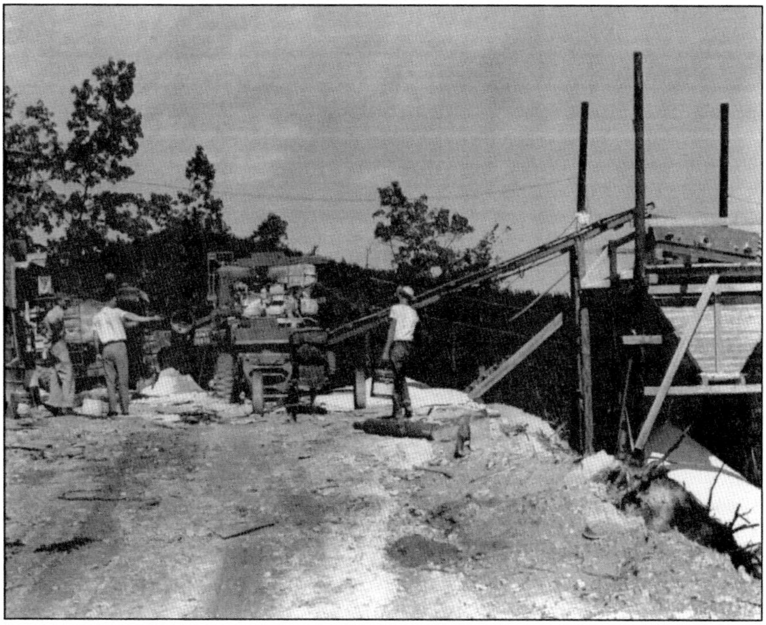

To pave all those Fannin County dirt roads takes gravel, so these workers at the Lance Quarry are busy supplying that need in the 1950s. Despite their efforts, many busy roads remained unpaved into the 1970s. (Courtesy Wilson and LaVerne Cobb.)

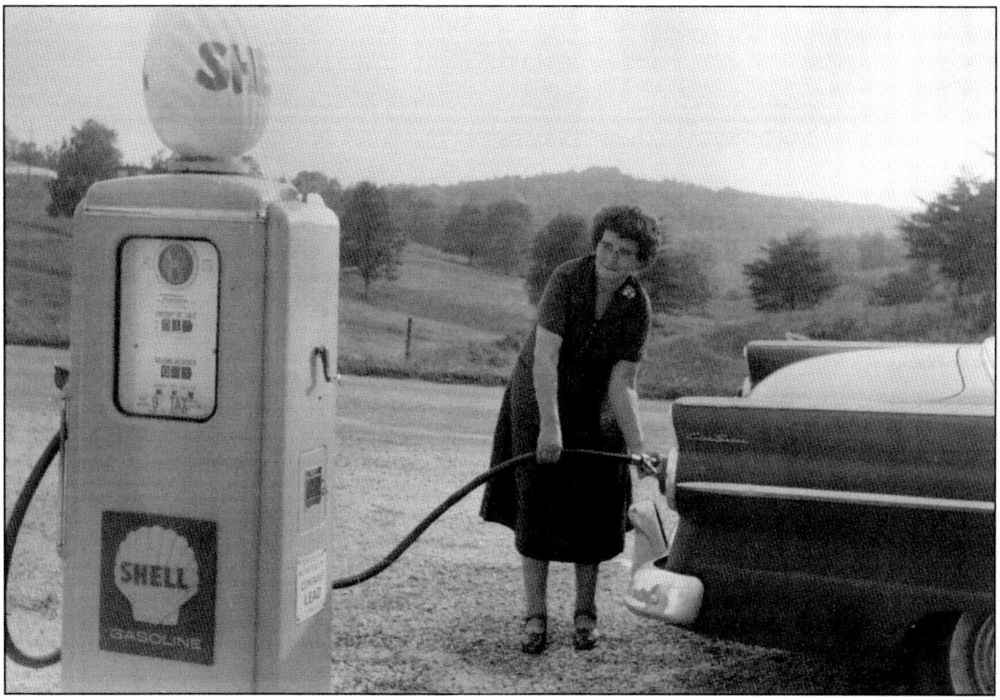

At the only station in mid-1950s Mineral Bluff, Mary Langley pumps her own gas because the elderly owners could no longer physically provide the service. Self-service was enough of a novelty at this time that it was worth taking a photograph to record it for posterity. (Courtesy Georgia Archives, Vanishing Georgia Collection, mur097.)

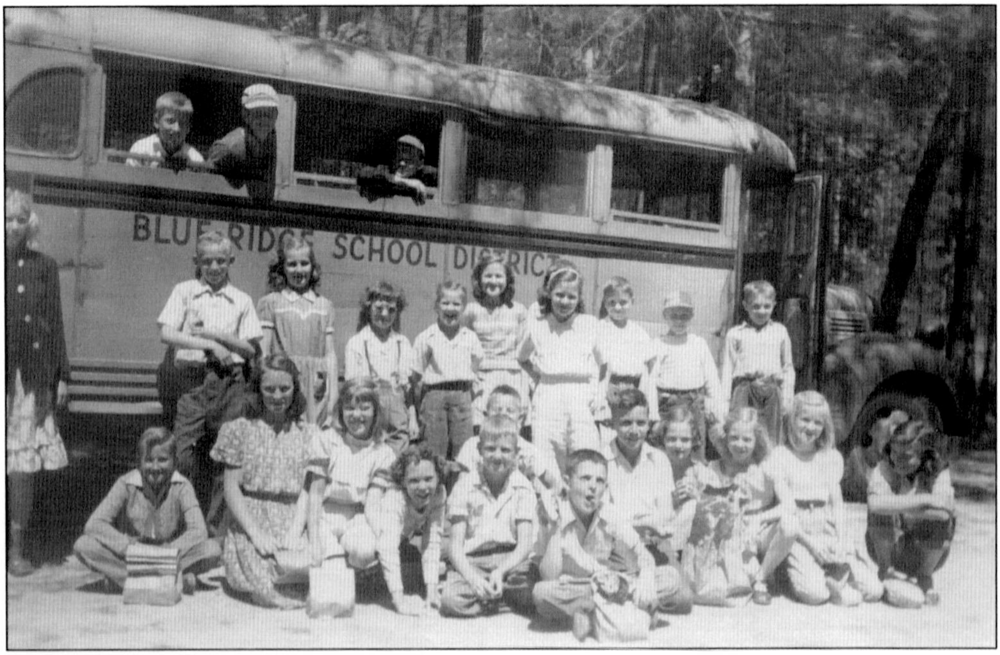

Is there a better symbol of the postwar period than a bus full of baby boomers? (Courtesy Michael Eaton.)

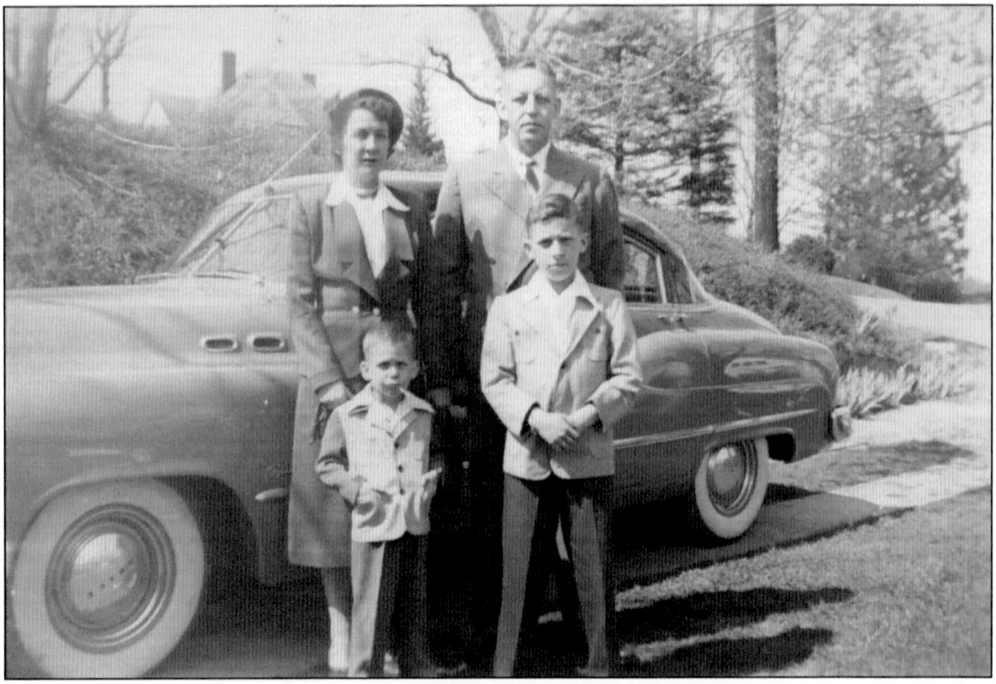

Steve Eaton poses with a sucker in his mouth and his hands defiantly in his pockets. His brother Lloyd, mother, Suella, and father, Joseph Milton "J.M." Eaton Jr. are ready to board the two-tone Buick for a trip to church on Easter 1951. (Courtesy Michael Eaton.)

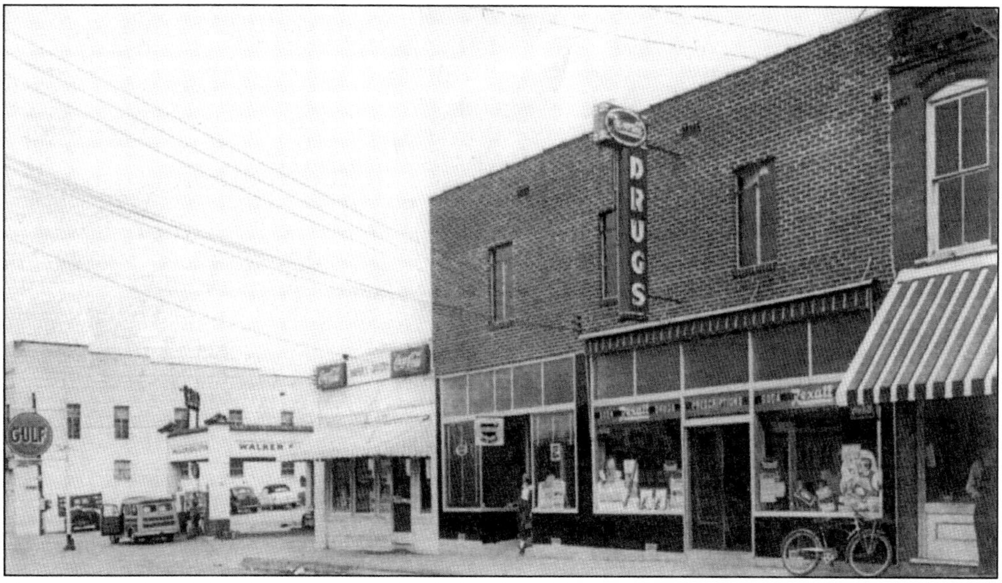

Downtown Blue Ridge drowses away the 1950s. East Main Street in this era was devoted mainly to retail stores, while county government, banking, real estate, and related pursuits dominated West Main Street across the railroad tracks. (Courtesy Wilson and LaVerne Cobb.)

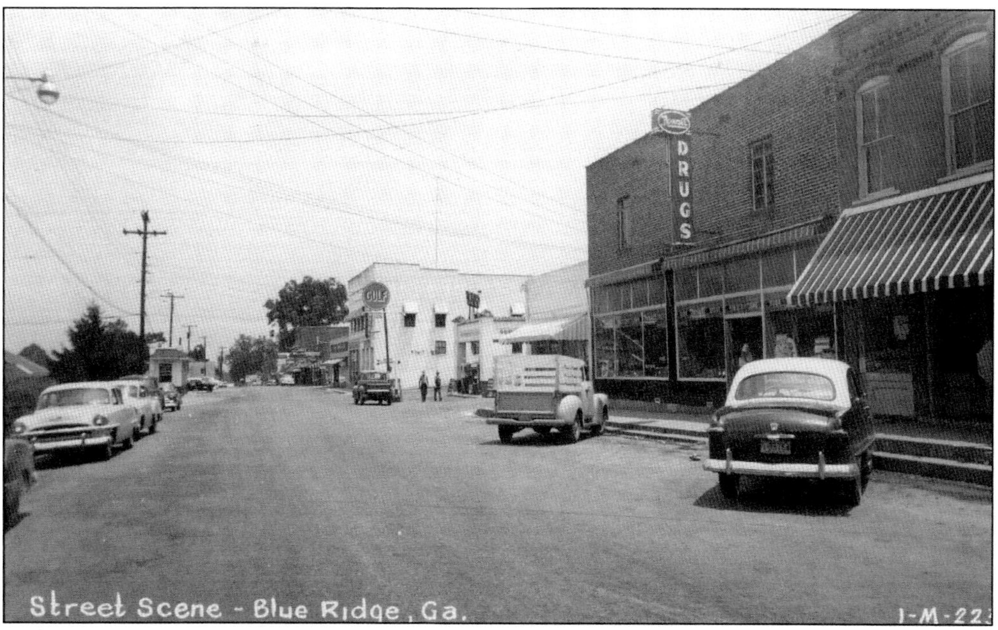

Perhaps on this afternoon in Blue Ridge everyone has gone inside to watch that newfangled television. (Courtesy Don and Carolyn Hall.)

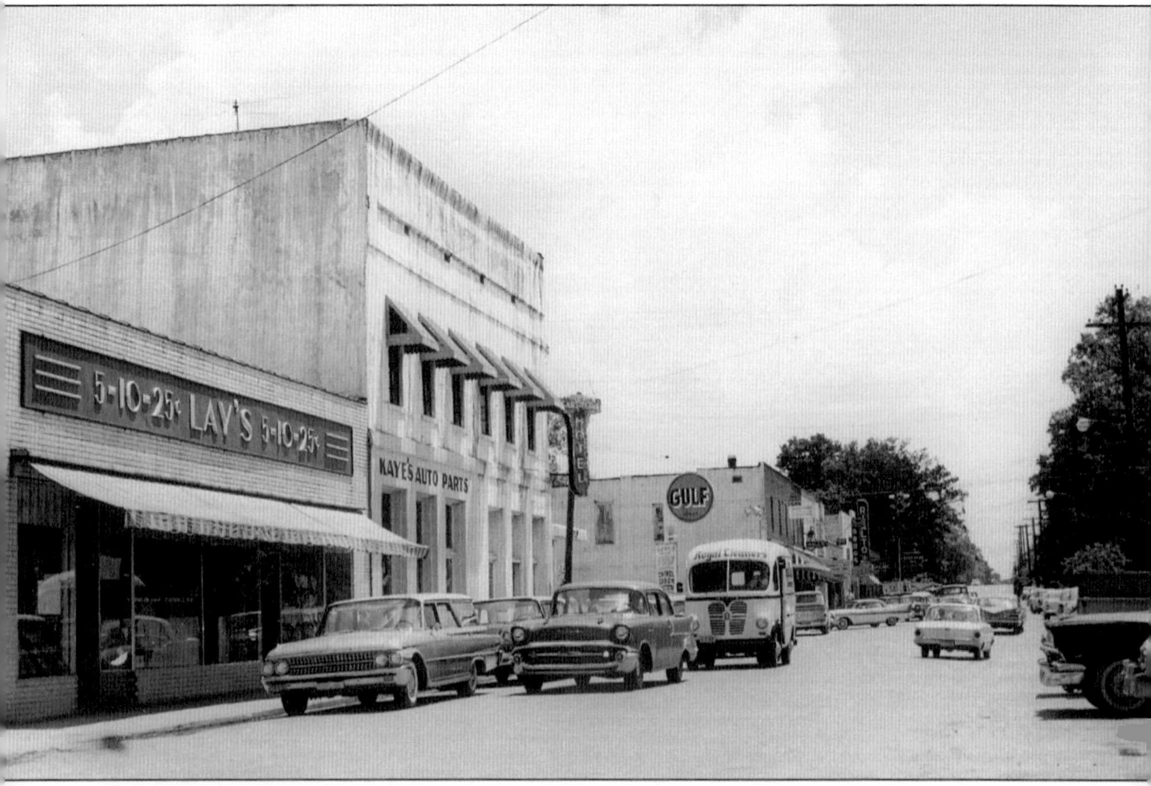

This photograph shows downtown in Blue Ridge, looking south along East Main Street in the early 1960s. (Courtesy Don and Carolyn Hall.)

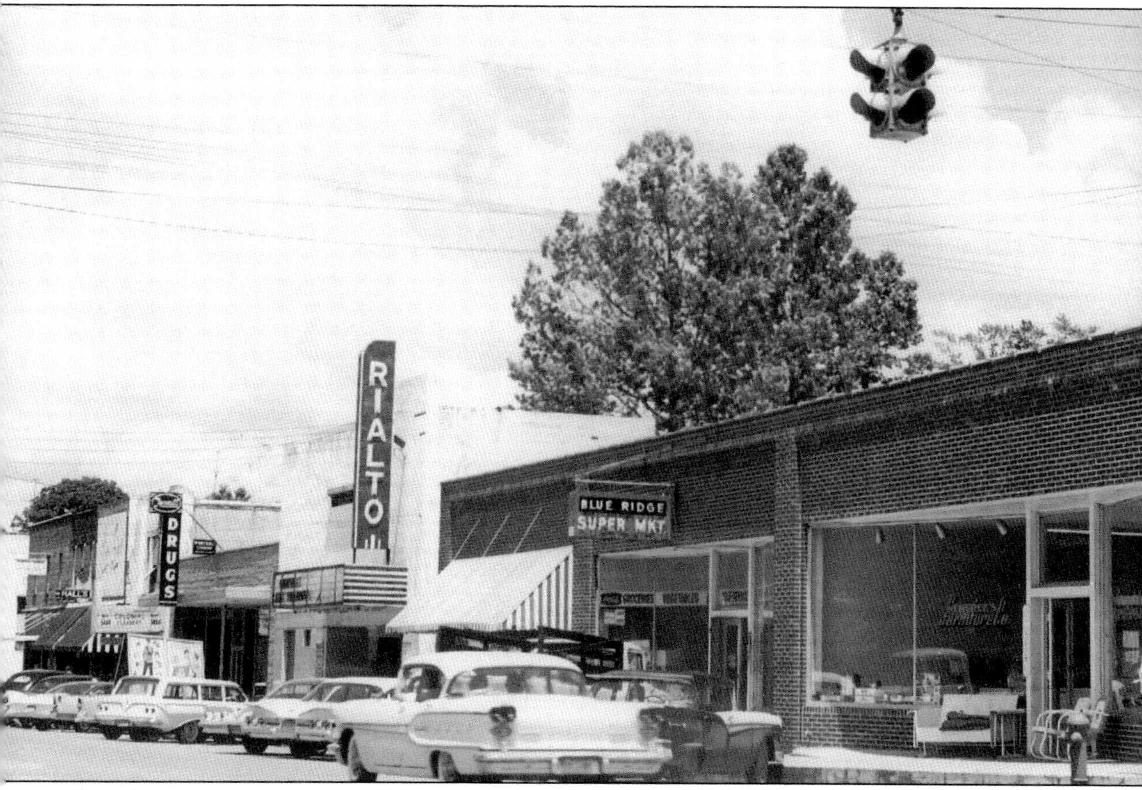

This photograph shows downtown Blue Ridge in 1961 on East Main Street, looking north. (Courtesy Don and Carolyn Hall.)

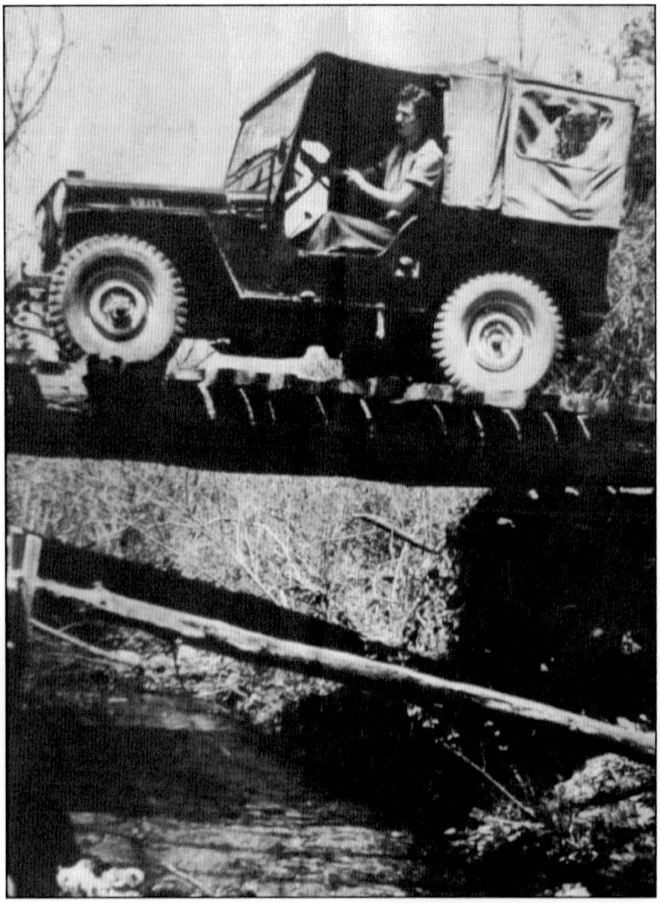

Rural mail carrier Versie Jones was remarkable not only for the rugged route she traversed in the upper end of southern Fannin County but also because she held a "man's job" in the early 1950s. The Sunday magazine section of the *Atlanta Journal-Constitution* newspaper did a story about her work. (Courtesy the Baugh House collection.)

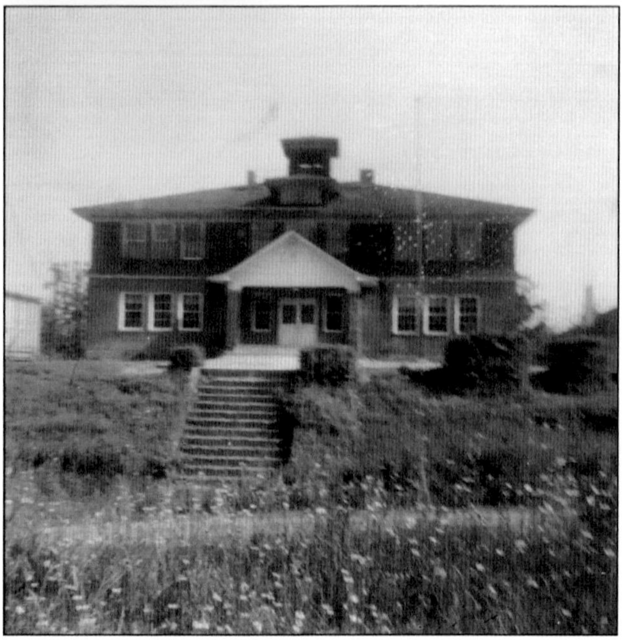

Fannin County High School in Morganton seems little changed since it housed the North Georgia Baptist College in the 1920s, but things will be shaken up soon. In the early 1950s, Fannin County will get two new high schools, East and West Fannin, and this building will become Morganton Elementary. By the early 1960s, it will be demolished and replaced by a cookie-cutter long, low, modernistic schoolhouse. (Courtesy Georgia Archives, Vanishing Georgia Collection, fan019-83.)

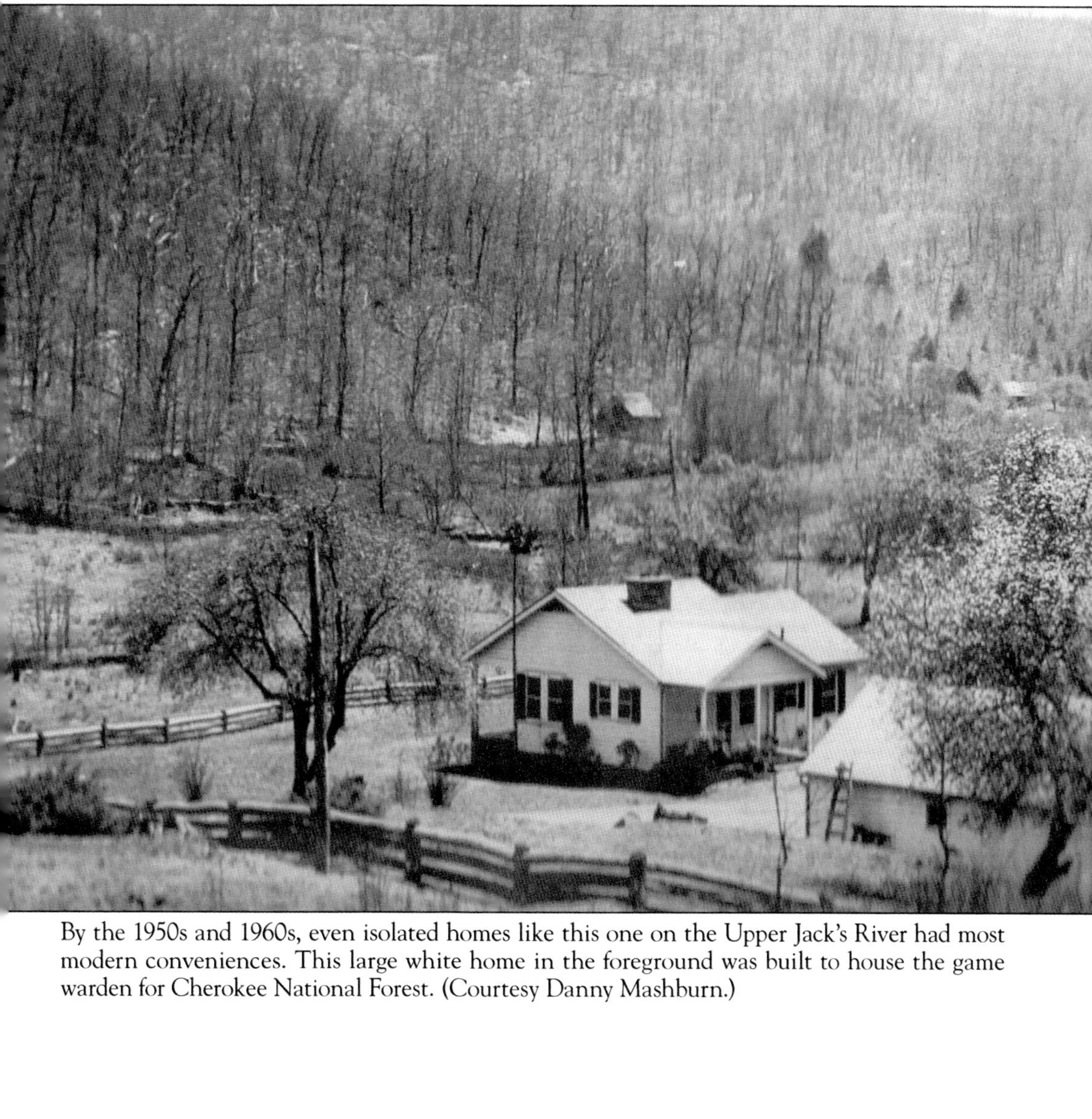

By the 1950s and 1960s, even isolated homes like this one on the Upper Jack's River had most modern conveniences. This large white home in the foreground was built to house the game warden for Cherokee National Forest. (Courtesy Danny Mashburn.)

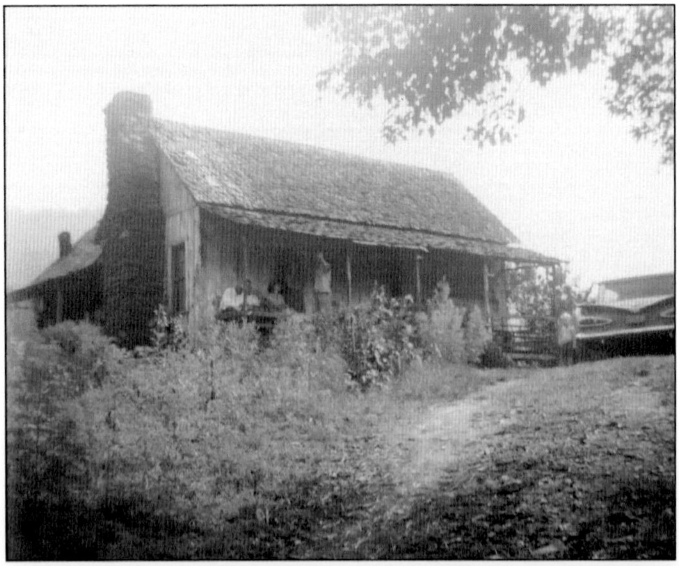

Externally, a few houses retained much of their pioneer character even when cars with jet-inspired fins were parked nearby. This is the home of Larkin Garner Davenport and his wife, Lizza Jane Talley Davenport. (Courtesy Vickie Forrester.)

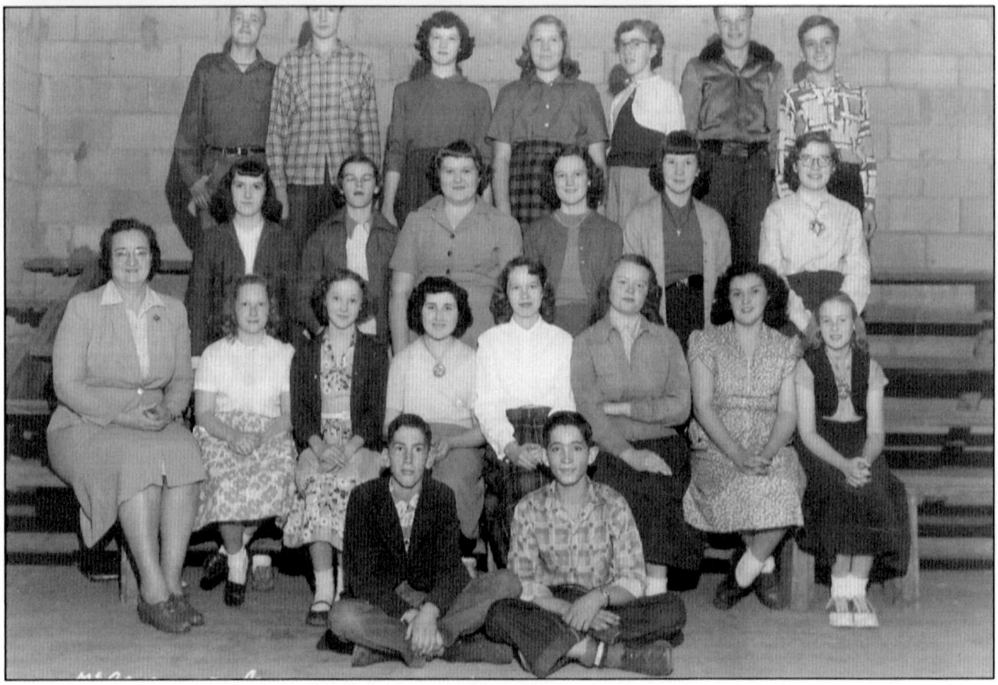

McCaysville is shown here on February 11, 1954. Edna Weeks taught eighth grade at this school and later taught freshman English at West Fannin High School. She loved to throw themed parties related to the literature the class was studying. She also pioneered techniques to help kinesthetic learners—one student built a scale-model working guillotine for a study of *A Tale of Two Cities* by Charles Dickens. Pictured from left to right are (first row) Roy Montieth and Jerry Panter; (second row) Edna Weeks, Jeannie queen, Shelbia Jean McArthur, Barbara Davenport, Kathryn Bradley, Peggy Ratcliff, Christine Dickey, and Joan Kearley; (third row) Betty Lou Hyde, Shirley Thomas, Peggy Hyde, Mary Alice Payne, Ruth Ann Coffey, and Carolyn Jones; (fourth row) Frank Poteet Roger Tatum, Margie Godfrey, Evelyn Flowers, Willa Ruth Holmes, Clinton Seagraves, and Tommy Walker. (Courtesy Shelbia and Nick Wimberley.)

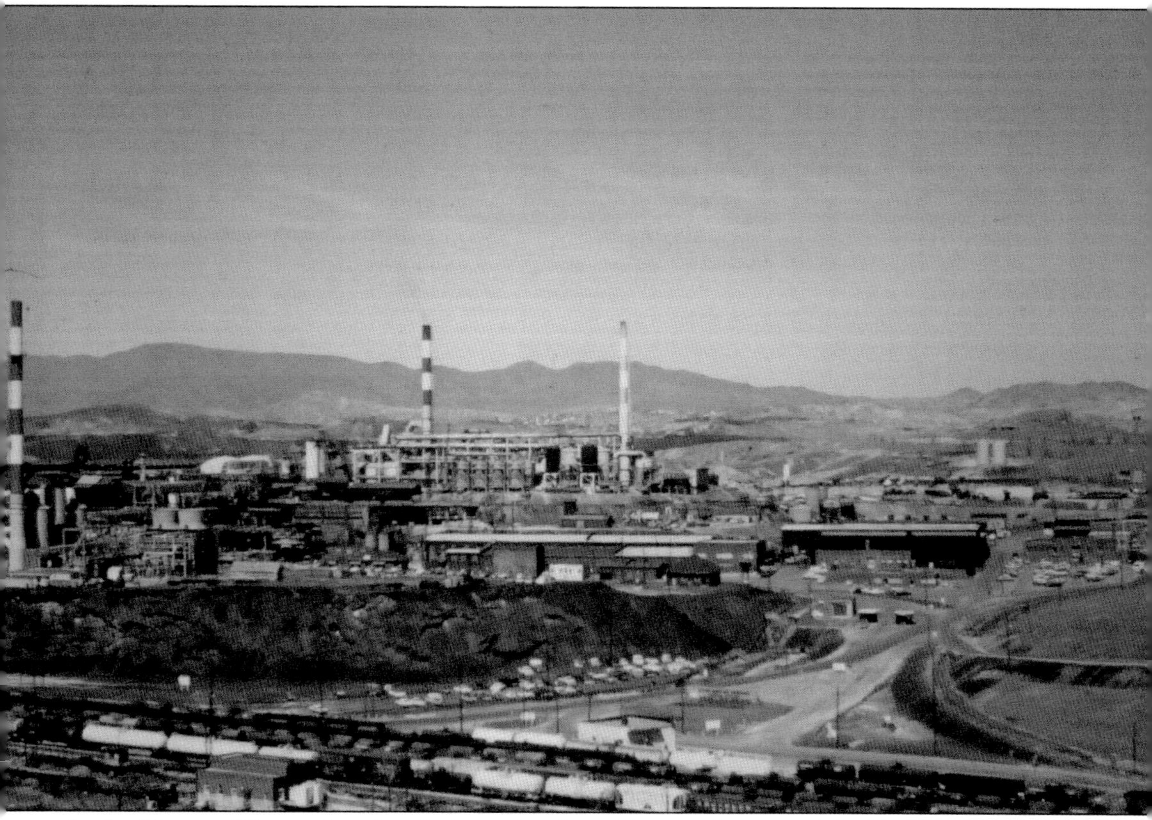

As the Vietnam War ratcheted up in intensity, the sulfuric acid output of the Tennessee Copper Company became more vital to the defense industry. Without sulfuric acid, it is hard to make nitric acid. Without nitric acid, it is just about impossible to make gun cotton, nitroglycerin, and other high explosives. During the late 1950s and early 1960s, students in the Copper Basin area did not bother with the usual "duck-and-cover" routine to protect against atomic war. Students believed that the school was a Russian target and that many large bombs could be heading their way. (Courtesy Ron Henry family.)

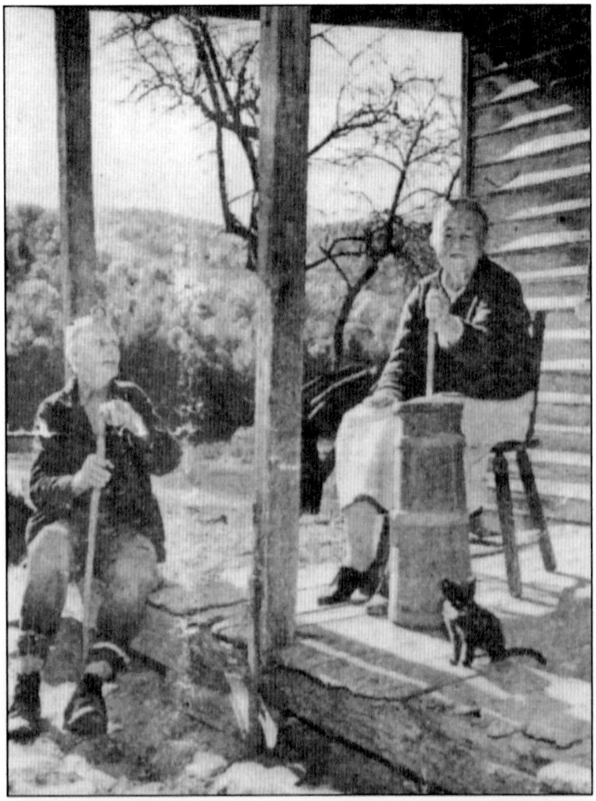

Some people kept to the old ways. Allen and Molly Edmondson of Margret were featured in an article in the *Atlanta Journal* the day after they celebrated 72 years of marriage on November 12, 1949. Molly was still spry enough to churn her own butter. (Courtesy Betty Parker.)

Dr. C.G. Lloyd planted the original orchard in 1924 that became the Mercier's operation. Bill and Adele Mercier bought the orchard in 1943, producing their first crop in 1944. The Mercier family originated in an apple-producing region of southern France, so it should not be surprising that the business has thrived. The old apple barn is visible to travelers on Georgia Highway 5, where it can be glimpsed across the ponds that flank the Mercier parking lots. (Courtesy Adele Mercier.)

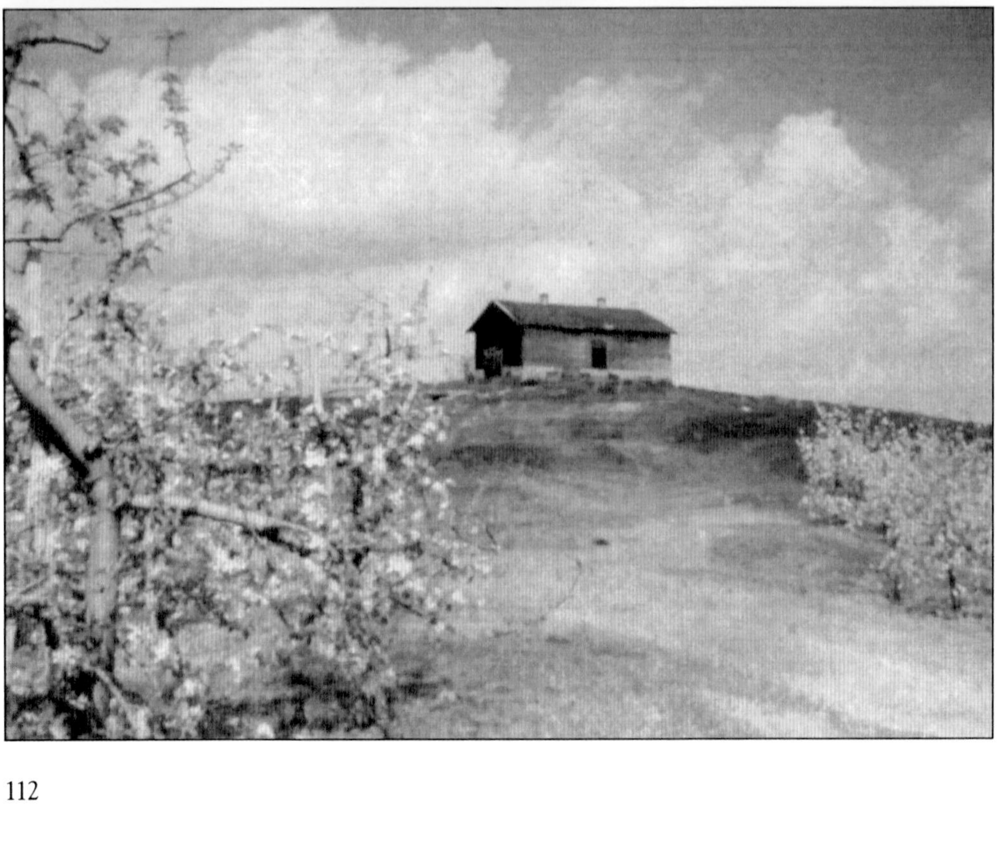

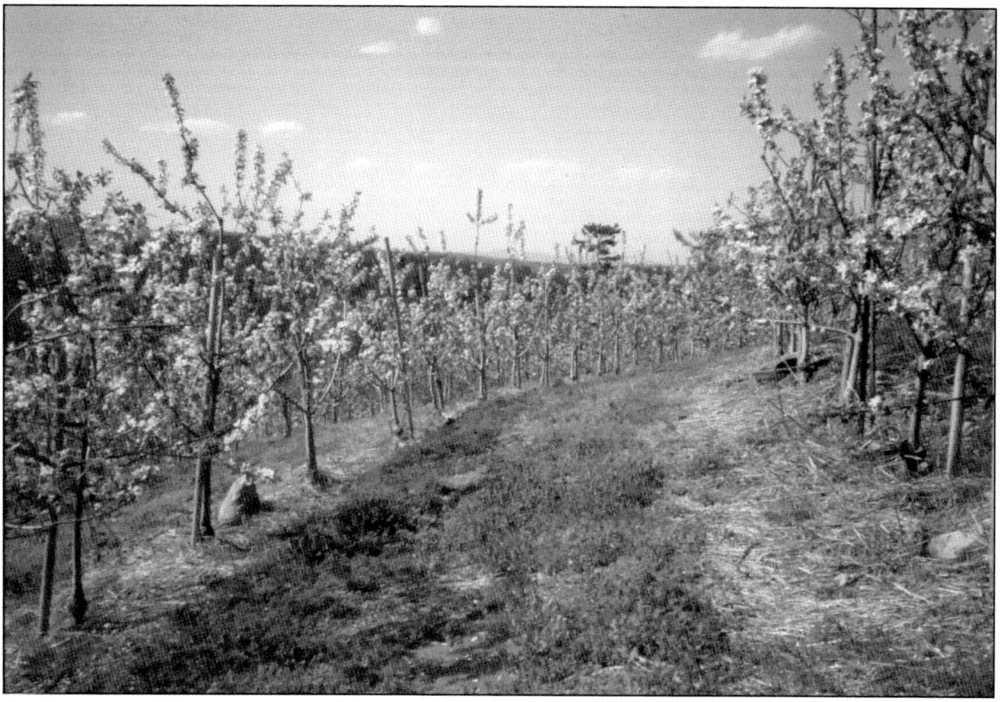

Apple trees in bloom are one of the most beautiful sights of an Appalachian spring. (Courtesy Adele Mercier.)

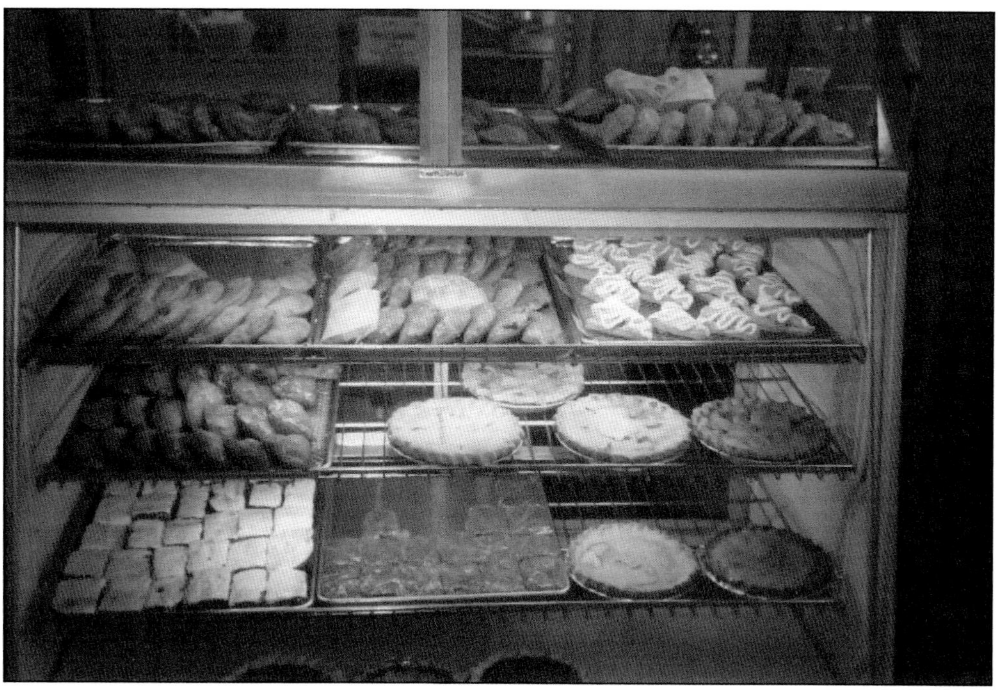

Mercier's fried pies and baked goods are among the best to be found anywhere. (Courtesy Adele Mercier.)

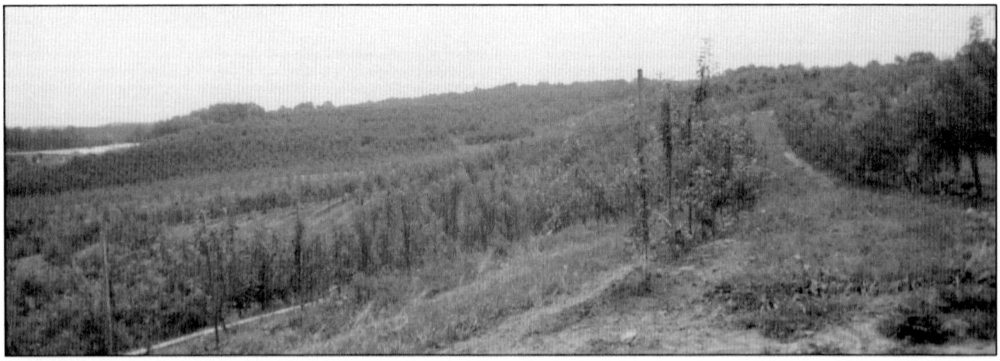

Young apple trees sink their roots deep into what was once depleted soil. Bill Mercier was a former county agricultural agent, and his son Tim majored in horticulture, earning a master's degree in plant pathology. (Courtesy Adele Mercier.)

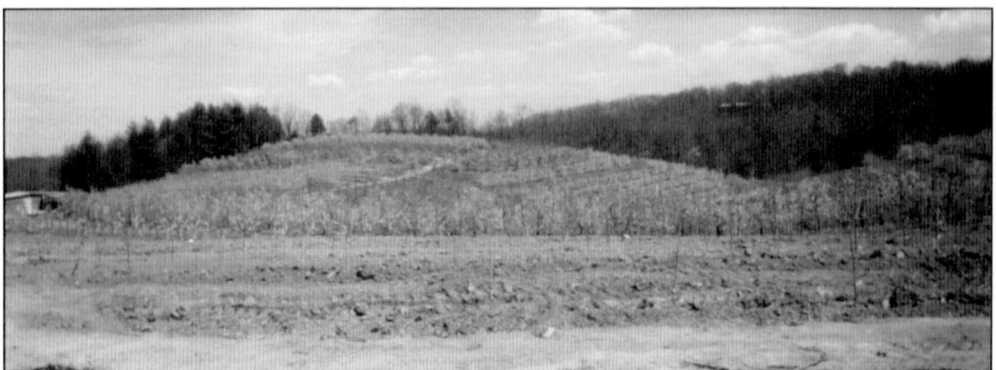

Gently rolling hilltops in the Mercier orchards would attract the eye of artists and nature lovers. (Courtesy Adele Mercier.)

Seven

The Times are A-Changin'

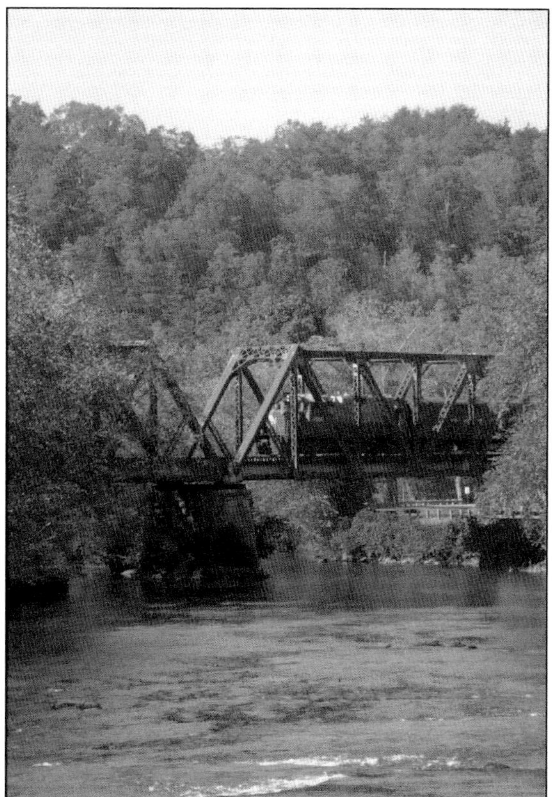

A train heads south from McCaysville to Blue Ridge. Note the white streaks in the Toccoa River. They are the left side of a V-shaped rock fish trap that oral history asserts was built by the Cherokee. (Courtesy Ron Henry family.)

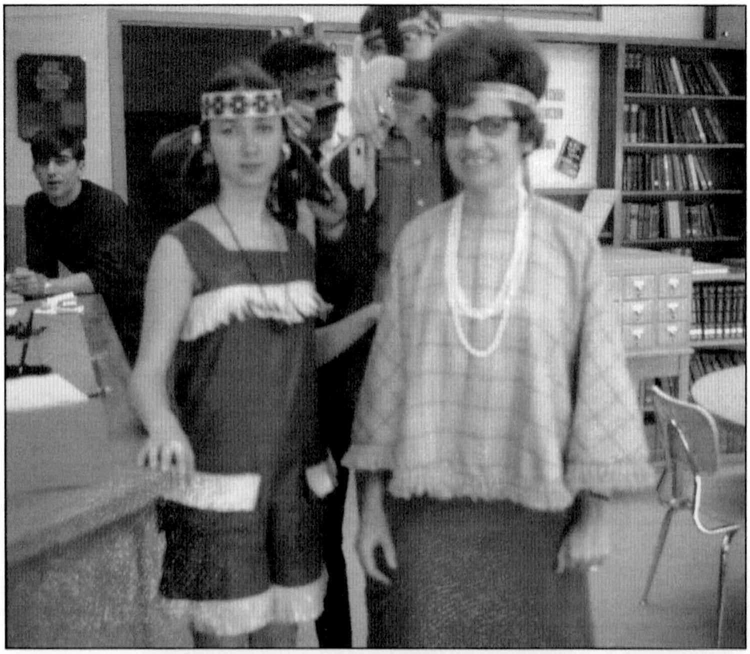

Thomas McClure (back left) looks on with bemusement at the celebration of Indian Day in the West Fannin High School library around 1969. Lesa Williams is in the fringed dress, and Jim Mercier peeks over her shoulder. Mike Dale is perhaps the next person peeking through. On the right is Ethelene Dyer Jones, who was the librarian/ media specialist at the school. (Courtesy Ethelene Dyer Jones.)

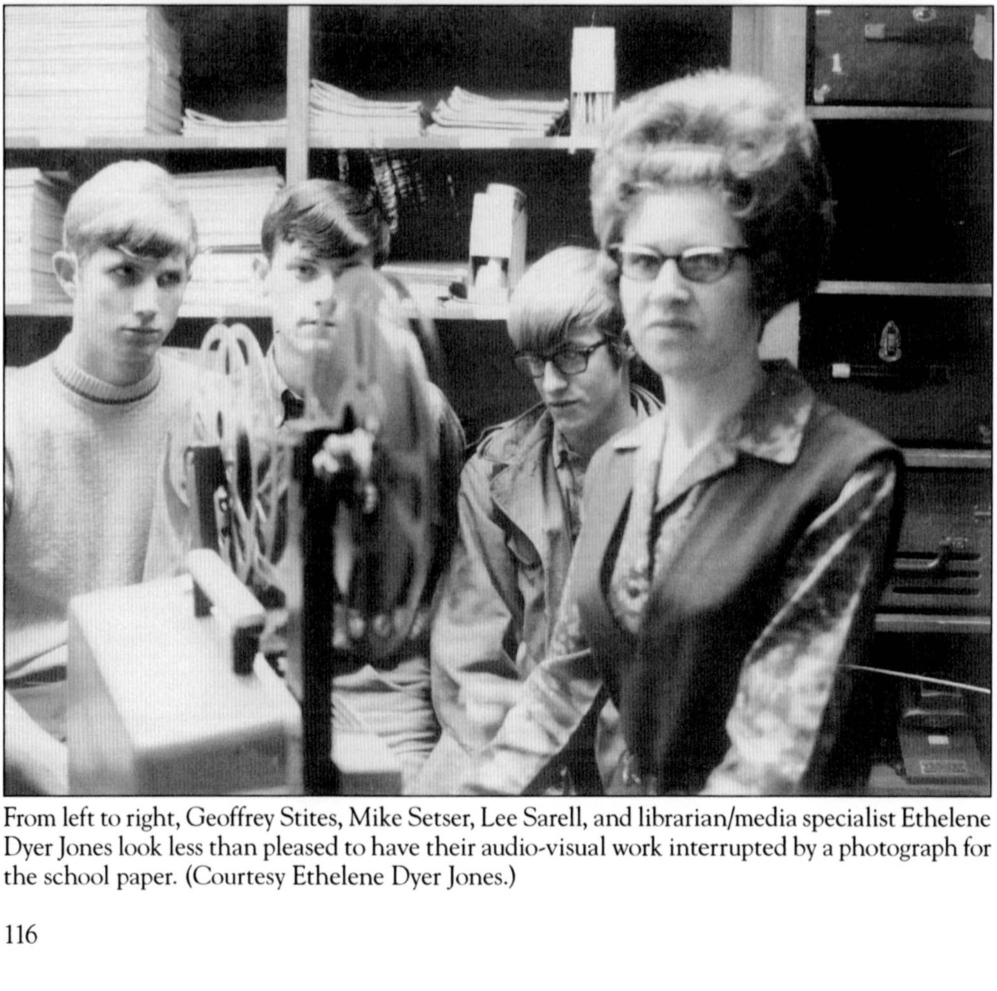

From left to right, Geoffrey Stites, Mike Setser, Lee Sarell, and librarian/media specialist Ethelene Dyer Jones look less than pleased to have their audio-visual work interrupted by a photograph for the school paper. (Courtesy Ethelene Dyer Jones.)

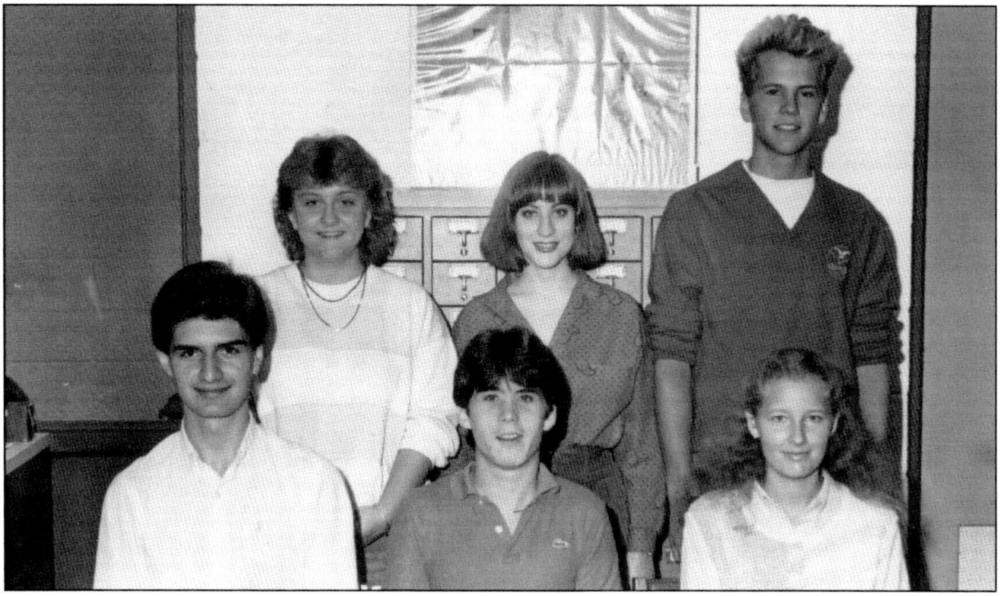

In the late 1970s and early 1980s, media assistants at the Fannin County High School Library formed a local chapter of the Georgia Association of Media Assistants (GAMA). They then dominated several contests at the state level for many years. Students got involved in researching family and area history, making multimedia presentations, and even helped the chamber of commerce prepare its first presentation to prospective businesses. The students, pictured here from left to right around 1986, are (first row) Pres. Michael Collins, Vice Pres. Kevin Harris, and secretary Robin Ballew; (second row) treasurer Tammy Porter, reporter Leigh Ann Sanders, and parliamentarian Martin Eliasson. Eliasson was an exchange student from Sweden. (Courtesy Ethelene Dyer Jones.)

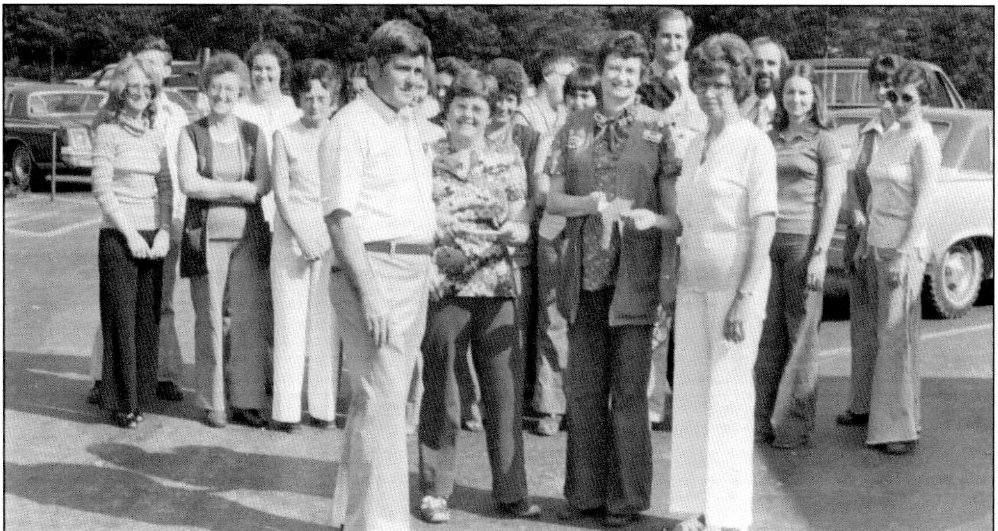

Around 1977, the community team from the local Levi's manufacturing plant in Blue Ridge presented a check for the media center to Frank Henson, principal of Fannin County High School, and media director Ethelene Dyer Jones. Henson is standing to the left of the center in a white shirt, while Jones is to the right of center in a white outfit. Also pictured with the team from Levi's are members of GAMA. (Courtesy Ethelene Dyer Jones.)

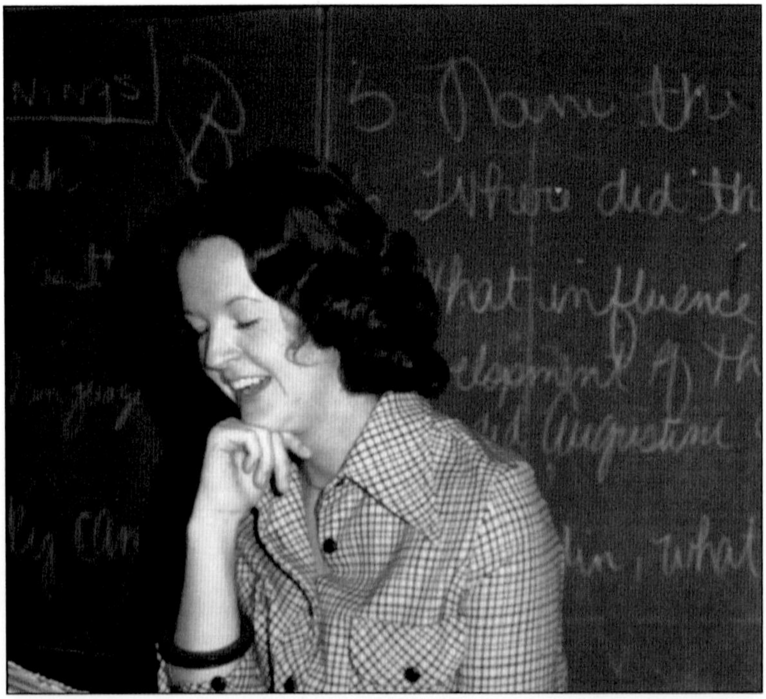

Sandra Mercier, an English teacher at Fannin County High School, went on to serve as Fannin County's first female superintendent of schools. After retirement, she was elected to the school board. (Courtesy Ethelene Dyer Jones.)

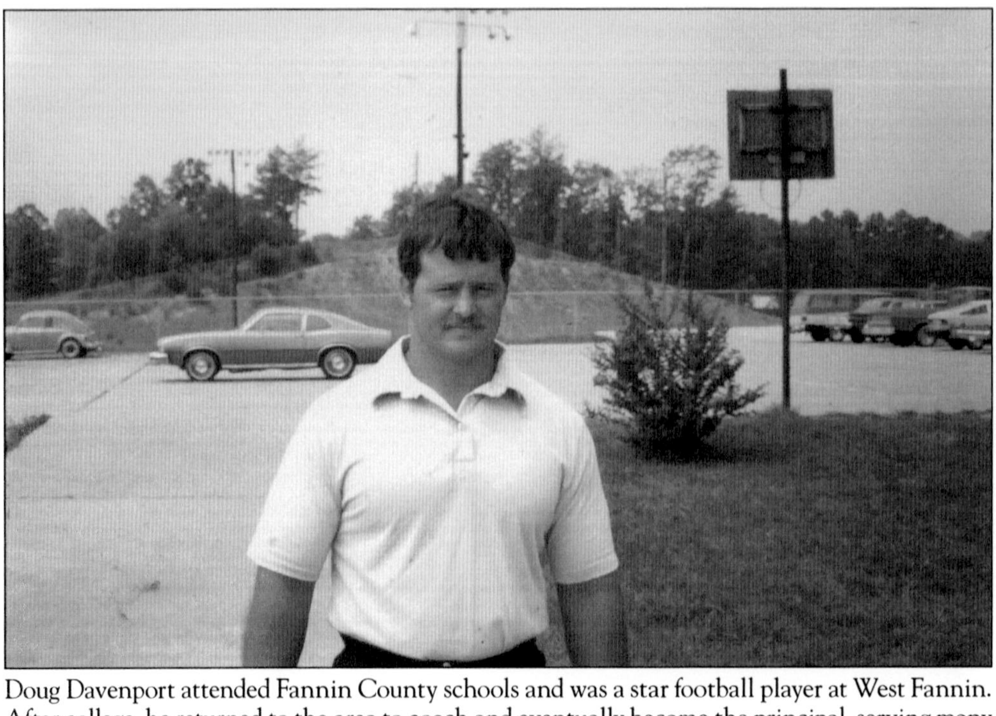

Doug Davenport attended Fannin County schools and was a star football player at West Fannin. After college, he returned to the area to coach and eventually became the principal, serving many years at Fannin County High School. (Courtesy Ethelene Dyer Jones.)

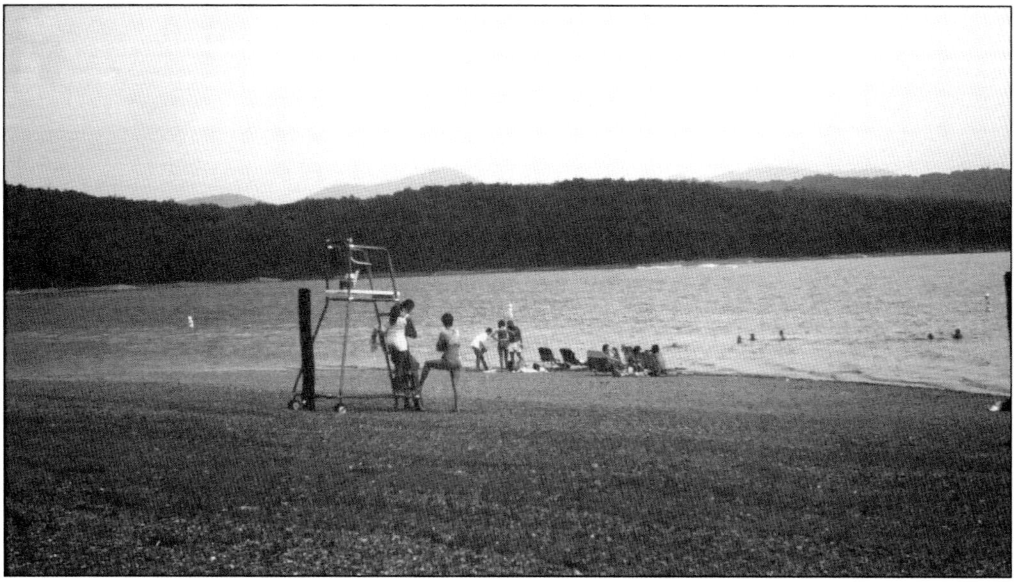

Swimmers and sunbathers enjoy a day at the "beach" (or at least on the rocks) at Morganton Point recreation area in the 1970s. (Courtesy Ethelene Dyer Jones.)

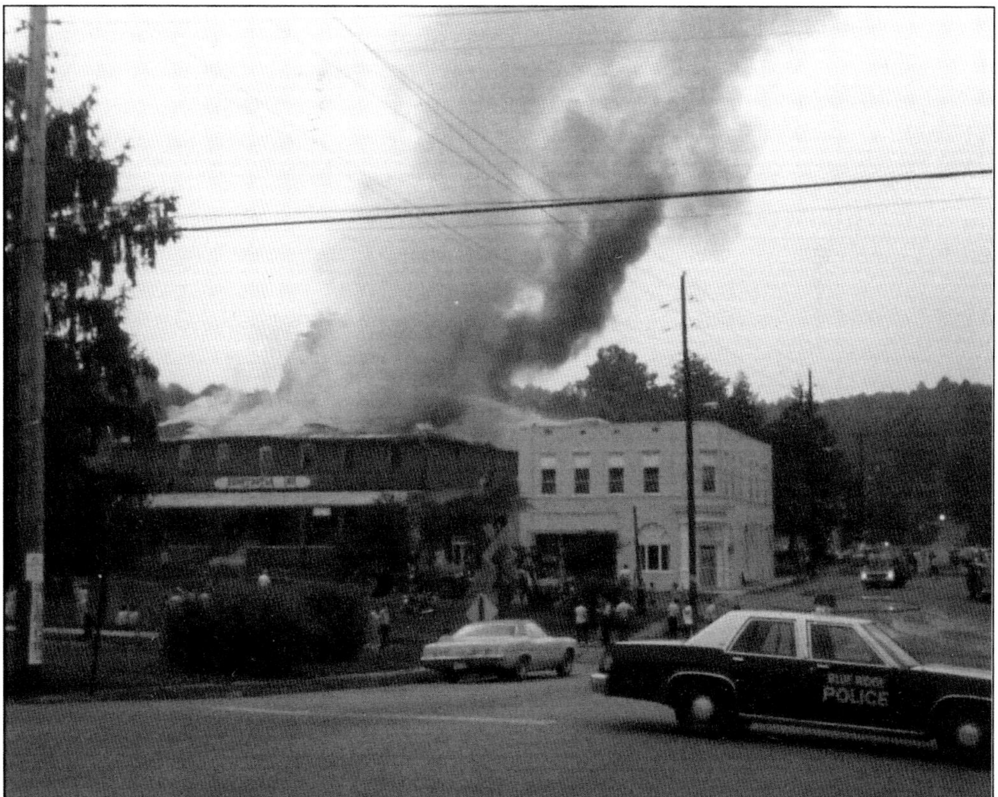

The historic Blue Ridge Hotel burned to the ground in the 1970s. (Courtesy Teresa Haymore.)

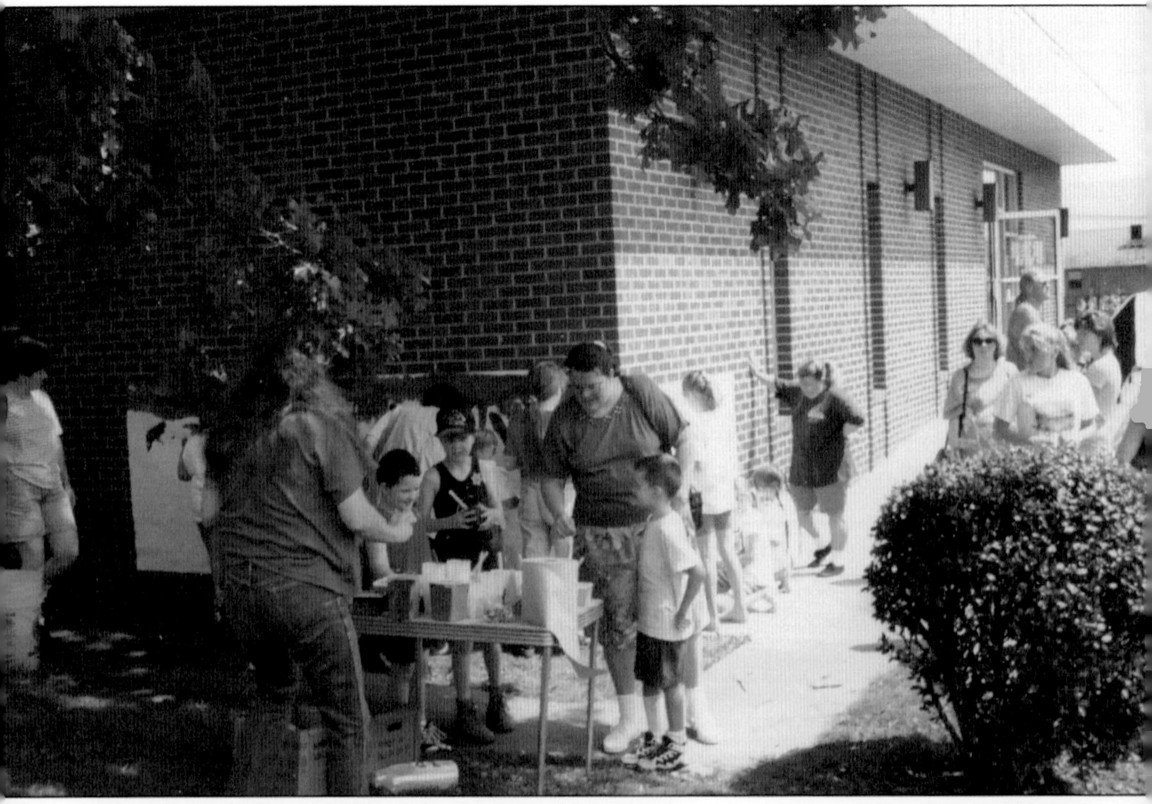

The Fannin County Public Library existed for decades in a small room in the courthouse. Eventually, this stand-alone library was built, but it was demolished to make room for the third Fannin County Courthouse to be located in Blue Ridge. The library now occupies a suite at the front western corner of the courthouse ground floor. Here, library patrons enjoy a children's summer reading activity. (Courtesy Teresay Haymore.)

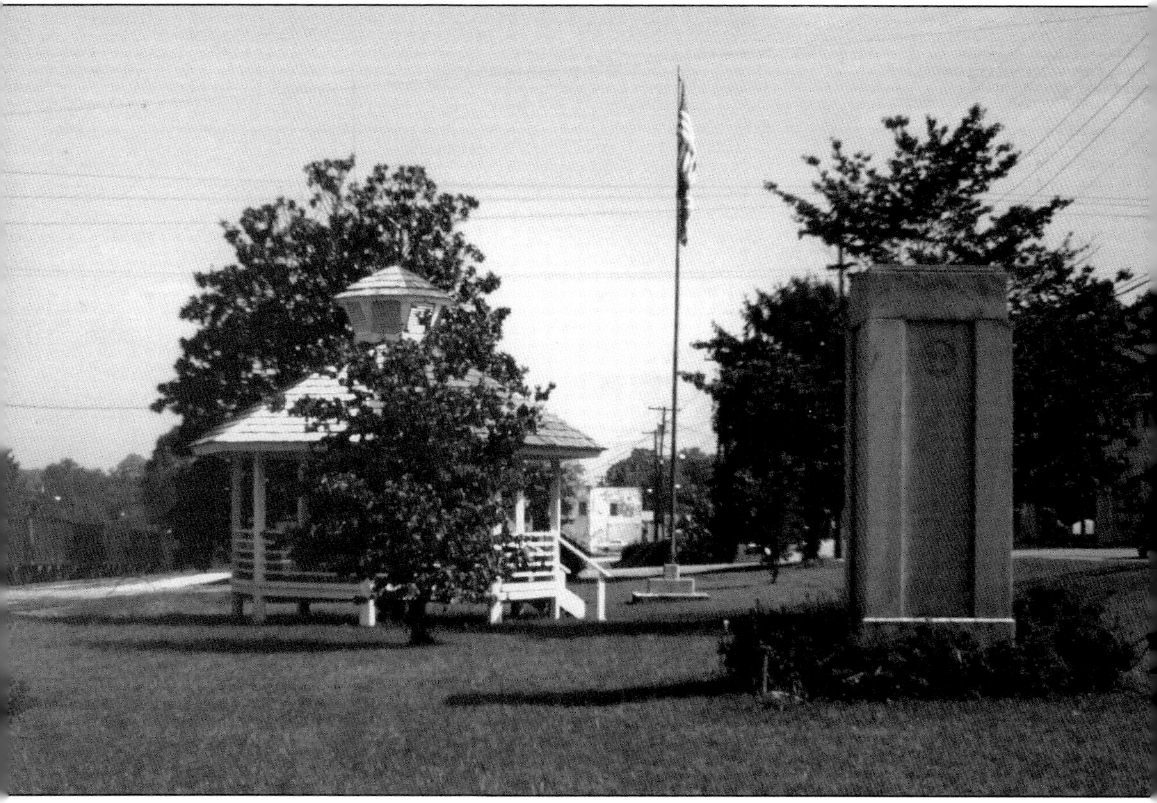

The Blue Ridge downtown park now boasts a wooden gazebo near the war memorial. The flagpole has been replaced, but the concrete base for it has been in place for nearly a century. (Courtesy Ethelene Dyer Jones.)

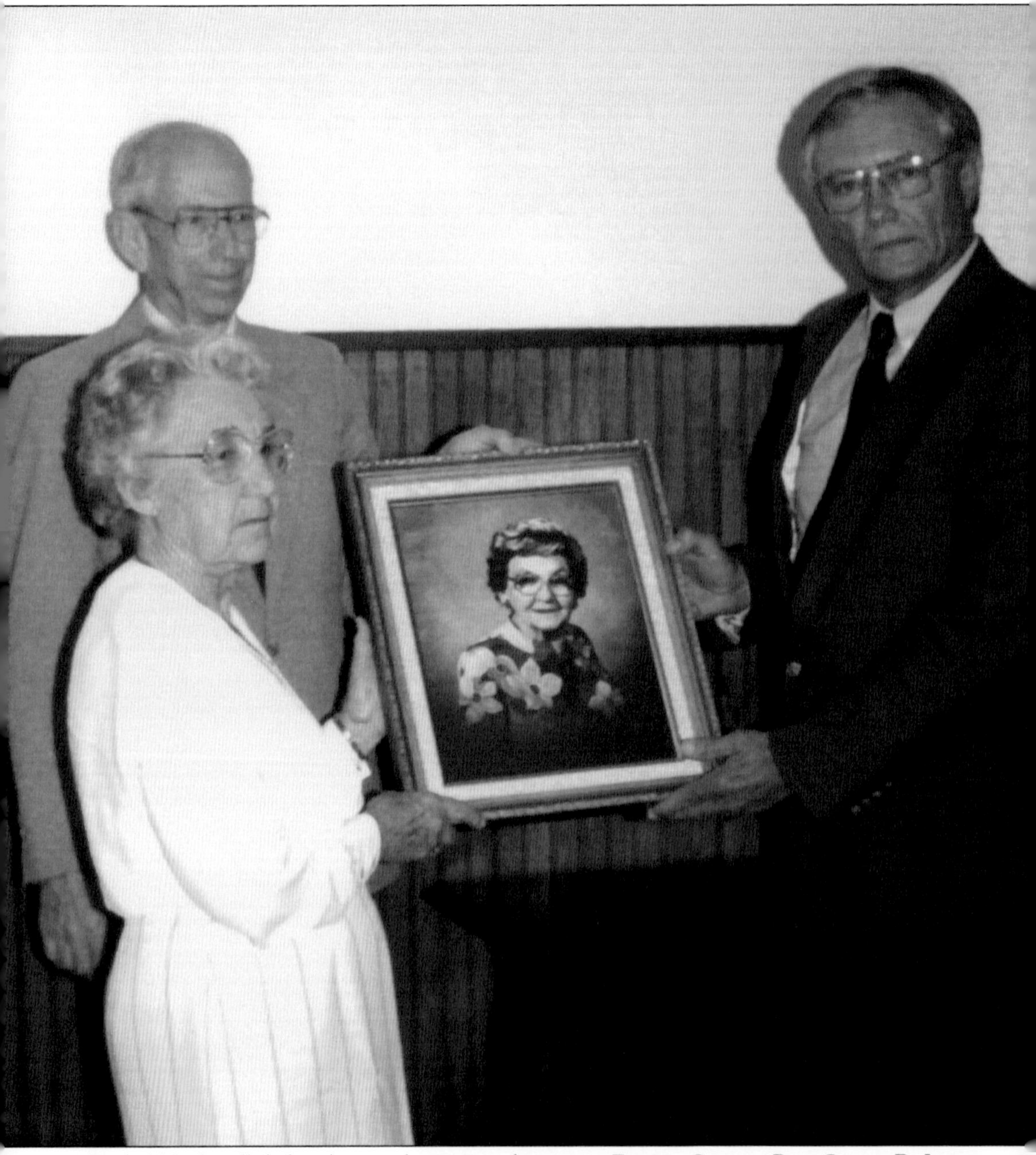

Rachel Higdon (left front) was a longtime educator in Fannin County. Rev. Grover D. Jones (left rear) served a dozen years as a pastor, 16 more years as the Baptist Associational Missionary, and continued to be active in the community for many years. Here, they present a portrait of Bonnie Hidgon Reaves, designating the Epworth School Campus as a site for higher education in Fannin County. Receiving the portrait is Tom Smith, director of the local campus program for Truett-McConnell College. (Courtesy Ethelene Dyer Jones.)

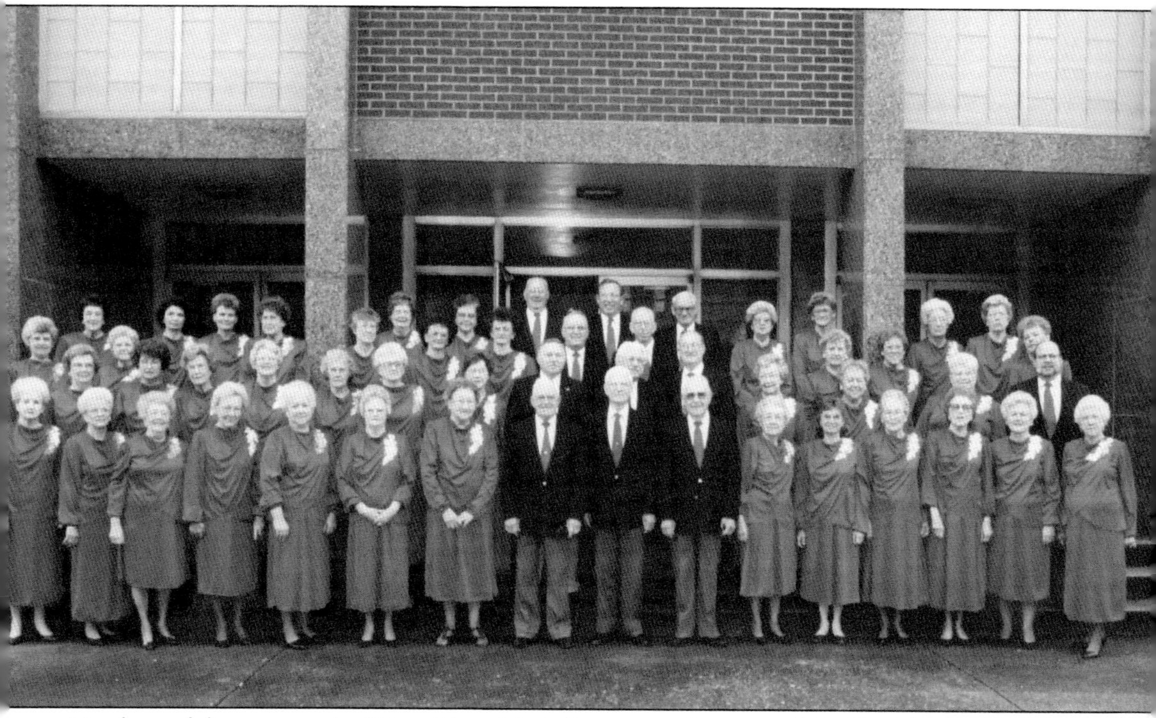

Members of the community Prime Time Choir line up on the steps of the First Baptist Church of McCaysville, Georgia, and Copperhill, Tennessee. Director Rick Grammer is at the far right of the second row. (Courtesy Ethelene Dyer Jones.)

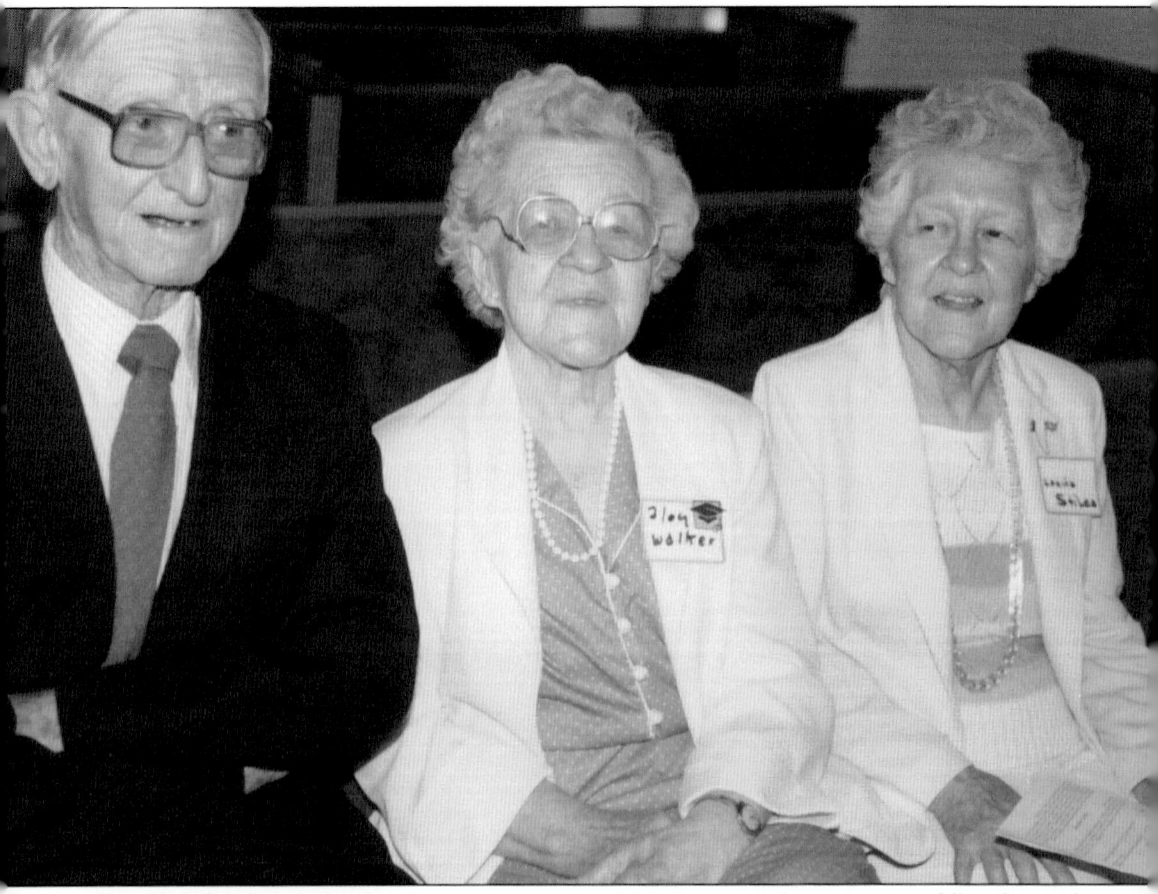

Rev. Paul Culpepper, longtime Baptist Associational Missionary and pastor, enjoys fellowship with distinguished alumnae Floy Stiles Walker and Louise Stiles at the dedication of the memorial marker for the Mary P. Willingham School. (Courtesy Ethelene Dyer Jones.)

Dale Dyer is shown announcing to the Blue Ridge Kiwanis Club that the long-awaited history book *Facets of Fannin* will be delivered in November 1989. The Kiwanis Club gave assistance to the project. Dyer, president of the local Kiwanis Club at the time, served as codirector of the project along with Ethelene Dyer Jones (no relation). Jones was the editor and her husband, Rev. Grover D. Jones, did a great deal of the needed research. (Courtesy Ethelene Dyer Jones.)

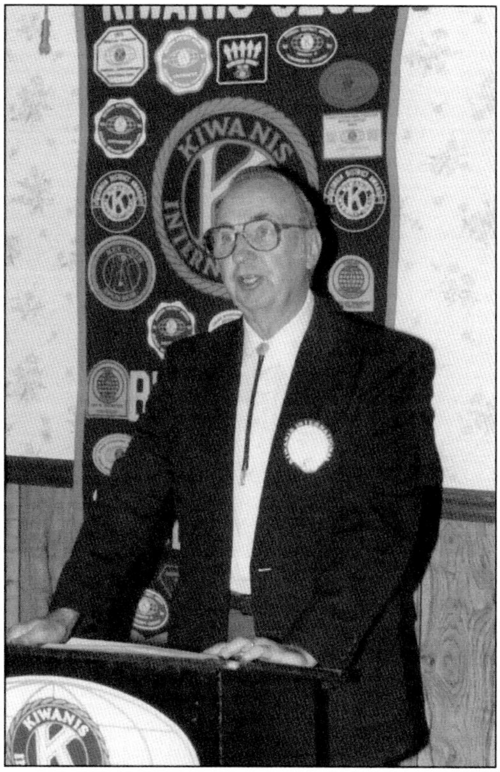

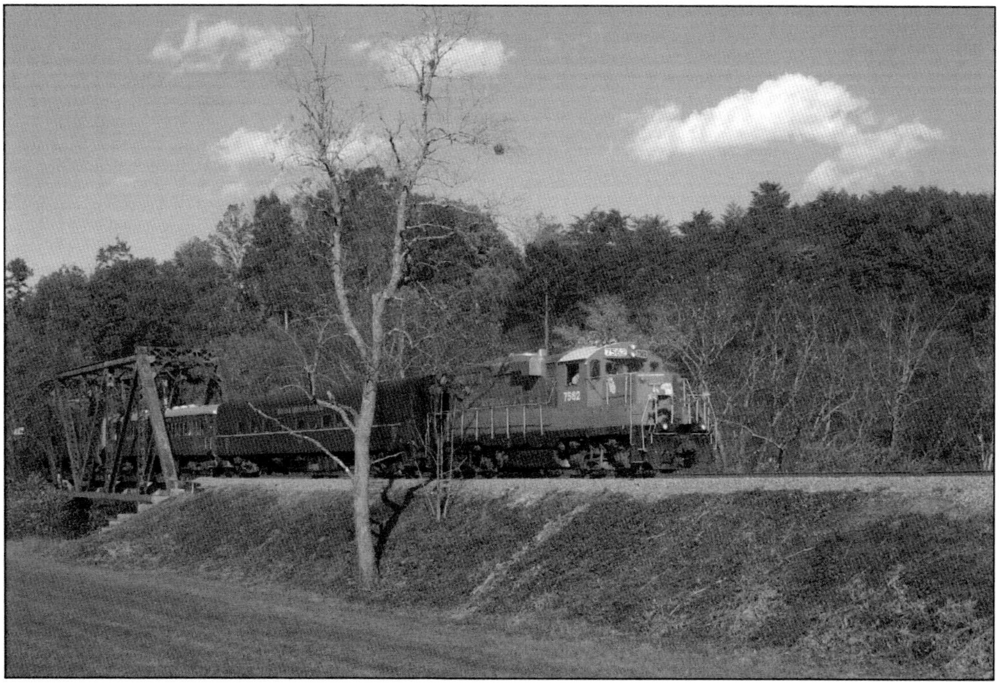

An engine of the Blue Ridge Mountain Scenic Railway has just passed over the Toccoa River near Horseshoe Bend south of McCaysville, headed back to Blue Ridge with a load of happy tourists. (Courtesy Ron Henry family.)

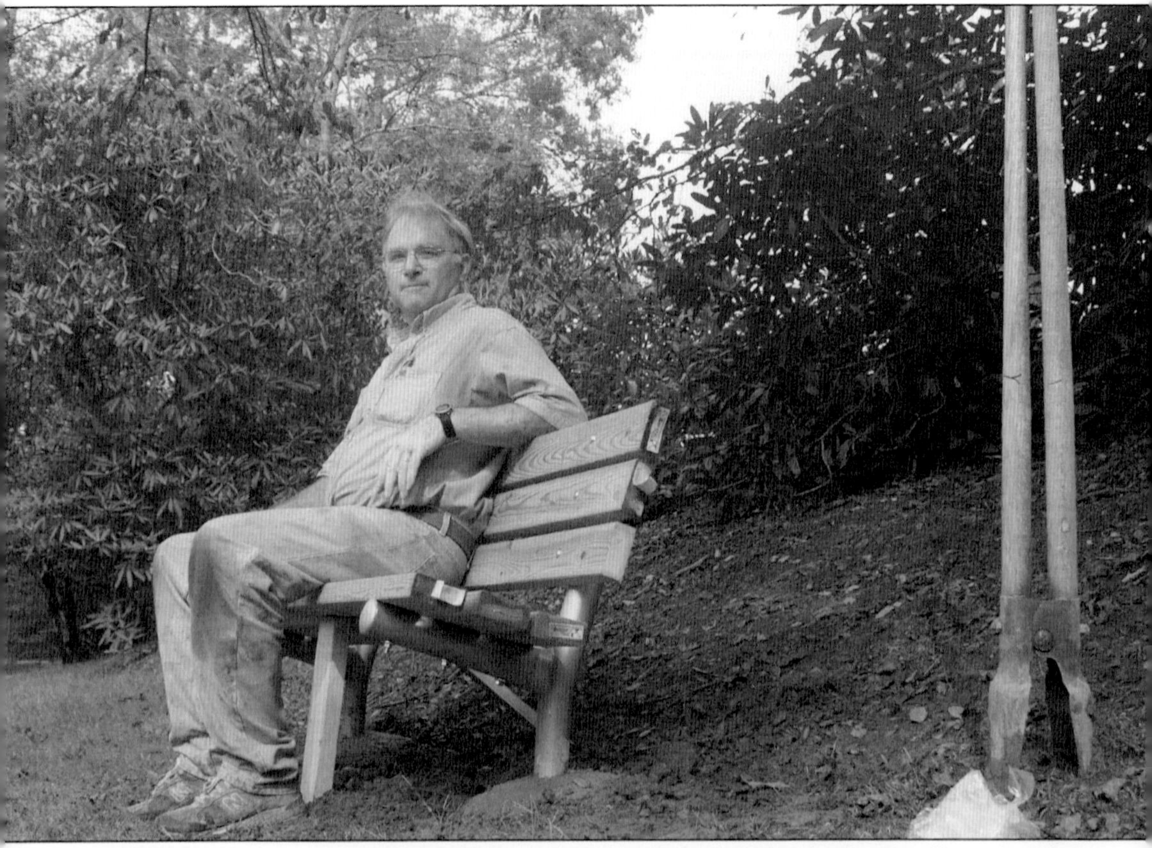

Ron Henry, photographer and park initiator, takes a well-deserved break after installing a bench at Horseshoe Bend Park along the Toccoa River. After his death, this park was renamed in memory of him. (Courtesy Ron Henry family.)

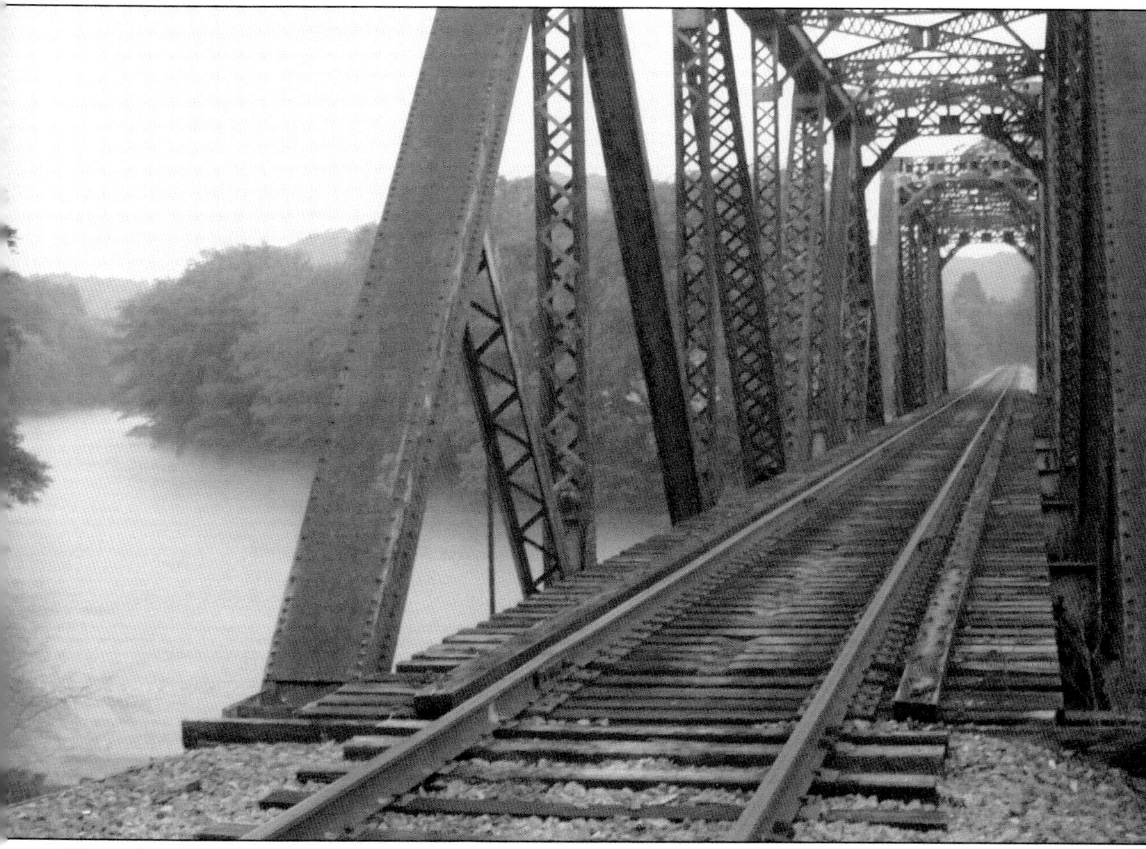

The rails crossing the Horseshoe Bend trestle are reminiscent of the old Irish blessing: "May the road rise to meet you, may the wind be always at your back, may the sun shine warmly on your face, may the rain fall softly on your fields, and until we meet again may God hold you in the palm of His hand." (Courtesy Ron Henry family.)